The E Word

Kaplan's Guide to Passing Exams

by Stuart Pedley-Smith

British library cataloguing-in-publication data

A catalogue record for this book is available from the British Library.

Published by:
Kaplan Publishing UK
Unit 2 The Business Centre
Molly Millars Lane
Wokingham
Berkshire
RG41 2QZ

ISBN 978-0-85732-205-0

First edition published 2010

Printed and bound in Great Britain.

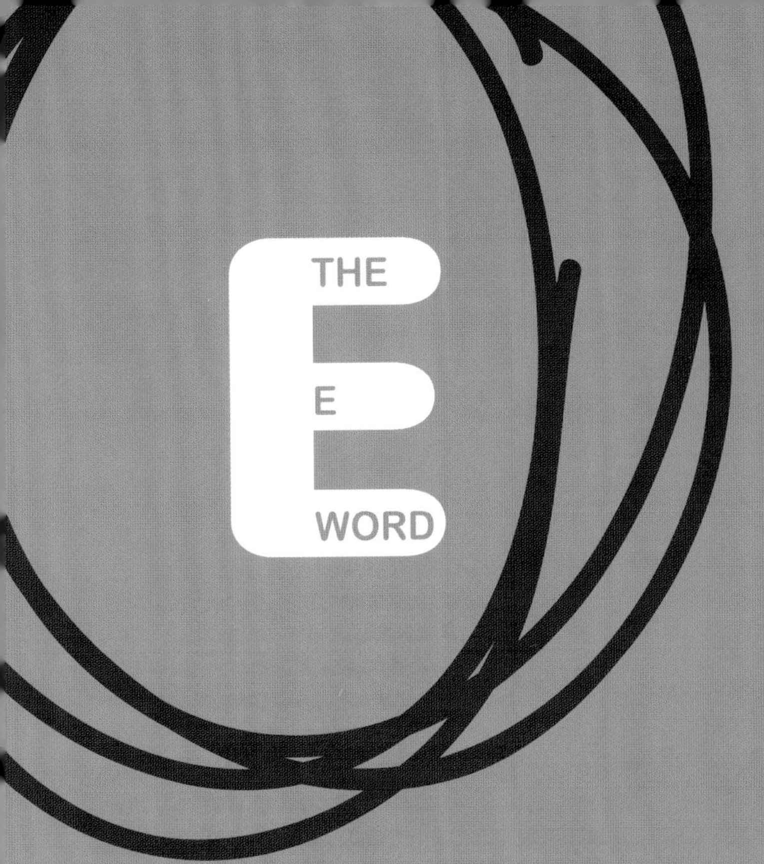

chapter 1
Why you should read this book

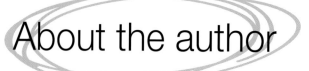

About the author

Stuart Pedley-Smith

Stuart Pedley - Smith is a qualified accountant and has been a senior lecturer at Kaplan Financial for more than 15 years. He specialises in learning skills and examination techniques, writing articles and delivering lectures both in the UK and overseas on these topics.

During his time in the classroom he has taught thousands of students and has learned a lot about people but most importantly what you need to do to pass exams.

All people are different: they all have different skills and abilities. Some seem to grasp concepts and principles far easier and will be thought of as intelligent and some have to work a little harder to achieve the same results. But exams are not intelligent tests; they require a whole range of skills most of which can be taught and so learned.

About this book

This is a book about passing exams. It is for anyone who has to sit an examination and wants to improve their chances of passing. The techniques described have been developed whilst working in the professional education sector where the most important objective is to get people through demanding and difficult professional examinations. It has a simple message, anyone can pass examinations with the right attitude and the correct techniques.

The techniques themselves have been tried and tested many times and are proven to work. They work at all levels of the exam system be it for entrance exams, GCSE's, A level, degrees or professional exams.

The E word interviews

At the end of certain chapters you will find an interview with individuals who have a specific interest in exams or the exam process. These interviews or conversations are not so much about what is in the book, but what people thought and felt about some of the issues within the chapters. The purpose is to further explore some of the issues raised and to introduce thoughts and ideas other than my own.

At the end of chapter 2 there is an interview with a mother of two children currently taking exams. Chapter 3 has an interview with an examiner, chapter 5 a secondary school teacher and chapter 8 a student currently taking final level professional exams.

The book includes an abridged version of these interviews but if you would like to hear them in full please go to http://kaplan-publishing.kaplan.co.uk/eword. Here you will not only find the recording of these interviews but recordings of interviews with other people who all have something to say about exams.

Acknowledgments

The purpose of this section is for me to thank everyone who has helped me in the writing of this book. But it is incredibly difficult to thank people in proportion to their contribution. Some of the ideas were almost certainly the result of snatched conversations at the photocopier or from asking probing questions of some of my colleagues and noting their responses. Yet there are some people who I would like to thank that either helped with a specific task or contributed in other ways in making this book possible.

So thanks go to everyone who kindly read the manuscript and offered me excellent advice. Sue Davis, Jenni Hudson, Karen Quinton and Graham Hambly.

Particular thanks to Lucy Henman, and friends. Lucy not only showed an incredible attention to detail but worked diligently and thoughtfully bringing ideas and opinion from her own world. She shared her personal experiences of learning which helped me see things from a different perspective.

Thanks to Zoe Robinson who is always constructive, eloquent and tactful and manages to find the time to talk to me on the phone often at length...To Julie Hughes for her support and confidence that there was in fact something worthy of publishing. And to Gregory Leigh for his guidance as to how the book could be improved, providing both criticism and praise in equal measure.

And to people who have inspired me and given their thoughts and ideas freely, including my friend and colleague Chris Cain who introduced me to the world of exams and exam skills and who taught me so much. Perhaps most importantly that the student is always the most important person and what they want should remain ever present in your mind.

Finally, a big thank you to all my students who perhaps unintentionally but never the less have taught me so much......

This book is dedicated to my wife Julie and daughter Bethany because without their love and support the book would still be a dream instead of a reality.

Table of contents

THE
E
WORD

Fast track reading

This book has been structured so that you can find out specifically what you want without reading the whole book. So should you wish to be selective about what you read, use the fast track guide below to help.

Do you want to know more about how the **exam system works and what exams prove?**

About exams

Do you want to know more about the **skills and techniques that will improve exam success?**

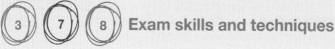

Exam skills and techniques

Do you want to know more about how you learn and **how to learn more effectively?**

Learning

Do you want to be more motivated and develop the right attitude so that studying becomes easier?

Motivation and attitude

The book also follows this simple formula

Knowledge + Examination skills + Mental attitude = Exam success

Take the techniques discussed in chapters 5 & 6 to understand and learn the relevant knowledge for your chosen subject. Add to that the exam skills in chapters 3, 7 and 8 and finally add the right mental attitude highlighted in chapter 4. The result, exam success.

Why you should read this book

I have thought long and hard about my motives for writing this book. As I watch my daughter Bethany, who is 14, grow and develop I can't help wondering whether the education system and the way it rewards success is best for her. When I think back to my school days, which were happy but largely unimpressive from an academic point of view, I don't remember feeling under pressure at any particular point, I just went to school. It may be my memory that is at fault or that it was just my perspective as a child, but it all seemed simple and straightforward.

My concerns for Bethany are not about what she is being taught or how she is being taught, neither is it about the school she goes to. It is more about the expectations that are placed on her by me and society in general with regards to what she needs to achieve in order to be considered a success. A large part of her life has already been affected by one simple thing: her performance in the exam room. Often from the results of a two or three hour test, (exam always sounds more serious) much will be assumed as to what she is capable of, and, at times form a judgment as to who she is.

And she is just 14, so what about the rest of us. How have and will our lives be changed by the results of a three hour exam?

This book is for anyone who has to sit an examination and wants to improve their chances of passing. The techniques described have been developed whilst working in the professional education sector where the key and, most important objective is to get people through demanding and difficult professional examinations. I have achieved this consistently for many years and so make no excuses for the simple message that this book carries. Anyone can pass examinations with the right attitude and the correct techniques.

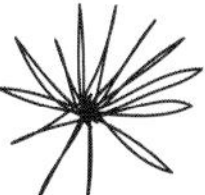

Anyone can pass examinations with the right attitude and the correct techniques.

I believe the techniques that have been used in the professional education exam market for many years, are transferable to all examinations.

In this book I am not trying to come up with a significant concept or learning technique that I can proclaim to be new. I would not be so bold or so naive. I believe that most people already have the necessary skills in order to achieve the success that they desire, be that in exams or life in general. I also believe that most solutions to problems and techniques to solve them are already well understood and recorded in detail somewhere. The internet must hold the answer to everything if only you ask the right question!

Neither is this book intended to be an academic thesis nor a round-up of all the available theory and it is acknowledged that one bit of research doesn't make a case.

I would like to think that this book will provide a focal point and motivation for people. It is a collection of concepts and ideas gathered from some of the best thinkers and writers on personal development and learning. My part has been to bring together these thoughts with some of my own and present them to you in a way that is easy to read and understand. I hope that the techniques will prove invaluable to you in dealing with the rigours of the modern exam focused world and will help you and others achieve the success you richly deserve.

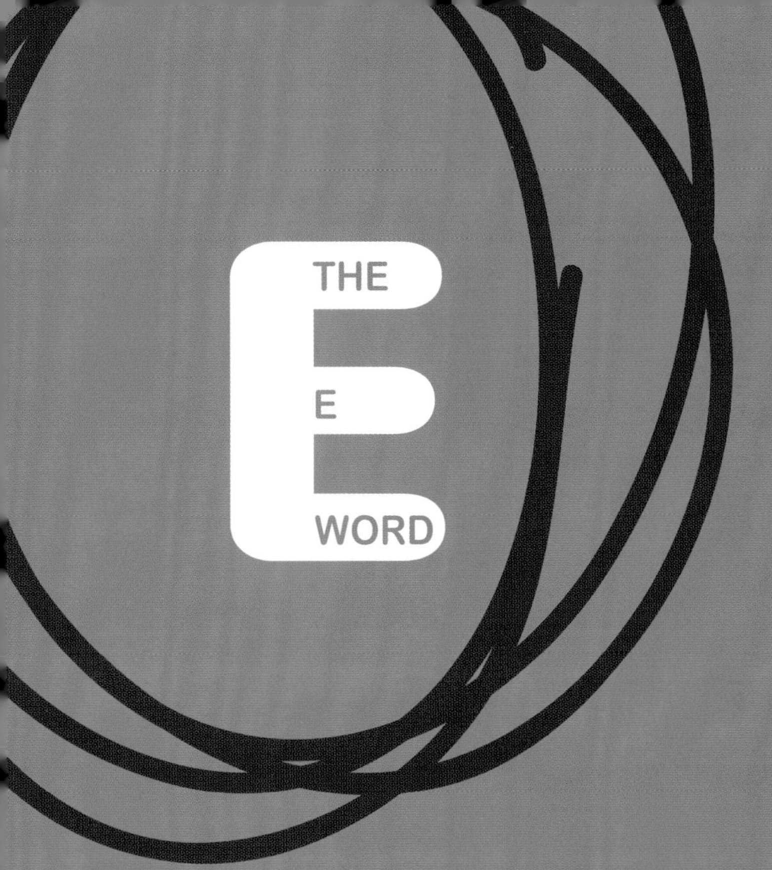

chapter 2
The system – how examinations work

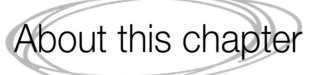

About this chapter

Although I have met people who like exams on the whole most people don't. So it seems appropriate that a book about exams should contain some debate as to the motivation behind sitting the exam in the first place. What is so important to you, that you are willing to give up much of your free time and work incredibly hard to achieve?

As each year passes succeeding in the exam room seems even more important and the gap between those with qualifications and those without gets larger. But at what price, what impact are the pressures created by this exam mentality having and is it worth it?

In order to pass examinations it is useful to understand the system by which you will ultimately be judged. This chapter ends with a look at the framework of marking guides, syllabuses and model answers that examiners use to assess performance. The idea is simple: if you understand what they are looking for and the system in which they operate, passing the exam becomes a whole lot easier.

What gets measured, gets achieved

We live in a society where increasingly all things have to be measured: your weight, your health, your age, your intelligence. People measure all of these things and more. They then put you in order, comparing you with other people. This order is how you are perceived by others and, perhaps more worryingly, how you perceive yourself. It is here that examinations play their all important role. They provide a form of measurement: a way of differentiating good from bad, successful from unsuccessful.

League tables

There is another element of this measuring process that is worth identifying. Once an order is established it becomes possible to identify who is at the top and perhaps more worryingly who is at the bottom, by publishing a league table.

In the world of education the league table has become a tool by which parents, employers and students judge the quality of the education they will receive or have received. And with the publication of national statistics, showing that more students pass their GCSE, A levels or degrees than ever before, the league tables show clearly that the nation is getter brighter!

This system of measuring applies to companies, schools, hospitals, sport and, of course, even people. People who pass examinations are successful and people who don't are not and climbing the table becomes the key objective.

And there's more.....once you have a table, you can look at people's relative position in the table and make predictions. You can decide whether a person will go higher or lower. The interesting thing is that this is all perfectly logical, rational and sensible. In fact, it is hard to think how we functioned as a society before we had league tables.

We live in the era of the league table.

Now you may at this point think that I am about to argue that we should stop this league table mentality and return to a time when decisions were left to the judgment of trained respected individuals within an accepted framework of collective responsibility. On the contrary, I can't help thinking that the measurement process, does have merit and can have purpose if only it were used properly. League tables in themselves are fine, it's the way that people interpret them that is the issue.

Let's consider some of the merits of league tables:

- The criteria for why a person or organisation is number one is known and in the public domain; although it could be argued that people don't look at the criteria or even understand it. The fact that someone is at the top is often sufficient.
- An easy and logical means of making decisions. The best school is the one at the top of the league table so that's where we should send our child.
- A method of communicating to those within an organisation exactly what the objective is and what they need to achieve to be rewarded.
- By asking questions of people who have moved up the league table, you may learn how it can be done.
- A process for measuring improvement.

So, there is much value in a table that separates winners from losers.

We have always had league tables to some extent in sport showing winners and losers. They create a competitive environment and a winning attitude. When people become obsessed about something, they are clear in what they want and what specifically it will be like when they get it. They have what is called a "well-formed outcome": a very clear picture of success as it would appear to them. That picture may be to see themselves at the top of the league. This in itself can be hugely motivational and may well be one of the unconscious techniques used by champions. But has this created a "win at any cost" mentality: is this the reason we have drugs in sport, where people will put the winning above their own personal well-being? Is this the reason footballers will appeal for fouls when in fact none took place?

So leader boards and league tables, like so many things, are not good or bad they are good and bad, probably in equal proportions.

To continue with the sporting analogy, for some people, maybe those who get a buzz from competing and winning, league tables can be very motivational representing the standard by which they measure success. But what about the people who want to or have to play who are never going to get to the top and are faced with the reality that they are always going to be lower down the pecking order? Are they destined to be second rate, there to make up the numbers, underachievers in everything that they do? This is where this measurement process falls down. It is not motivational for the vast majority of people. In fact it can be the exact opposite; it can be very de-motivational as it can provide evidence of their inability to be successful and exactly how much of a failure they are.

There is one final insult, not only do you start to believe it, you begin to behave as if it is true and others begin to treat you as if it is true.

You are so much more than your position on a league table.

League tables are in everyday use. Have you ever had a conversation where you have been asked what you do for a living? Does the person have a genuine interest in the answer or is it perhaps simply a way of labelling you, putting you in order so that they know how to treat you and also how they should behave?

This reminds me of a story…

A recent skiing holiday in France was the backdrop for this interesting conversation. Newly arrived in their chalet, one of the families in our group was greeted by a well-spoken gentleman who, with an outstretched hand, announced, "Hi, my name is Richard. I am an airline pilot, what do you do?" The response was a perfect foil for this ranking question: "Nice to meet you, Richard, could I ask do you own the plane or are you just a driver?"… Fantastic.

I have taken much inspiration from people I have met and books that I have read over the years. One such text that I make several references to throughout this book is *Frames of Mind* written by Howard Gardner in 1983 which is said to have had a profound impact on thinking and practice in education. I am reminded here of something Gardner says:

Pay one's respect to school and test results but do not let them dictate one's judgment about an individual's worth or potential. In the end what is important is an individual's actual achievements in the realms of work and personal life. These judgments can and should be made directly, not via the proxy of a test score.

To me, this can be used as an inspirational slogan and a useful belief for you to see beyond the simple ranking judgments that we are all perhaps guilty of making from time to time. It is a plea to look beyond the test result. But do we? Or are we inclined to look for a more objective way of summing up an individual? In many ways this is more truthful: "Yes, of course they have many qualities, but you can't deny the simple fact that they failed the exam."

Gardner's statement is inspirational, and should perhaps be written on the back of every exam results slip handed out or as the footer to the email containing the results. It does not, however, suggest that you should or can ignore the test results. It suggests that you should "pay [your] respects". For some people, this may, as Gardner suggests, be little more than a cursory glance at what someone has achieved in the exam room. But for some, perhaps many employers, it will be a defining judgment.

Education, Education, Education

League tables are certainly evident when it comes to examinations, in particular examination results. The media publish their own tables showing the "raw examination" results. It is argued that the performance of the school can be seen in its examination success, full stop. In fairness to the likes of the Sunday Times and others, they suggest that it is perhaps only one aspect and parents should also consult OFSTED reports for guidance on other aspects of particular schools. I have to say that, although statistics can be very misunderstood, there is a wonderful clarity in this exam results only approach. This is, however, where the league table mentality begins to take over. Parents wanting to make the right decisions read them in order to provide guidance as to whether their child should go to a particular school. A-level students wanting to find the "best" university look at them to ensure that not only will they end up with a degree but a valuable one. And in industry, senior managers and board directors will look at them to ensure they are sending their key people to the best MBA provider.

You're momma sure does care about your education, son.

Forrest Gump, movie

It may not be the main focus for the decision and yet what parent, when given a choice, would send their child to a school that, according to the latest government statistics, is bottom of the ladder, or which top employer would send their most valuable assets, their people, to a training provider at the lower end of the scale? So it is unfair perhaps to blame the school or university for wanting to be at the top of that league table if ultimately it is one of the main criteria by which they are judged.

Concerns regarding this exam mentality are already being expressed.

NEWS A recent report from academics at Durham University..... found that schools routinely drilled 11-year-olds to pass the tests. It questioned whether such "teaching to the test" had led to sustainable improvements in pupils' understanding of English and maths.

"Without question, national tests dominated classroom teaching of both subjects in these schools for a large part of year six," the report said

Source – The Times, December 2005

This is an ongoing debate and you could argue a healthy one. The answer as with many things is that we should strike the right balance and from the rhetoric we get from both sides it does not seem we have found that yet.

Do examinations prove anything?

If you are going to spend hours working towards a qualification, it is important to consider what you will actually end up with. Examinations are tests which aim to determine the ability of a student. They are set in order to identify that the student has acquired the necessary skills as deemed appropriate by the examiner or examining body.

Although they can take many forms (simulations, case studies, computer based, etc.), for the purposes of this book I am mainly addressing issues that arise from a handwritten, timed exercise where questions are asked and predetermined answers are expected.

So, here is our first introduction to the structure of an examination.

The structure of an examination

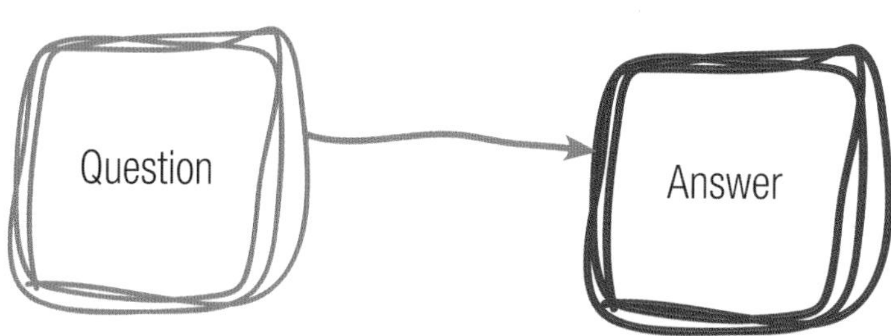

A bit obvious, I know, but it does demonstrate the simplicity of what is required to pass an exam. To pass an exam you have to get the answer to the question as identified by the examiner – or at least satisfy the main requirements of what he/she is looking for. This also highlights a very different way of thinking about examinations and is the basis for "the exam focused approach", something that we will develop in later chapters. Why don't we learn the answers to the questions rather than learn everything?

So, if you pass the exam, what have you proved?

In passing an examination, you have proved that you knew the answers to questions the examiner set. To be precise you have only really proved you knew enough to get a pass mark. But you have certainly not proved that you understand everything about that subject and you have not proved you could work unsupervised in practice: knowing what to do is not quite the same as doing it. You have in fact simply passed. So, when people pass examinations, it proves something, but perhaps not exactly what you thought. This is not to say that examinations are easy or to underestimate their importance, but simply to clarify exactly what has been achieved and so begin to clarify what skills are needed.

There is a tendency to suggest that people who pass examinations are clever or intelligent. But what do we mean when we call someone intelligent? This can of course be a circular argument. If you pass an exam you are thought to be intelligent, so intelligence is passing exams. In fact, one definition of intelligence is that you have a high IQ (Intelligence Quotient). Your IQ can be established by taking an IQ test, they are widely available on the internet. But what is an IQ test if not some type of exam. *

*Footnote – It is fully appreciated that an IQ test is far more than a simple test. However don't forget that Alfred Binnet originally developed the IQ test to identify children with learning needs and not to create some sort of an exclusive club.

How often have you heard the statement that he may have passed lots of exams but he has no common sense? There is in fact no universally-accepted definition of intelligence, so, for the time being, let's assume that being intelligent means you can pick up information easily and answer questions correctly. These skills are certainly required in passing any exam. More on intelligence later…

As long as learning is connected with earning, as long as certain jobs can only be reached through exams, so long must we take this examination system seriously. If another ladder to employment was contrived, much so-called education would disappear, and no one would be a penny the stupider.

E M Forster

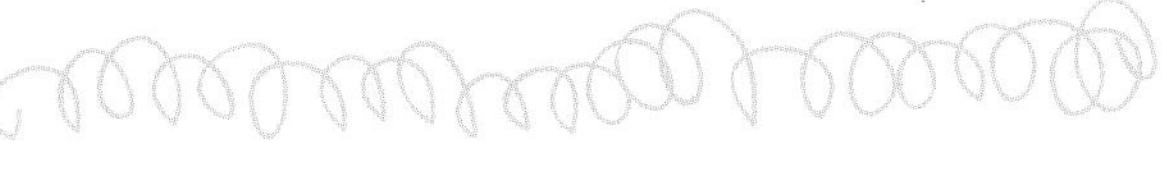

Examinations do prove lots of other things

What we can say is that an average student who passes an exam will have proved they can apply themselves to a task in hand. This requires, amongst other things, concentration and motivation. They have also proved they can work within a timescale, not just on the day of the exam but in their approach to studying. These attitudes and skills are important; in fact, many of these are used far beyond the examination hall.

How many students go to university and study a particular subject, only to take a completely different career path after gaining their degree? The attitudes they develop and the skills they learn are a by-product of the knowledge acquired and yet in the long run they may be the most important. So, in order to pass an exam, perhaps we should take a closer look at the attitudes and skills that are tested rather than the knowledge itself. We will do this later in the book.

Motivation

Motivation can be thought of as the wants, needs and beliefs that drive an individual towards a particular goal or perceived outcome. If you can focus on a given task, then there has to be a sense of value in achieving the result of that task: it must satisfy something deep inside. If this were not the case then you would simply give up halfway through. This would suggest that we need to be motivated in order to pass an exam and that motivation has to be personal.

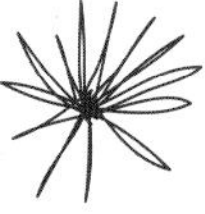

In order to be motivated there should be a want a need and a belief. The secret is to identify exactly what you want, what you need and what it is best to believe.

Concentration

To concentrate is to direct your mental powers or your efforts towards a particular activity, subject or problem. It implies that you should focus on the task in hand and learn to avoid distractions. For some people, concentration comes easily; for others, it might involve removing all distractions by locking themselves in a room. Some people's concentration may be improved by taking more frequent breaks or listening to music. By identifying what is best for you and the environment in which you perform more effectively, you have the beginning of an understanding of your own learning style.

A study conducted by Russell Poldrack of the University of Texas, Austin, has thrown some light on concentration and how the brain works.

Poldrack explains that the brain learns in two different ways. One is called declarative learning. This is the learning of facts and events that can be recalled and used whenever required. The second involves habit learning which is more to do with the process of learning and involves repetition and trial and error.

Poldrack goes on to say that although both of these types of learning are useful they tend to compete when distraction occurs and the habit learning is the more likely winner. In general, therefore, distraction is almost always a bad thing and so should be avoided.

Time management

Time cannot really be managed; it is outside our control. All we can do is spend our available time more effectively. This probably translates as spending the time available on specific tasks that are helpful to you in achieving your objective.

When a student begins a course of study, there are effectively two stages. The first is the learning stage; the second, the revision phase. You have to learn to manage time in both these areas of study.

Stages in learning

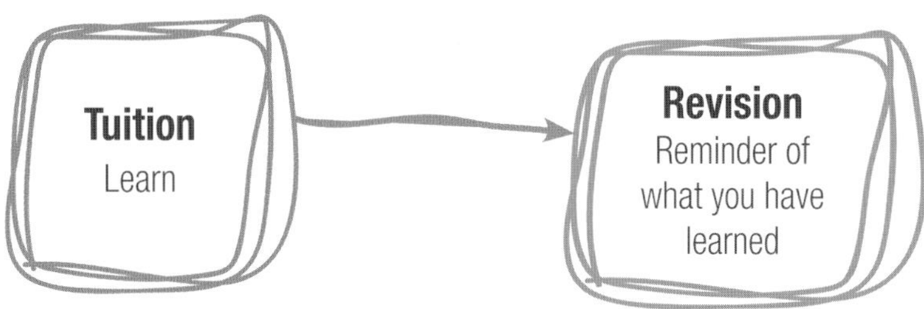

So, it might be a good idea to learn techniques that will improve your concentration, motivation and time management. This will help with the learning process and thus provide a more efficient way of transferring the knowledge from the page into your head. The chapters that follow will give some really useful tips and techniques as to how some of these areas might be improved.

Does exam success make you happy?

If I think back to my own examination successes, I don't remember being happy when I learned that I had passed. The emotion that is most prominent was relief, in the sense that I would not have to sit that exam again and I could move forward. You see, not everyone is motivated in the same way. What you feel is partly the result of how you are motivated - more on that in chapter 4.

So, if you want to be happy, do you believe that passing examinations will make you happy? Interestingly, happiness, which can be elusive at the best of times, is not guaranteed with the passing of an exam. So what does it give you? Well, how about a great sense of achievement? It is a statement to others that you have worked hard and have succeeded in what you wanted to do. Secondly, it will build your self esteem and help you develop a type of confidence that only comes from being successful in a chosen field. Others will congratulate you and, as a result, treat you differently. Thirdly, it will open doors to opportunities that simply would not be possible without the piece of paper that carries the statement "Congratulations, you have passed".

And, lastly, it is a tangible and permanent reminder of success that can never be taken away.

Examinations don't guarantee happiness but they do give choice and make many more things possible.

Do any of these result in happiness? Of course not, but then nothing does guarantee happiness; happiness is personal, created by each individual and dependent upon their aspirations and motives. So, exam success does not guarantee happiness, but it will give you a sense of achievement, confidence and provide opportunities that would not normally arise. And that in itself is a cocktail for success.

Exam success will give you choices

If league tables are not always helpful and exam success does not guarantee happiness what should we do? Well, here is my view and in many ways the basis and motivation for this book. In the short run we cannot change the system, league tables of one form or another are here to stay and will continue to be used by others to judge and make decisions about people. Yes, the criteria may change, new targets may be introduced but the process itself will remain intact. It would give me great pleasure to take the moral high ground and suggest that none of this exam stuff matters – the only thing is that it does.

I remember reading once that successful people are people who identify the criteria by which they are judged and simply look to satisfy that criteria. What an excellent goal, be the person you are going to be, follow the dreams that you have, but first and foremost get the exam results!

Exam success will give you choices, it will change how others look at you and perhaps more importantly it will change how you feel about yourself…

But first and foremost get the exam results!

We all start from the same basic raw material; we all have skills, some things we are better at and some things that we are not so good at. This is partly our genetic make up. What we need to do is make the most of what we have. You may not be the best mathematician in the world but you still need to pass the maths test.

So if examinations are so important what do we need to do to be successful? Is there a magic formula?

Most people think that passing examinations is about knowing the answer, so in simple terms all you need is knowledge of the subject. However, knowledge alone is not always sufficient to ensure success. I have known students more than capable of passing given what they know of the subject and yet they have still failed the exam.

But what else, why did those students fail? Perhaps they ran out of time or simply misread the question. This would suggest that exam skills are also a very important part of our formula.

And finally what about the student, who has good exam skills, has worked hard and learned the subject, yet lacks self confidence, constantly doubting their own abilities, and so produces answers that seem unconvincing and sometimes are simply wrong because they change their minds at the last minute? They may even run out of time – not because of poor time management but because, halfway through the exam, they had such strong feelings of self-doubt and an inability to put down the correct answer they began to sweat and were unable to think straight: exam nerves set in.

For me exam success is about three things:

- knowledge of the subject – obvious, but important to state
- examination skills – the approach and specific techniques that will help, both before and during the exam
- mental attitude – a belief in yourself, an ability to cope with stress and the motivation to succeed.

Knowledge + Examination skills + Mental attitude = Exam success

And although a simplification of the exam process it underpins the structure of this book.

What impact are examinations having?

There was a time when children did the 11-plus, O-levels and A-levels. That meant that there were only 3 formal levels of assessment before higher education. Also, the information regarding the results of these tests was not as much in the public domain as it is today; the "league table" had yet to be developed. There is no doubt that we receive far more information than we ever did in the past. This public accountability is probably the result of a more aggressive media, the development of the internet and perhaps the public's lack of confidence in government institutions and professionals. Schools were selected less on their exam results and more on word of mouth, where your siblings went and proximity to where you lived.

We have a very different world today. Children who go on to higher education now have potentially 5 formal levels of assessment and this is even after the key stage 3 tests were recently scrapped. The results of how schools perform are in the public domain for all to see. This means that parents can make more informed choices, in theory at least. Most often, though, the league tables are confusing as the government continues to change the criteria as to what makes a school successful. This confusion may result in parents taking little time to review the facts and simply look at the top five schools in the league table, not really thinking about what was required to get to the top. It is fair to say that any league table should be considered alongside other important sources such as Ofsted reports, school profiles and school prospectuses. But how many parents have read the Ofsted report for their child's school?

Although to some extent this is my world and so I could offer a view, I do not for one minute think it would be the answer, just an answer, and so for the purpose of this book I will side step the "which one is right" debate. Instead I will take the more pragmatic view, that in the short run at least, examinations are going to play an ever-important part in an individual's development from the ages of 5 to 25. And, as the labour market becomes more competitive and the pace of change accelerates within the workplace, it is hard to see the role of formal qualifications decreasing, no matter how old you are. In many ways this shift towards increased testing and measurement was another factor in the writing of this book. If examinations are going to play such an important part in all our futures then we should at least try to make the whole experience a little easier by learning new techniques and strategies for coping.

Examinations are going to play an ever important part in an individual's development.

Those in higher education are no longer immune from these pressures. Those living university life, have to deal with the added responsibility of having to pay off their loans together with the uncertainty of actually getting a job at the end. Oh, and yes, you do have to pass with as high a grade as possible, and high grades are on the increase. According to a report by the Commons universities select committee in 2007/8, 13.3% of students receive a First, the highest grade possible – twice as many as a decade ago.

New students face £23,000 debt

Students starting university courses in 2009 can expect to graduate owing £23,000 according to the Push student debt survey.

BBC news 18th August 2009

Stress and examinations

Stress is a condition or feeling experienced when a person perceives that "demands exceed the personal and social resources the individual is able to mobilize" (mainly attributed to Richard S Lazarus).

Stress is one of the unfortunate by-products of this league table, result-orientated process. Yes, it is good to have a target to work towards, but if you believe that the target is beyond you, then, when threatened, the body will react. The body will release hormones that would normally be required to help us flee from a potential predator. These hormones increase blood pressure, produce sweat that cool the muscles that would be required in a physical confrontation with danger. The problem is when threatened in the modern world without the physical release, these reactions generally result in all the above physical changes and what we commonly call stress.

Who ever heard of a child with stress? Years ago there were very few but now it seems a common occurrence. ChildLine, the children's charity, had this to say following research undertaken in 2004: "The number of young people calling ChildLine because they are struggling to cope with the pressure of exams has risen by over 50% - the biggest annual increase since the charity began taking calls."

The stress relating to examinations can be so severe that it can result in suicide. Unfortunately it did not take a search on Google long to come up with the specific instances where children had taken their lives due to poor exam results or simply the belief that they had not been successful.

RESEARCH

A study from the Centre for Family Research at Cambridge University (August 2004) says 66% of parents believe their child is more stressed than they should be. The Soothing Family Life report claims stress at school can also cause problems at home.

A framework of skills

If we are creating a more stressful environment, and the environment is here to stay, we must provide a framework of skills that can be used to help. One of the great attributes of human beings is the ability to learn how to survive no matter what the circumstances.

Most people assume that to pass an exam you need to have the answers to the question and that this requires knowledge. This, of course, is true but, without the skills to deal with the time pressure and the stresses that the examination process brings, knowing the answer is only part of the solution. In chapter one I identified three elements of exam success, suggesting that knowledge was not necessarily the most important part; perhaps now you can see why mental attitude was included and why, along with exam skills, it should be ranked equally with knowledge as being a key determinant of exam success.

- Mental attitude – dealing with stress, motivation and attitude.
- Knowledge of the subject.
- Examinations skills – both before the exam and during.

We will look at stress and strategies to cope in more detail in chapter 4 and exam techniques in chapter 8.

Having discussed what exams prove and the impact they may be having, this next section considers the framework in which examiners work. I don't think it appropriate that we look at any individual examining body or examiner here. All we need is to establish the process that an exam paper will go through and what specifically you can do in order to help the marker give more marks.

Examiners are only people

I have read many examiners' reports and none have said that they wish to make the exam so difficult that no one can pass. Examiners are standard setters, guardians of quality; they are not trying to make things hard for the student. They are professional in their approach and would consider equality and fairness to be important. They want to ensure that every student who has a script marked will be treated in exactly the same way. Marking and assessing students' scripts is an important business that is taken seriously by all involved. Some examinations are, however, harder than others and, as a result, some students will pass and others will fail. If you think about it, one of the things that makes an exam valuable in the first place is that it is recognized as being difficult to pass. So don't think of the examiner as the enemy: they have a framework and a set of rules to follow, and they will follow them, as this is the best way to ensure fairness.

Examiners are not the enemy, find out exactly what they want by reading any articles or guidance notes they produce and then do exactly what they say.

The guidelines

All examiners will have a syllabus, or, at the very least, a framework . It establishes what has to be included and to a certain extent what is not. Off the back of this, there will be a more detailed syllabus and teaching guide to drill down into specifics. All examinations will have some form of a syllabus. Most examiners will start by looking at what can be covered and begin setting the exam paper with these boundaries in mind. The only problem with this approach from a student's perspective is that different examiners will consider different areas to be more or less important.

For example, the statement, "Students are required to have a good knowledge of the mountains in Italy," could be examined in many different ways, and, although some clarification of what the examiner does want will take place, there is always some degree of interpretation.

So, although a quick look at the syllabus will give the student some ideas as to the topics that should be studied, the best place to find out what is meant by "a good knowledge of the mountains in Italy" is to find a past examination paper with a similar question and read the examiner's answer. Not only will this provide you with the relevant knowledge, but you will find out exactly what the examiner wanted. Working from past examination questions is a major theme of this book and a significant factor in passing exams. Where you are faced with a "brand new" exam and so no past papers exist, there will often be a pilot paper and this will have to be your guide. It won't be as comprehensive but is better than nothing.

The marking process

Following the examination, all scripts will be collected and counted to ensure none are missing. They will then be sent to the respective examining body for distribution to the examination team, normally headed by an examiner who takes responsibility for the integrity of the process. The examiner will then generally arrange a markers' meeting with members of his/her marking team to discuss issues arising. This might include clarification of alternative acceptable answers not mentioned in the examiner's answer, technical queries and any specific issues regarding interpretation of the question.

One of the things to bear in mind is that, when markers mark, they are themselves going through a similar process to students. They have to read the question (carefully), and they have to understand the requirements. In fairness, they do have the answer and are not sitting the exam under exam conditions, a situation that, as we are aware, does result in considerable stress. They are, however, engaged in the marking process in deep concentration for many hours, aware of the responsibility to the students to ensure a fair mark is awarded. It is when in this deep state of concentration that students should be aware markers can switch off. They will be looking at script after script and after a while they can begin to blend into one. This is not a dig at markers, just an acknowledgement that students have to be aware that this can happen and so should present the information in a format that is more likely to grab the marker's attention. This can be as simple as leaving white space (gaps between paragraphs) to ensure that the marker does not skip over a very valuable and mark-worthy point. It also identifies why it is so important to write neatly. Markers do get bored with marking and if they cannot read what you have written they are not necessarily going to go out of their way to do so. And why should they?

The criteria for equality – marking guides

Apart from a model answer which incidentally can have several different possible solutions all considered acceptable, the markers will have a marking guide. The purpose of the marking guide is to create some degree of consistency in the marking process. It also helps clarify some of the more important elements of the answer. Remember, the main focus for the examiner is equality and fairness and this is a useful way of helping with that objective. The marking guide will contain information on exactly where marks are awarded for specific tasks.

For example, if the question asked:

Can you calculate the number of patients that should go to the Doctors in January and discuss why this might be different from last year? **10 marks**

The marking guide would break this question up into separate sections.

Calculations of the number of patients	4 marks
Discussion	6 marks

The marking guide can of course be even more detailed, providing specific aspects of the question that should receive marks.

These marking guides can be a very useful study aid. As examinations are time pressured it is really useful to have an understanding as to where you should spend your time to maximize the marks. They may not always be available, but when they are they provide invaluable guidance as to exactly what the examiner is looking for. More on the use of marking guides later.

In conclusion

It was important in a book about exams that it started with a debate as to their importance, what they proved, the impact they are having and how the exam system works.

The fact that league tables may be flawed and that people use them as a way of helping them make decisions is not really the issue. People will always look to differentiate one group from another, be it by the football team they support or the colour of their skin. In the society in which we live and at this point in time, the score that you get in an exam does matter and qualifications are important. Rightly or wrongly people will judge and form opinions about you, using only your qualifications as a guide.

But even when you pass the exam does it prove anything? As we continue to see an ever-increasing number of students passing exams, does this mean that students are improving or does it mean that the exam is getting easier? This is just one of the problems with examinations, even when you pass, what it proves is open to interpretation.

So do exams prove anything… yes, they probably do. They prove that the student can be self-motivated, able to concentrate and perform to an acceptable standard within a time constraint. These are life skills and can result in success in many other areas. And although exam success may not result in happiness it can provide you with a great sense of achievement, build your self esteem and open doors to opportunities that would not otherwise be available. In short exam success gives choices, what you then do with those choices is up to you.

The modern examination system is having an impact upon children, parents and students. There are more examinations than ever before and stress has become an acceptable consequence, almost the norm, so what can be done?

You may think that I am about to suggest that the system is flawed and needs changing, which in fact might be the best long-term solution. It is not, however, the point I wish to make. My objective is far less ambitious, I simply want people to recognize that these problems exist, and, secondly, that the best short-term solution is to develop a sufficiently robust mental attitude to 'cope' and that this, along with good examination technique, will be enough to get you through.

The E Word Interviews.

A Mother

Q Could you introduce yourself and tell us about your interest/involvement in the exam process?

Yes I am a mother of two boys, one aged 15 who is just about to take GCSE's and my eldest son is 17 just about to take A levels and looking forward to going to university.

Q Do exams prove anything?

Exams are obviously a proof of a standard of work and passing means that you are capable of achieving that standard, does passing prove you are intelligent, I am not sure, but exams do represent a standard and level of skill that in the context of say driving a car needs to be verified, we wouldn't want people driving on the road without having passed the necessary test. So yes exams are important, in certain places.

Q Are your children constantly doing exams, constantly assessed?

My two are in the independent system and so don't sit the SAT's exams, but they are constantly assessed in other ways throughout the year.

Q Are they conscious of this level of assessment or is it just the norm?

I think it's the norm for them now, they expect to be tested on all their work, although they are constantly moaning about all the exams they have to do but they accept that they have to do them. They do sometimes feel hard done by because studying and preparing for exams affects their lives, every evening they have to cover work ready for exams, they don't really have a time when they don't have something to do. There is always one exam or another that every week they have to revise for. So it has a huge impact on their life outside of school and on our family life as well.

Q What are your expectations of them?

Starting back with my eldest son, when he took his entrance exams into the senior school, he had actually been at the junior school, he failed. He felt that he was a failure and although everyone came up to him and said how sorry they were, this somehow made him feel worse. But then motivated to prove that he was capable of much more, he has worked extremely hard and has subsequently gained excellent GCSE results.

I suppose we had an expectation that he would do it and we knew he could, but he took it on himself to do the work.

Q Thinking back to your own time at school, what are the key differences for your children?

The thing that strikes me is how much harder they seem to have to work than I did, especially going back to GCSE's. We started a two year course and did not have exams until the end of it, where as now they are constantly having modules that they have to sit, course work that has to be in all the time, it just seems to be one round of exams after the other.

I can't remember any pressure when I was doing my O' levels or my A levels it all seemed to pass in a happy blur....It's not however necessarily worse, just different.

Q When choosing a school, what were the criteria you looked for and how important was the academic success of the school?

The criteria I looked for mainly for my eldest son , was that he would be happy. At his previous school he wasn't coming along very well, they said he was slow, that he was a typical boy not concentrating and we felt that he had more to him than that and so we applied to a school that had smaller classes. My youngest son did not have to apply as he was already at the school.

What I had heard about the school which was largely hearsay from other people was that this was a good school and when I asked what that meant they said that their children were happy , which was my main criteria. They had smaller classes which we felt my eldest son needed because he did lack concentration. It also offered a lot of sport and the pastoral care was very good. I didn't really look into anything else other than he would be happy there.

Q Do you think that the sacrifices you have made as a family will be worth it?

Only time will tell wont it if it was worth it. I can see how much it has brought on my children, the confidence it has given them. It has also given them a lot of other things. They have to get up early so they are quite disciplined, they have to cover a lot of work in a short space of time to be prepared for all the exams that they sit, so they have to be organised. So it has given them a lot of life skills above and beyond education.

Q Do you think they have an appetite for learning or will they be glad when it's all over?

I think they will be relieved when it's all over but then they are onto the next lot aren't they, it doesn't stop there, GCSE's into A level, A levels onto university and if they want to go into the professions there will be professional exams. I think they just go along with the flow now really.

They have a little moan every now and again but they know that's what's expected of them and that they will be judged by the results they get, not by us but by the universities and employers. My eldest has to get 2 As and a B and anything less is not acceptable, so he has got to rise to that challenge and do it. I think they know themselves really, it's drummed into them at school.

I certainly don't expect it of them.....

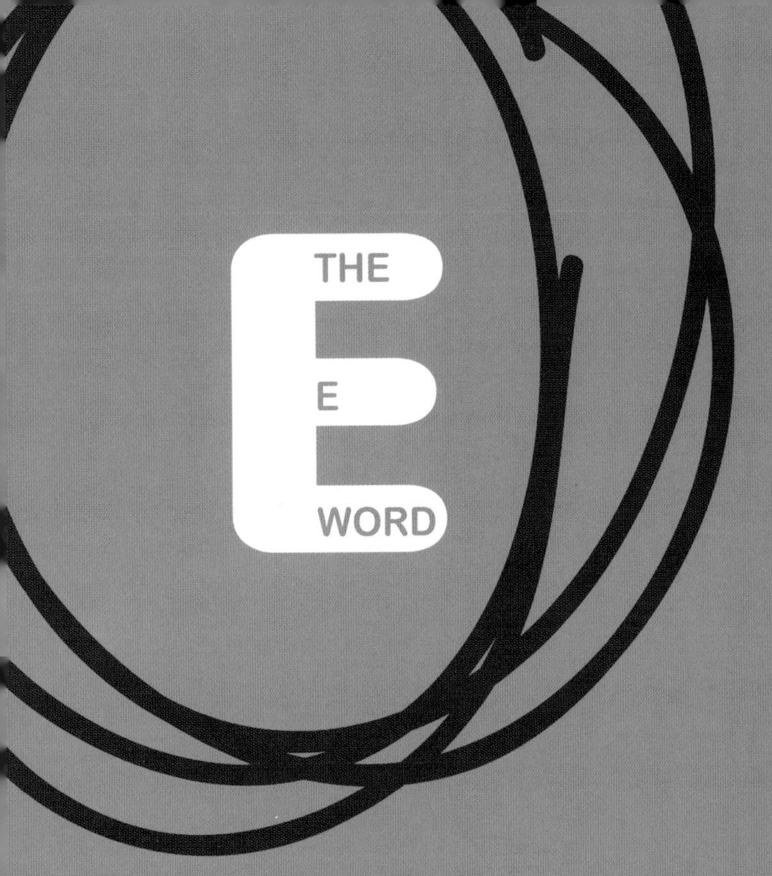

chapter 3
What's stopping you from passing?

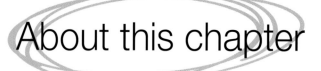

About this chapter

Lots of books on examinations will list out why people fail examinations. This often includes not reading the question properly, not managing time, etc. While much of this is sound advice, and I have included methods to avoid these types of mistake in chapter 8, we need to start at a more fundamental level: by looking at you.

It's not that you keep putting off studying; you are going to do it next week, when you have a little more time to concentrate. Perhaps you think you already know all the answers so see little point in taking advice from others, or maybe you believe that on the day of the exam all the answers will come into your head as if by magic, a "what will be will be" attitude and so what's the point in studying? You've either got it or you haven't. Do any of these sound familiar? Taking a look at yourself from a distance can be very illuminating and can help identify areas that are acting as barriers to exam success.

It is also time to question and maybe change the approach you are using to study. The method you used in the past might have been fine, but is there a better method of studying that gives you an improved chance of passing, is there a more exam focused way to study? I think there is...

In this chapter, we meet some characters that may be familiar to you, and introduce two very different methods of improving your chances of passing exams: the traditional approach and the exam focused approach.

Who you are, how you behave and how you think

Every now and then I think it is important to look at yourself and think about how others may see you. This is perhaps easier said than done. If you ask someone, "Do you think I am confident?" first, they may not give you an honest answer, and, second, the answer they give may jar so much with your own perception that you argue with their comments and so little is achieved.

So rather than thinking of yourself may I introduce you to the following characters? They are not you, but are representative of extreme personalities that I and my colleagues have come across over the years. So, read a little about them and think about whether some of their personality traits are similar to yours. Do you think about exams and yourself in the same way they do? If so, make a mental note and understand how what they think and how they think can have a detrimental effect on their exam performance. Remember, these people are not real and they are not you...

The Vicar (David)

David is the Vicar; he is happy, confident, and almost serene. When people talk about the exams he seems relaxed and little bothers him. If there is something presented in class that is complicated and hard to understand, he probably won't understand it, yet, in discussions with his fellow students afterwards, will appear unconcerned. While others worry and go home to learn more about this difficult topic, David is happy to carry on chatting and does little work on the area. Others around him believe that to have so much confidence he must be a genius; he must be one of those people who picks things up very easily at the last minute.

This is, of course, not true. David is not a genius: he just has a very powerful belief that what will be will be. He believes that if he is meant to pass, he will pass, so what is the point worrying about it? He is also very confident in his own abilities and thinks that if he reads something it must be in his head, and so on the day the information will come flooding out. In fact, revision is probably not helpful, because the information will "fall out" while he is practising questions and so will not be there on the day of the exam. He believes that he thrives on pressure and so, when faced with an exam question he cannot do, he will look up to the sky and pray for divine intervention and the answer will be delivered as if by magic. Yes, he has worries when he can't do something, he has those niggling self doubts, but, if you always hold the belief that it will be better next time, then the problem you have now will disappear and so is not a problem at all.

David however cannot avoid the facts and, when the exam results arrive and he has failed, what does he do? Well, the Vicar remains true to his character and can be heard making comments such as, "I was, in fact, very pleased with my exam result, given that work pressures meant that I hardly did any studying. I am sure next time I will get it."

Now, the Vicar has many great qualities, and people who suffer from exam nerves could do worse than use some of his techniques. However he has a simple failing: he thinks that exam results are pre-ordained; he thinks that if he is meant to pass, he will and, if he doesn't, there will be a reason. He will then look for that justification: the exam was too hard, I was not taught that, the examiner is clearly mad - none of it is his fault. The problem is, however, that his belief in divine intervention stops him studying; it stops him going back over the area he did not understand and working at it until he does. So, although he feels relaxed and happy whilst studying, he lacks that nervousness and pressure that is necessary sometimes to be successful.

Exam results are not pre-ordained, success is in the hands of each individual and so to believe what will be will be is not helpful as it removes the good pressure that is required to learn something new or challenging.

Marvin

Marvin has never been lucky; in fact, he is probably the unluckiest person on the planet, or so he believes. He will never see the good things he has achieved, only the bad ones: he is a glass-half-empty sort of a guy. Marvin believes in luck, and, a little bit like the Vicar, thinks that events are predetermined and whatever those events are they will be bad and will happen to him first. When Marvin looks at his friends, they are all much cleverer than him; they pick facts up quicker and seem more confident. He walks around looking at the floor and generally feels sorry for himself.

The facts, however, tell a very different story. Marvin does very well in the tests and comes out above average. If he did in fact pass all his examinations first time, he would think that the only reason he did well was because he worked so hard and that others achieved similar results with little effort. Marvin is motivated, he does want to succeed and so does in fact work hard and thus deserves the success he gets. When he does fail at something, he seems to get pleasure in telling others how right he was: "See? I told you I found this hard." He was also heard to have a conversation with one of his teachers suggesting that, although he had passed everything first time, he was convinced he would fail this time because the law of probability suggests that you can't pass everything all the time and so failure was guaranteed.

Learning is not a fun process when you think you are going to get the hardest exam paper and all the questions on the paper will be the ones you haven't revised.

The first thing is to recognise that this state of mind is not helpful and neither is it true, however looking on the dark side can be useful on occasions. Creating the expectation you are going to do badly will make success even sweeter when everything turns out fine. Just make sure that when you look back on the event you recognise your success and don't once again make it look like some sort of failure.

Alec Smart

Alec is oh-so-clever; he is naturally talented and thinks he knows everything. He has proved this to himself on many occasions. He has a high degree of self-confidence and has achieved some exam success already. Alec is, in fact, about average. He does work reasonably hard but is so self-opinionated he finds it difficult to accept advice from others. He thinks that when he writes an answer in the exam the marker will score it highly because what he has said is correct. What he fails to appreciate is that it may not be what the question asked for or the examiner wanted. To Alec, though, that doesn't matter. If he does not do very well, that is because they are wrong and, in some circumstances, even stupid. He is also likely to miss the important aspects of a question by jumping to a conclusion and so, once again, tells the marker what he thinks is important, not what was required. His hand writing is generally scruffy but that's okay because lots of clever people have poor handwriting, doctors for example, and it is the marker's problem to sort that out. They get paid to mark his answers regardless of the quality of his presentation.

Now, being an independent thinker is excellent and having self-confidence and your own opinions that you can support by argument would be considered excellent qualities. However, having some degree of humility and taking the advice of others can be equally important, it's just that Alec can't do this. So when Alec is given advice he generally fails to take it.

Improve your handwriting, look carefully at what the question is asking, pay attention to how many marks there are within the question as it gives an indication of how much to write – these are great exam tips, and Alec will simply ignore them all.

Mandy Monday

Mandy Monday is a busy person: she has lots of other interests, is always doing something, and is never idle. Very rarely does she sit back to reflect and sees little point in planning; in fact, she never has the time. Mandy is very efficient at dealing with problems. If the phone rings, she always answers it; when someone wants to see her, she always makes time; however, sometimes, she simply fails to achieve the one task that she wanted to do that day. Mandy is a student who wants to succeed, the only problem is that because she is so busy she never gets round to doing anything and constantly puts off studying. She is the ultimate procrastinator. She would always be starting her diet on Monday and so it is with studying. She wants to study and makes every effort to do so and yet this effort never seems to translate into an effective study session.

So, Mandy is not a lazy person, far from it. She does, however, get her priorities confused. Dealing with things as they arise is efficient. It is, however, not particularly effective. To be effective, you have to achieve your goal or objective and that is to do well in the exam. So Mandy is lacking in focus: her desire for exam success is not powerful enough to change her behaviour. If it was, she would find herself ignoring the phone calls and concentrating on studying. Many students suffer from the Mandy Monday syndrome; they will tell others that they want to study, that they want to pass, and yet never seem to get around to it. The final characteristic is that in order to avoid feeling bad Mandy will tell herself not to worry she will start studying in earnest on Monday…

Mandy would benefit from clear objectives, a large helping of motivation and a timetable to remind her when things need to be done. But unfortunately she is too busy to sort it out.

Peter Perfect

If Peter Perfect was married to Mandy Monday, they would either be the world's most perfect couple or hold the record for the fastest divorce. You see, Peter is the perfectionist: he is highly motivated and focused. In fact, when he sets his mind on doing something, he will think only of that thing to the exclusion of everything else. Not only does Peter focus on his objective with a passion, he will also achieve it with the very highest degree of accuracy and quality. Peter believes that if a job is worth doing it is worth doing well. His parents taught him this rule and it is the philosophy by which he lives. Peter does, in fact, sound perfect. Having a high level of attention to detail and getting things right are excellent qualities, but not always, and not always in examinations.

The problem is that Peter cannot see the bigger picture: he fails to appreciate that sometimes you simply cannot work to such a high standard in the time available and so you have to "do your best" in that time. When studying, Peter is unable to leave a section of the text until he fully understands everything. He will constantly go over and over things until he has mastered it. At this point you might be thinking, so what is wrong with that? Well, nothing, if you have limitless time, are always in the right frame of mind to study, and don't ever get tired. The truth is that you may not grasp something first time and going over it at that point is not always helpful. It takes far longer because you are in the wrong state of mind or may simply be tired. Better to accept that you have not understood that area, mark it accordingly and come back to it, perhaps with the help of a teacher or when feeling more responsive. Peter does, however, eventually grasp the issue but it takes an age. As a result of staying with this one point until he feels he fully understands it, he is unable to keep up with the workload and so gets behind the point where he should be.

You see, Peter is not a genius; he is just a normal intelligent student with a personality that demands perfection.

Peter has more problems in the exam. When faced with a question that has an answer, he simply has to solve it. Time passes without him noticing and, as with studying, although he may ultimately get it right, the clock will beat him and he will fail to complete the test paper, leaving many easy areas in the exam untouched. Some of the answers to other questions could have been answered in a fraction of the time and scored higher marks.

A word of advice

Dear David, Marvin, Alec, Mandy and Peter

You all have many great qualities and personalities that will enable you to be successful in whatever career you choose. David, your self confidence and ability to put off worries and pressures can be helpful not only in exams but also life in general. Marvin, when you look at a situation, you tend to think that something will go wrong and so make contingency plans, this means you are always prepared. Alec, so self-confident and forceful in your views, you may become a leader of people. Mandy, you have a strong work ethic and are highly motivated.

And finally, Peter, your attention to detail and your tenacity in wanting to get the right answer is a much valued skill in the work place.

Yet all of you need to adapt the way you think and behave if you are to succeed in examinations.

David, examinations are not predetermined: the effort you put in will change the result. Don't rely on divine intervention, by working hard you are more likely to achieve your goal of exam success.

Marvin, you are a good learner, your results prove that. Luck can play its part, but not so much as you think. Developing a positive attitude will help your ability to learn and make the whole process easier. If you think of yourself as lucky, you will begin to notice a difference in how you feel.

Alec, humility is the breakfast of champions. Have confidence in your own views but pay attention and take the advice of others and don't be so quick to judge, they might be right.

Mandy, you need to set your objective more clearly and use your instinctive motivation to achieve it. At the moment, although you want exam success, it is not important enough to you.

Peter, in examinations you do not have all the time in the world and so sometimes you have to do the best job in the time available. This may mean leaving a question without proving the answer. You will have to learn the skills of time management and prioritisation

The perfect student

The perfect student, of course, does not exist. But, if he/she did, they would recognise the personality traits that are not helpful in the exam room and adapt. They would not change who they are but perhaps change how they think.

The approach and techniques

Another reason that some people are unsuccessful in examinations has less to do with who they are or how they think, but more to do with the approach they take and the techniques they use. These could be referred to as exam techniques or study skills. Let's look at these in a little more detail by breaking them down into three separate areas:

- the overall approach to examinations
- the techniques used to learn (learning skills)
- the techniques that can be used both before and during the exam (exam skills).

The overall approach to examinations

This is more to do with the strategy of passing rather than the operational aspects. We need a master plan that we know will take us in the right direction. In this section, we consider two different approaches: one "the traditional approach" and two "the exam focused approach".

The techniques used to learn

These might also be considered learning skills. They are the little tricks that can help us learn more effectively. They involve gaining a greater understanding of yourself and how you learn as an individual. These are discussed more fully in chapter 6.

The techniques that can be used both before and on the day of the exam

These are the really powerful exam skills: how to revise, how to read the question properly, how to write an answer and how to manage time. These are dealt with more fully in chapter 8.

Traditional approach

The traditional approach to education and passing examinations is perfectly logical and practical. It is a process best described by the use of a diagram:

The traditional approach

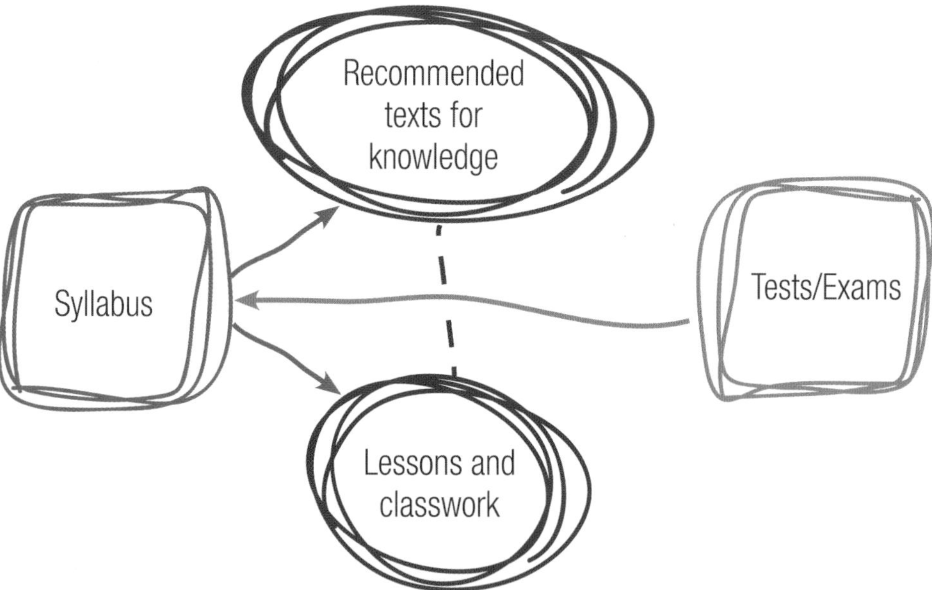

The syllabus contains the framework and boundaries for what is and is not examinable for a particular subject. It is written to provide guidance for all concerned: examiner, publisher, teacher and student. The logic goes like this: the examiner needs to read the syllabus in order to ensure they do not ask questions on areas that are beyond what is required at this level. They then produce draft questions that are of the necessary standard based on each area within the subject. Now this is not always as simple as it sounds as examiners need to make sure the questions are neither too difficult nor too easy. As well as the examiner, there is normally an assessor, someone who will review the question for quality and consistency. Both follow standard procedures and guidelines that should result in exam questions being produced, year in and year out, that are not only within the syllabus but of the necessary standard.

Where material is specifically prepared for a particular examination, the publishers will review the syllabus and begin writing material. They will want to ensure that what is included and explained within the text is clear and easy to understand. Also, they will not want a text that contains examples that are beyond the required skill level or are outside the scope of the syllabus. The teacher will then use the syllabus and the textbook to prepare the lesson plans as part of the preparation for classroom delivery. This is an age-old process and generally works very well.

The student may be encouraged to read the syllabus to be clear themselves as to exactly what can be examined and what they should study. The examination is very much seen as a test of the student's ability and knowledge of the subject. If the student produces an answer broadly in line with the examiners then they will be considered proficient in that subject.

So what's wrong with the traditional approach?

Imagine you are about to begin studying for a new subject, one that you have little or no knowledge about. Let's also assume that you are studying from home. What do you look at first? Maybe the text book, you turn to the contents page and look at the 22 chapters that you are required to read and understand. Perhaps you then get a blank pad of paper, a pen and a coffee and begin by reading chapter one. This is the chapter headed introduction to the subject. You probably make notes as you go through so that you have something to read that summarises the main issues raised.

This could well be a very successful process, and you might feel you have gained a good understanding of what is required, the difficulty of the subject and learned some new and interesting facts and concepts. All you have to do over the next few months, prior to taking the exam, is work your way through the next 22 chapters making notes as you go. Time plays an important part in this study process: in theory with limitless time you could learn everything in the book... or could you?

It's all about focus

We now need to start to understand more about how the brain works and people learn. Faced with a list of 22 chapters, it becomes very difficult for the brain to take everything in at once, so it becomes necessary to break the chapters down, separating the important from the less important. But how do you do that? Which chapters are the most important, and, even when you have identified what you consider to be an important chapter, what topic or point should you concentrate on within that chapter?

The complexity of learning

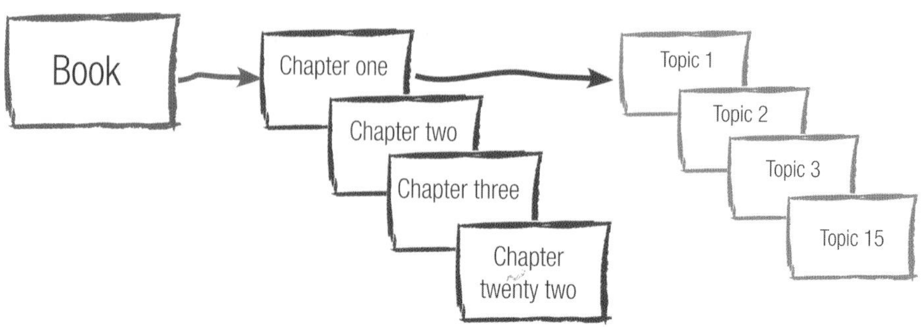

So, although the brain has a huge capacity to learn and absorb, it is going to need some help. But what can you do, using the traditional approach? Well, you will probably begin ranking the importance of the topics using two criteria: one, the thickness of the chapter, and two, the level of difficulty of the topic. This may sound strange, and you may not fully appreciate that you are doing it. The logic, although a little flawed is that it must be important if there is a large amount written about it and, secondly, if it is difficult to understand you need to spend more time on this area whether it is more important or not. Let us also assume that you begin to run out of time and therefore have to make some difficult decisions: do you leave some chapters unread and, if so, which ones? What will happen if you get a question that relates to one of the areas that you missed out?

This often leads students to the opinion that they have to learn everything to avoid taking any risks. Many teachers and lecturers will advise against not covering "the whole syllabus".

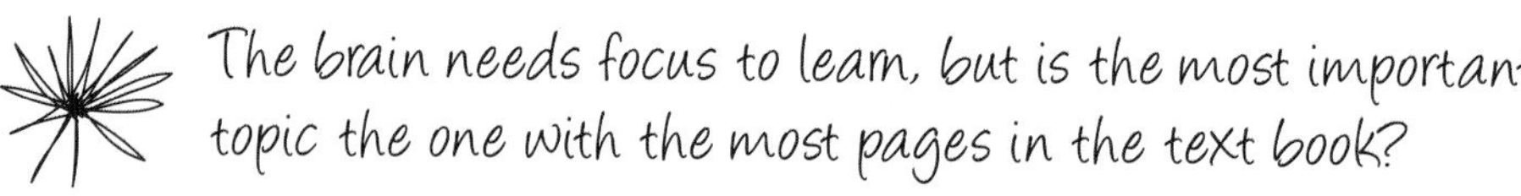

The brain needs focus to learn, but is the most important topic the one with the most pages in the text book?

The brain is desperate for some form of differentiation: in order to begin the learning process, it needs to be able to differentiate the important from the unimportant, it needs FOCUS. This is where the traditional approach begins to break down. The syllabus may give some rankings, and this can be very helpful, but how many people will spend their study time in proportion to the written guidance? They will almost certainly spend time on the difficult areas and the ones that are covered more in the textbook. Whether you want to or not, it will prove necessary to choose specific topics and spend more of your time on those areas in preference to others.

This process of reducing large areas into small ones is called chunking. Not only is this a very useful technique for learning, it has many applications when it comes to memorising.

We are concerned more in this chapter not with the process of chunking but with which topics to choose. Once you have identified the topic, the brain can begin breaking down the topic into even smaller chunks until they can be learned and mastered.

The revision period

The examination date is set in stone, and so, as you move into the three weeks before the exam (the revision period), you should now be revising all of the areas you have learned. Instead, you may still be wading through some of those chapters. You may also have convinced yourself that there is little point in practising questions until you have learned everything. This is a fatal mistake. If you go into the exam room without going through a sensible period of revision which would include lots of question practice you are considerably reducing your chance of examination success.

Think about other areas where it has been necessary to learn. Driving a car or learning to swim perhaps. Would you go swimming for the first time having only ever read how to swim? My guess would be that you would have watched people swim, perhaps read a little, booked on a course with an instructor who would get you in the water and make you practise swimming.

So why would you think about sitting an exam without practising? The practice can take many forms; it does not have to be a full three hour mock. Simply looking at the questions will help your understanding of what the examiner is asking so that you can prepare more accurate and informed answers. It does, however, involve a point where you put the text book away and start to do examination questions.

There is one very interesting aspect to the traditional approach to examinations that is worth exploring.

Let's assume that you did not quite manage to read and make notes on every chapter, you simply did not have time. So, you left out some of the areas that you did not think were that important, based on a feeling perhaps, or, as I suggested before, the size of the chapter. You did some revision, maybe reading over the notes you have made and looking at a couple of questions. And so, as prepared as you will ever be, with the confidence you have studied everything that you could using the syllabus as your guide, but having spent little time on practising exam questions, you enter the exam room. Although reading and making notes is an excellent way of learning, to be effective you need focus, you need to have "a geography" to your knowledge. There needs to be mountains and rivers, you need to know which areas are more important than others. If all your knowledge is flat, it all feels the same to the brain and this makes it hard for you to access that information when required. Exactly how you get this clarification as to what is important or not is in the next section, exam focused learning.

You turn over your examination paper and start to read the questions. Most of the questions are on areas that you have read about, so you feel you can at least attempt them - all except question 2, that is. This is a 25 mark compulsory question based on an area not well covered in the textbook and not one that you looked at in any detail. You made no notes on it and so have no idea what to do. You begin to panic and feel ill-prepared for the whole exam. Your internal dialogue, the little voice in your head, starts telling you that if you can't do this question, chances are you are going to fail… and so the pressure builds.

The post arrives early, and you are well aware that the results could be out today. You open the brown envelope and pull out the computer-generated slip that contains your grade. Marginal fail, your worst fears have been realised. After a few days of feeling down, you start to think about what you are going to do next. Perhaps you should not continue with this exam, it is clearly too difficult – remember question 2? You simply had no idea as to what this question was asking. You must have to be really clever to pass, and it is clear that you are simply not good enough!

This is of course one response, but what if you decide to give this exam one more go?

And this is the really interesting thing about the traditional approach. You have learned one major lesson. Rather than start with chapter one, you will make sure that you study the chapter that included the subject matter examined in question 2 of the exam you just sat. You are not going to be caught out with the same question twice. When you come to resit the exam this will be one area, should it come up again, that you will be prepared for.

The most important lesson you have learned is to practise the question you could not do in the exam last time. Now that's focus.

So, maybe there is a better way of learning than starting with the syllabus, which does not always provide sufficient guidance as to what is important and what is not. Why not start with the questions: questions that have been examined in the past, questions that are on areas that the examiner thinks are important, questions that you can practise and use to assess your performance?

This is the principle behind the exam focused approach.

The series of events I have described above as to how the individual studied assumes they are studying on their own. Many students will of course be in a classroom environment with an experienced teacher delivering the material in a way they think best. I would still, however, argue that when it comes to passing examinations, focusing your effort on the examinable areas will improve examination performance – with or without the teacher.

Now, this may be a contentious point and my intention is not to be critical of teaching methods or the broader considerations of education and teaching. A teacher is attempting to do so many more things than to get people through examinations. They are there to facilitate learning in a more holistic way. They are looking to engage the student in the world around them and not simply prepare them to regurgitate facts so that they can pass an exam. This book, however, is not about teaching. It is about the best way to prepare students for an examination, and I would argue that the best way to do this is by focusing on the important areas and those important areas will be ones that have been examined in the past.

My Mama always said you've got to put the past behind you before you can move on.

Forrest Gump, movie

The exam focused approach

Start with the end in mind

This process, although simple in my opinion, is also profound, as it deals first with what you want and then with what you should do to get it. What you want is to pass the exam, not to learn everything and then check what you have learned. I realise that some people may not agree with this, but in the exam-passing world it is true.

The model then works backwards from the objective, to identify exactly what is required. The interesting thing is that we do not end up with the syllabus. This is in stark contrast to the traditional model, which starts with the syllabus and works forward.

The sub-heading *Start with the end in mind* was a term developed in order to clarify what this model was all about. It was not until later that I came across a very similar saying "begin with the end in mind". In Steven Covey's powerful and influential book, The 7 Habits of Highly Effective People (published 1989), Covey suggests that we should create a powerful and meaningful image or picture of the end of our life, and use it as a frame of reference or criteria by which everything else is judged. By creating this visual focal point, the individual can see what they want and this gives direction and motivation sufficient to influence the thoughts and actions they have today.

We can apply the same simple idea to passing exams. Although learning is a wonderful thing we don't want to learn for learning sake; we have another objective and that is to pass the exam. The exam focused approach uses the objective of exam success and works backwards. Knowing what your objective is also helps clarify what you are trying to learn. You will never be able to learn or understand everything, but you may be able to learn enough to answer a question.

Having identified our end goal, we then work backwards asking the question, How do I do that?

- End goal - I want to pass the exam – How do I do that?
  ANSWER: Obtain the pass mark – How do I do that?
  ANSWER: Pass the exam question – How do I do that?
  ANSWER: Practise past exam questions on the examinable areas – How do I do that?
  ANSWER: Identify examinable areas – How do I do that?
  ANSWER: Analyse past questions, ask an expert and read examiner's guidance.

We have now identified the key steps to exam success, and these should provide us with the focal points that will guide our study.

The exam focused approach

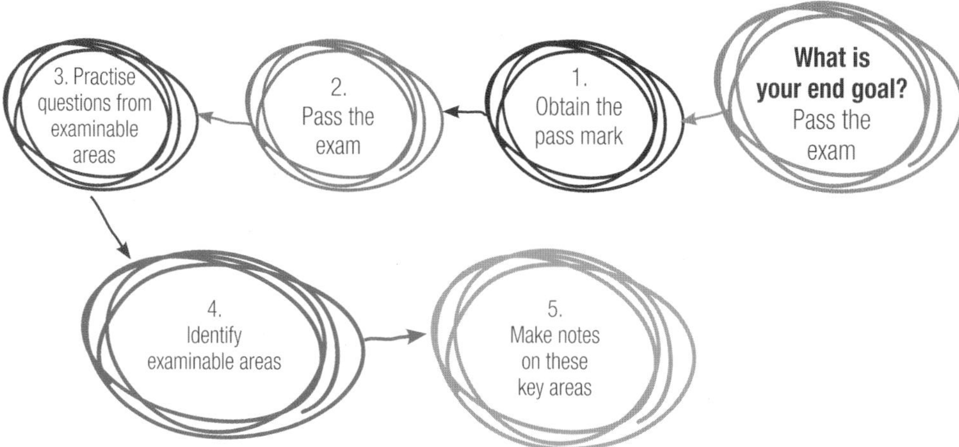

1. Obtain the pass mark

This is perhaps the first and most obvious question. The pass mark will be different for every exam that you study. You would also imagine that this would be a very easy figure to find out. For example, the pass mark for GCSE is somewhere between 16% and 50%. In 1995, following an investigation by the Times Educational Supplement, it was discovered that pupils scoring as low as 16 percent could be awarded C grades in one Edexcel maths GCSE paper and an A* grade with only 47 per cent in an AQA business studies paper. The analysis also revealed that pupils could achieve a C grade with 20 percent in AQA GCSE maths, 25 percent in classical Greek or 28 percent in physics.

Degrees are usually graded with 70% and above being the class or grade boundary for a First, 60% to 69% for a 2.1 and 50% to 59% for a 2.2 and 40% for a 3rd.

So what seemed like a perfectly reasonable question, "What mark do you have to get to pass this exam?" is perhaps not so straightforward. In the absence of an absolutely definitive answer to this question, I am going to assume that 50 percent is the pass mark. Just think about that for a second, that's 50 percent... WOW! That means you can get the exam half wrong and still pass. Maybe passing examinations is not as hard as it at first seemed.

The idea that you don't have to be perfect to pass can be something that you should hold on to as you work through your course. When faced with topics and subjects that seem impossible to understand and when you begin to doubt your own abilities, simply keep reminding yourself that you can get 50 percent wrong and still pass.

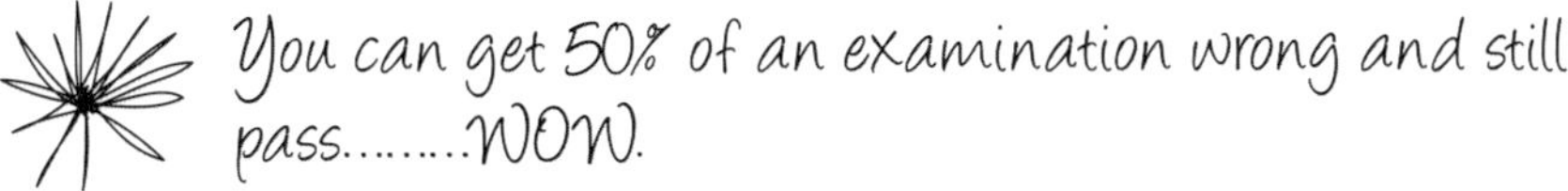

You can get 50% of an examination wrong and still pass.........WOW.

Now, although this fact is reassuring, it only works in certain circumstances. You must attempt all of the questions! If you do not attempt 100 percent of the paper then your odds are reduced considerably.

- If you miss out 10 percent of the questions, then you have to get 56% of what you do to pass.
- If you miss out 30 percent of the questions, then you have to get 71% of what you do to pass.

So the message of the 50 percent rule is that you must attempt every question.

2. Pass the exam

In order to pass the exam you have to turn up on the day, complete your answer booklet with sufficient content to score more than 50 percent (see above). Let's just think how easy this would be if we had the actual exam, yes, the one that you are about to sit next. What if you log on to this site, www.yourexamquestion.co.uk, and there it is, the exam question?

How good would that be, rather than studying from the textbook or attending any lectures, you simply have to practise this question. What would your chance of exam success be then? Think how much better it would be if you had the answer as well. You could look at the answer and know exactly what the examiner wanted. By then practising this question over and over again when it came to the exam you would be able to produce the perfect answer. You would score 100 percent.

Just joking! Of course the web site does not exist, and I am sure you would not look anyway - it would be cheating, wouldn't it?

But this process is important if you are to understand the purpose of practising exam questions. We don't have the exam, but we do have past exam questions that the examiner has set. They will be indicative of the style of that examiner, the level of detail they consider necessary and will give some clues to the areas that are most important. This is a very important aspect to the exam focused approach, a theme that is continued below.

3. Practise questions from examinable areas

So we don't have the exam but we do have lots of exam questions from previous sittings and we can practise these. We still need to be even more focused, because we really want to start by practising only on the key examinable areas not all questions. How you identify the key areas is explored in more detail below, but, clearly, if we analysed the past questions this would give us a very good starting point. Keep things simple when you first do this. Look back at, say, the last four years worth and then go further if time allows. The further you do go back the less relevant the question may become, particularly if there has been a change in examiner or syllabus.

There are two further aspects that need clarifying with regard to practising past questions. You need to do this under both exam and non-exam conditions.

Exam conditions

Exams can vary in both style and duration. It is, however, important that you practise questions that are the same as those you will come across in the exam hall. This type of exam question is often called a mock, a simulation of what the real thing will be. We should also challenge one of the myths about mock examinations. They should not be thought of as predictive. After all, it is only one exam, if you did several and the results were very high or very low than it may give an idea as to what will happen on the day. The reason I make this point is because a lot of people don't like to take mocks because if they do and fail, it will mean they will fail on the day of the real exam. This is not helpful and not necessarily true. The mock may well be three to four weeks away from the real exam and much can be achieved in that time. Practising mocks is part of a process and the more you practise, the better you get. You don't stay the same. So why should you believe the result will be the same?

There are however a number of good reasons why you should practise on a mock. Firstly, you need to find out how you perform under time pressure. Being aware that you have to finish in the time available is not the same as actually finishing in the time. It takes practice.

I always remember an interview with Rolf Harris: he was describing how he used to produce drawings on live television using large paintbrushes and paint rollers, the type that would be used in decorating your lounge. Rolf had five minutes to complete the whole painting, and, remember, it was live so there was no opportunity to do it again. As most people are aware today Rolf is in fact a very talented artist and so producing the drawings was relatively easy. But he used to practise these paintings over and over again, not to perfect his art but to make sure he could finish on time.

This is a perfect example of the benefits of sitting a mock under timed conditions.

Another significant reason for sitting a mock is that you need to practise writing. If your exam is computerised then this may not be such an issue, but, for handwritten exams, you need to know that you can physically produce an answer in the time allowed that can be read and understood. This might be obvious but you would be amazed at the number of students who produce answers that cannot be read as the handwriting deteriorates towards the end of the exam. Once again, this practice will not only give you an opportunity to review what you have written but also allows you to look objectively at your handwriting and see if it can be read.

And the last reason for practising under exam conditions is that during this mock you will more than likely face a question or part of a question that you find difficult to answer. How are you going to cope with this feeling? Do you look at the question and think I am going to fail if I can't do this, or do you look at the mark allocation and think, this is only 10 marks, I can have a go at this question but will probably not pass it, maybe I can get 3 out of 10? This is called "managing ignorance": dealing with a situation that we have not come across before. This is a skill and needs practice. Once again, knowing that you should behave in this way is not the same as behaving in this way.

Non-exam conditions

This refers to a situation where you take a past exam question and read the requirements and then the question itself to see if you can do it. If, after some thought, you feel that you are not sure what the question is looking for or in fact even how to start it, then you simply turn to the answer and find out. This has got to be the easiest way to find out exactly what the question is about, what specifically the examiner meant by the terms and expressions used, and what the answer is. This you would obviously do before you attempt questions under exam conditions as many of the things you will learn from looking at past exam answers will help when it comes to the mock exam.

There is then, however, some work to do. Read the question again, this time noting exactly what the answer said whilst carefully underlining the important points. You need to be able to understand the answer, if not, then study the topic again sufficiently so that the answer makes sense.

From the key points that you identified in the answer, you need to make notes. They should be short and to the point, you are simply trying to reduce the answer to the very essence of what is required to pass.

Then look at another question, can you answer it? If not, then look at the answer and go through the whole process again. Then look at another question, can you answer that one? No? Then go and look at the answer…

This is a process and, in going through each of the questions, you will become more and more familiar with the answers and the examiner's style. You will begin to notice that certain questions crop up time and time again – if not exactly the same, consistent themes will emerge. And here is the point: if you have looked at say twenty past exam questions, are confident that you know the answers and can produce them when asked, you are ready for the exam and cannot be any better prepared. Studying from the syllabus will never give you this level of focus or readiness.

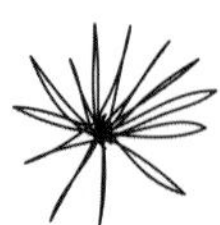

Look at twenty past questions, be confident that you can produce those answers again; you can never be better prepared for the exam than that.

So which are the twenty most important questions? They should be the twenty questions based around the key examinable areas – see below. However, a good start would be to simply list out the last twenty questions going backwards in time. It is important to state here that, when I talk about past questions, I am thinking more about questions that are 15 to 50 marks in length rather than short form or multiple choice. Practice and repetition are key: if you keep going over the twenty questions, eventually you will simply begin to remember some of the answers, and also, more importantly, remember the process that led to the answer.

4. Identify examinable areas

Analyse past questions

The most examinable areas are those areas that have been most frequently examined say over the last 4 or 5 years. Note that this can change if there has been a new syllabus and/or a new examiner. The example below assumes all questions are of equal importance, i.e. there are no compulsory questions. If this is not the case, then you have to pay more attention to the compulsory topics rather than the options. The first way to identify the areas is to prepare an analysis.

Let's consider the following example:

The topics for a particular subject range from A to J, 10 in total. The analysis looks at the exams over the last 5 years and there are 5 questions on the exam each year.

	2009	2008	2007	2006	2005
1	**A**	E	G	J	D
2	**A**	F	I	I	**A**
3	C	G	C	H	H
4	D	**A**	H	**A**	H
5	J	H	**A**	B	I

Key areas are:
A is the key examinable area; it has come up in every single exam.
H has come up in 4 out of 5 of the last exams.
I has come up 3 times but not recently.

Minor areas are:
C,D,J,G which have come up twice and B,E,F (only once).

This now gives us focus: we must look at topics A, H and I first. Every single angle relating to topic A needs to be learned, practised and mastered. It is going to be in the exam. H and I were not examined last time but are clearly key areas; they are very likely topics for the next exam and therefore must also be considered key examinable topics this time.

If we think of time as fixed, then we must choose what we do in that time. The exam focused approach prioritises time and ensures we cover the most important first.

Key areas and time

If, as sometimes happens, time simply disappears then we are still in a better position with the exam focused approach because we have at least covered the most likely exam topics.

The exam focused approach is about focusing on what are the most important areas, the areas that you simply must learn. After that, you are free to explore the other topics. That doesn't mean you have limitless time on the examinable areas, because you don't. You still have to cover all three key areas and some, if not all, of the minor ones. So you will have to set a maximum amount of time for each area and may, in fact, find you have to move on before you have fully grasped everything; it's all about time and priorities.

The best way to prepare for exams is to focus on past exam questions.

But this is just question-spotting

The criticism often levied at the exam focused approach is that it is simply question spotting and that, by trying to guess exam topics, you are taking a big risk because what if something comes up in the exam that you have not predicted, what will you do? It is also associated with lazy learners, students who can't be bothered to learn everything and so only learn a small amount of what is required. The first criticism is often put forward on the basis that the alternative "traditional approach" enables students to cover everything, but it does not. Students still end up guessing but, as suggested before, they guess on the basis of the size of the chapter or even the toss of a coin. And, as to the lazy student, it is often said that the smartest people try to find the easiest way to doing something. Well, what's wrong with that? This is just the easiest way, not the route a lazy learner takes.

The exam focused approach is just a better way of focusing your time, or would you rather leave it to chance?

Questions give focus

In 1974, Tony Buzan wrote his now famous book Use Your Head. This book has been translated into over 27 languages, published in 100 countries, and has sold well over a million copies - this is one popular book. And, although I would recommend you buy this, the reason I mention it here is because of an experiment that is referred to in the book to explain the power of the brain and how effective mind mapping is.

Tony Buzan tells us of two sets of students. The first were told that they would be tested on the whole book. The second were told that they would only be tested on the two or three major themes in the book. Both groups were in fact tested on the whole book, which one would think to be unfair to those that were told to only focus on the main themes.

To the surprise of many, the students who 'focused' only on the major themes did better on questions pertaining to the whole book as well as those only pertaining to the themes.

According to him, the themes act as 'grappling hooks' to which the knowledge attaches itself. The knowledge forms strong associations with the themes, enabling the knowledge to be more easily understood and recalled. And here is the link with the exam focused approach, not only does focusing on key examinable areas provide direction as to what topics you should study and where you should start to study, but it also helps you learn more about the less examinable areas.

I will just repeat that, because I think it is so important.

You also learn more about the less examinable areas.......

How? Well, because when you are studying the key examinable areas and questions related to those areas, there is always something relating to other, not so important, less examinable topics. Past questions may be on similar topics, but they are not the same questions. And, because, as Buzan said, there is a central theme, the knowledge is more easily learned and remembered. Simple!

Read examiners' guidance

Analysing past questions is one way of spotting key examinable areas. Another is by reading any guidance produced by examiners. If at all possible it is a good idea to identify who your examiner is as this can sometimes reveal preferences that may result from their individual bias. Also, if they produce articles in any educational publications these carry more importance than articles produced by other authors. I realise that this may not always be possible as some examining bodies keep this information confidential or have a team approach to the exam production process. This guidance might take the form of articles or examiners' reports.

Examiners' reports can be found by identifying your examination body's website and then following the links to the necessary documents. As well as the examiners' reports many of these bodies provide the all-important past papers and marking guides. More on marking guides in chapter 8.

Start out by simply looking at the last examiner's report. Avoid getting bogged down in all the detail. Be ruthless: what you want is the summary of the topics examined and any information that will give weight to the importance of the question or the topic. For example, does the examiner say that he/she was disappointed that this question was answered badly, as it was examined in the past and is one of the most important topics in the syllabus. When you have the important topics, simply write them down with any anecdotal observations and look at perhaps two more reports.

This, together with your analysis of past papers, should be helping with the clarification as to what areas must be studied. There is one other way of finding out what is examinable and that is to ask an expert, a lecturer or teacher who has gone through this process in order to prepare their lessons. They should already know what the key areas are. You may also find some very useful sites on the internet that are a useful resource in finding information. www.examstutor.com is one such site that is well worth investigating.

One word of warning: although some of the sites will provide great resources they will generally provide the standard guidance towards study and will therefore recommend the traditional approach to learning. Stay focused on what you want and the approach that you are following or you will end up studying as you have done in the past.

5. Make notes on these key areas

What happens next partly depends upon how you are studying. The example below assumes you are studying on your own using a standard study text or textbook. If you are attending classes or lectures, then follow the same approach but use your course notes or lecture guidance instead of the textbook. You have the added advantage that you can also ask your tutor for guidance. Be careful though they may not approve of the exam-driven nature of what you are doing.

Below are the key topics identified earlier:

Key examinable topics

A

H – Assume this was also referred to in the examiner's report as being important and there is an article written on it.

I

Minor areas are:
C,D,J,G which have come up twice and B,E,F only once

Assuming that you are studying from a text book, you need to go to the contents page of the book and identify the chapter(s) containing the relevant knowledge relating to your key examinable topics. Highlight them so that they stand out as being important. You may need to familiarise yourself with how these topics fit into the other areas in the book. This can be done using a mind map. This is covered more fully in chapter 6. It may be sensible to study the introduction first, as this often provides an overview of everything. If you can and it makes sense to do so, study the highlighted chapters as soon as is practical, starting with chapter A as this was identified as being the most important. Make notes as normal (chapter 6 includes more guidance on note-taking) but have in mind at all times the question(s) that will be examined. When you get to the end of the chapter, the test becomes whether you can answer these questions.

Remember, if you can't answer the question simply go to the answer (usually at the back of the book) and look at it. This initially look should be an overview which may simply jog your memory or clarify what the examiner was looking for. If all is well then you can attempt to answer the question. If this initial review does not help, then you may need to read the answer more closely. As you do this, work through any calculations (assuming that there are some) and make sure you understand them. If needs be, go back and check your logic using the textbook. The important thing is that you make notes as you do this. i.e. what were the 5 advantages and disadvantages required to get this question right? Are they in the notes you made from the textbook? If not, they should be, so put them in. When you are happy that you understand the key aspects of that question, you can move on to the next one and go through the same process.

Now here is an important point: if you are running out of time, then leave the section only having looked at one question but with a note that you should follow up and look at the remaining 2 or 3 questions at a later date. Then move on and look at the next key examinable topic. You may not master each area before you move on to the next. Sometimes the deeper understanding required to grasp a particular topic needs time and may not become clearer until later in your studies. There is some evidence that one of the reasons we sleep is to help us absorb and reorganize the day's events. Whether this is true or not, there seems little doubt that a good night's sleep will help.

Structuring notes and key topics

Key examinable topic A

Notes
xxxxxxxxx
xxxxxxxxx
xxxxxxxxx

Question 4 June 2009 attempted.

To do - Question 5 (2008) and 4 (2007).

Key examinable topic H

Notes
xxxxxxxxx
xxxxxxxxx
xxxxxxxxx

Question 5 June 2009 attempted.

To do - Question 4 (2008) and 3 (2007).

Read examiners' report, note comments and read article.

Key examinable topic I

Notes
xxxxxxxxx
xxxxxxxxx
xxxxxxxxx

Question 2 June 2008 attempted.

To do - Question 2(2007) and 5 (2006).

You follow the same approach with the next category of topics. However, the time spent on these areas will be less and the notes less detailed.

When you get to the final category of questions, the notes may be even less important and you may only glance at the question and make some outline notes.

What you end up with is a set of notes based on the key examinable areas, with past questions having been attempted so as to provide a realistic idea of what you are up against. If you have not finished your studies, then the areas missed out are less likely to result in a problem on the day of the exam because by definition they are less examinable and so less likely to come up. The notes can then be summarised and reduced down even more. Ultimately, these notes will form the basis for revision and will need to be memorised.

Applying the exam focused approach

I have explained the exam focused approach above in the order in which it is developed. Obviously in practice you will not start with your objective, although clearly you should never lose sight of it! You should start with the analysis of past questions, this will help you identify what the key topics are and so provide the focus for your studies. Then begin to make your exam focused notes, ensuring that you are practising exam questions under both exam and non exam conditions. Your notes should be updated to reflect what you have learned from each question you have attempted.

The exam focused approach in practice

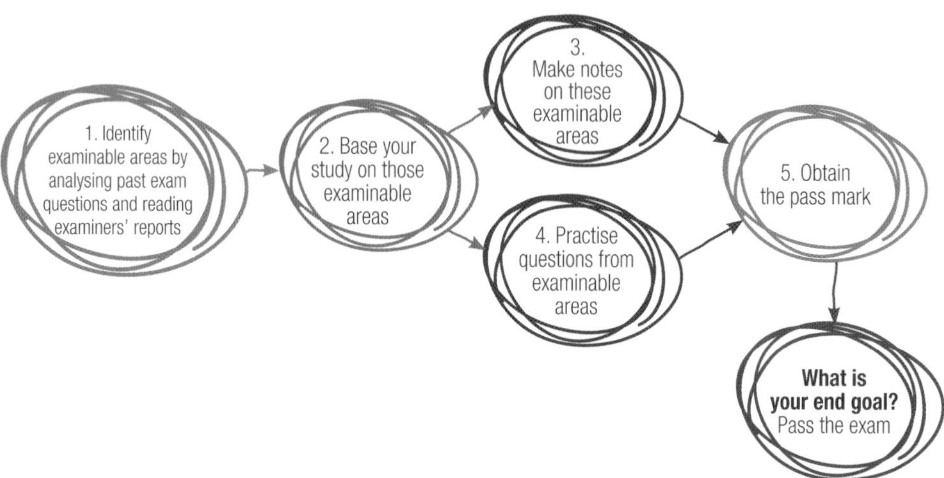

The exam focused approach does not guarantee success but, I believe, is so much more effective at directing and targeting your energy so that you can be confident that there is simply no better way to prepare for examinations. And, as with all other methods, in a competitive world if you don't follow this method and someone else does, do you honestly think that on the day you can get more marks? Think about it…

Over a number of years, I have presented many courses on the exam focused approach to thousands of students and the feedback has always been one of illumination and gratitude for providing structure to what at times seems an impossible task. It gives people clarity, direction and confidence that they can pass the exam; it gives them a new way to study, focus their attention and spend their time more effectively.

In conclusion

In this chapter, we highlighted that you can improve your chances of passing exams by recognising a little more about how you think and behave, together with the way that you study i.e. the approach.

Acknowledging the way that you think and behave is an important first step to improving what you do. This does not mean that you have to change your whole personality; in many ways this is who you are. But you should be aware that you keep delaying things, or believing that everything will be all alright on the day. Once you have recognized such things, you can adapt and make changes to ensure that you still achieve your objective, which, at the end of the day, is to pass the exam.

The exam focused approach may look like question spotting, but I would argue that it's an effective method of study that recognises that your objective is to pass the exam and that you have limited time to study. It is simply a method of prioritisation.

This is an important chapter for me as the exam focused approach changed the way I thought about the whole exam process. Simply recognising that it might be the way I was studying rather than the difficulty of the exam or my own abilities was a wake up call. I hope it is for you too.

The E Word Interviews.

An Examiner

Q Could you introduce yourself and tell us about your interest/involvement in the exam process?

Yes of course, I am an examiner for one of the accountancy bodies and my role is that I write the exam paper, the answers and also the marking guides. After presenting the paper to the examining body and going through quality control procedures, at the end of the process I am in charge of the marking and moderating of the paper.

Q Do you think there is a certain person who does well at exams or has a certain personality that helps when it comes to passing exams?

I think it's interesting because you do tend to see people's personalities coming through in their scripts that they submit for marking. For example you can tell if someone is confident in tackling questions. You can tell if someone is quite logical in terms of allocating time between questions and for that reason I do think personality is important. You have to be confident enough sometimes to reach an opinion or form a conclusion.

Q There are some specific personalities referred to in the book, have you ever come across a Peter perfect.

I think I am a Peter Perfect...... and I think there are a lot of Peter Perfects who take exams and I agree with the comments in the book in that the problem these people have is that they find it really difficult to move away from the question without finishing it to the best of their absolute ability. But people have to be realistic and to actually do well in a paper they sometimes need to leave a question and move onto the next one.

Q Could the traditional approach work?

I think it could work in some circumstances, but I think the exam focused approach is much better because it starts with what you are trying to achieve.

Q Do you think the exam focused approach is better or just different?

I think it is better, certainly for the types of exams I have taught for and the kind of exams I am the examiner for, students have to appreciate that even given the same syllabus, two examiners could write quite different papers based on that same syllabus. So without using the exam focused approach you are never really going to know the style, the length of the questions or what the favourite areas of the examiner are.

Q Should the examiner's role not be about more than the exam itself, shouldn't the exam be viewed in a broader context?

I think in a lot of cases it is, particularly where you are preparing people for a vocation, to be able to do a job for example. But I guess at the end of the day the examiner's remit is to use the syllabus to put together a series of questions and how much that can reflect the real world is probably debateable. An exam is an artificial situation so you can never ever really say that passing an exam will mean you will be successful in your career or in the work place.

Q What are your thoughts on using past exam questions as preparation to pass the exam?

I think learning from past exam questions is probably the best way to understand the syllabus rather than starting with the syllabus and trying to learn it all. Starting with the questions and seeing how the examiner has chosen to test the syllabus in a particular question has to make you better prepared to pass the exam.

Q Would you recommend that students look at examiners' reports and marking guides?

Definitely, the whole point of writing the examiner's report is to show students what was answered well, what wasn't answered well and so people sitting the exam in the future should learn from the wrong approach that students might have used in the past. The fact that we write examiners' reports and we know that they are not used very much is quite sad in a way because they are written to help students.

Unfortunately examiners' reports are very repetitive and I tend to say the same things every single sitting.

Q Is using past exam questions to identify examinable areas not question spotting?

I think it is a very fine line. I don't agree with question spotting or tipping because I find that when people do tip they are too narrow in their focus and I do think a lot of it is based on guess work.

You do however have to try to draw this fine line between trying to spot a question and thinking more broadly on what the main themes of the paper are and what the examiner likes to test on a regular basis. That is not the same as questions spotting. Think about examinable areas as themes or topics that are likely to appear again. The question requirement itself might be really specific and you will never know what that is but you can gauge quite well by looking at past papers what topic areas are likely to be tested, even if you don't know exactly how they will be tested.

Q Do you expect students sitting your exams to know everything?

I think it would be unrealistic to expect them to know everything but I do expect them to have a good knowledge of the main areas of the syllabus.

Q What goes through your mind when you are writing an exam question, a lot of students might think you are setting the question to trick them?

I think that students might be quite surprised to know that I actually want people to pass my paper; I don't want them to fail.

I try to pick scenarios that I think students will understand, that they won't have to sit and worry about. I definitely want students to comprehend the question scenario and the requirements. There is certainly no intention to try to trip people up and it's not just me that wants the paper to be fair. It's everyone who is involved in the setting of the paper, which could be up to twelve different people.

Q If someone passes your exam what does that mean?

To me it means they are technically competent because my paper has technical elements but it also means that someone has the ability to apply that technical knowledge so if they pass the paper they have demonstrated a proficiency in two things, one that they have learned the appropriate technical rules and two can apply them to the situation I have put them in the exam.

Q Does it mean they are clever?

Yes....

chapter 4
Motivation and attitude

About this chapter

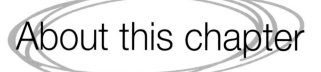

Just imagine if you woke up every morning jumped out of bed and said, "I can't wait to start studying today." How much would you learn if that was the way you felt? Well, that's what it would be like if you were motivated. The interesting thing is that motivation can be learned, just like anything else. With the right techniques you can improve your desire to study. In this chapter we look at the main driver behind motivation: goal-setting.

But this chapter is about more than motivation: it has a section on developing the "right attitude", which, although helpful with motivation, is not the same thing. A positive attitude (more explained on what I mean by positive later) is important to help deal with setbacks such as exam failure.

An attitude could be defined as a frame of mind. Well, one frame of mind that can cause problems whilst studying and during the exam, is stress. The final section discusses the impact of stress and looks to provide practical guidance on how you can cope.

But I am going to start with a discussion about luck, partly because people sometimes think that passing exams is not down to hard work, the right attitude or being motivated, but the fickle finger of fate.

You make your own luck

What makes one individual succeed when others do not? Perhaps they are naturally talented and deserve to succeed. Or maybe they have everything going for them, all the advantages and couldn't really fail. On the other hand, they could just be lucky? They are no better than anyone else; they were just in the "right place at the right time" or "dead jammy". You know the type: everything they seem to do works out in their favour.

But what exactly is luck? Does it exist? And can it play a part in passing exams?

Our destiny is only defined by how we deal with the chance elements to our life.

Tom Hanks about what the feather means in Forrest Gump

Types of luck

Lucky level one

The Machiavellian perspective of luck is that it is the sum of all the events that can impact on your life but which you cannot predict or control. If those events bring you good fortune, then you are lucky; if they bring you misfortune, then you are unlucky.

Personally, I think you need a little bit of luck in life. The train you got on by mistake that led you to meet the person who would become your wife or husband could be called good luck, fate or even destiny. The fact that you picked up the wrong bag one morning on your way to work and had to go back to your house and discovered the gas cooker had been left on, that was lucky. The country in which you were born, the parents that you were born to, the colour of your hair, the genes you inherited… And, as Malcolm Gladwell suggests in his book Outliers, luck can extend even to the year you were born. These are all lucky things, over which you have or had no control. Some are "givens", you inherited them, and others are outcomes that could have turned out very differently, even badly, had a particular random event, to which you gave no thought, not worked in your favour. This is what I call being lucky level one.

Lucky level two

So, if you wake up in the morning and find that all is well, feel fit, healthy and your friends and family are all fit and healthy too, then you should consider yourself extremely lucky (Lucky level one). You have a great start, events over which you have no control have dealt you a good hand.

The problem with luck is that it is often used as an excuse for poor performance; it may even give you a reason for not trying. If you believe you are unlucky and your calculator lets you down on the day of the exam, you might put that down to bad luck, although it possibly has more to do with poor planning. Perhaps you should have anticipated that your calculator might fail and so taken another one into the exam? Now if you had taken a spare into the exam and that in turn failed, that would indeed be bad luck (lucky level one). No one would imagine that two calculators could fail; it is an event outside your control.

Lucky level two is about the type of luck created by you. It is the result of hard work, effort and planning. This is why people say "there is no such thing as luck, you make your own." They are talking about this second level.

Luck is what happens when preparation meets opportunity.

Lucius Annaeus Seneca

If luck is the sum of events that you cannot predict or control, then this second type of luck is not luck at all. There are many events in your life that may appear to be out of your control, but in fact are not. With hard work, persistence and focus you can still get what you want. The job perhaps where there are hundreds of applicants, surely you have to be lucky to get that?

Well yes and no. Yes you need the luck to have gone to a school that gave you the opportunity to be educated in the first place, that was out of your control, you personally did not choose that school. But how you present at the interview, what you say, how motivated you are, the preparation you did before to find out about the company, all of that is within your control. When of course you get the job people may suggest that you were simply lucky. This is, of course, partly true, it's just that some of the luck was of your own making. Lucky level two is a kind of hard work lucky.

Hard work lucky

Perhaps you think you were lucky to study a particular topic the night before the exam that actually came up in the exam? I don't think that's luck. If you have identified your key examinable areas and have been working on them by practising questions, as suggested in chapter 3, then no, you weren't lucky.

Were you lucky that you finished on time, that you knew the answers to the questions set, that your answer could be easily read and was a pleasure to mark...? The answer to all of these is no, this has nothing to do with luck or to be precise lucky level one. This is how you make your own luck.

> The harder I work, the luckier I get.
>
> **Sam Goldwyn**

Lucky level two is the type of luck you create for yourself, a kind of hard work lucky.

Don't blame your bad luck

Perhaps you consider yourself unlucky because you are not as "smart" as other people. You might hear yourself saying, "It's alright for them: they're lucky, they have a really great memory and are very smart, so it's easy for them to learn." Now there is something in this. Some people have the ability to pick up facts and concepts more easily than others,

and this may indeed be an example of the good fortune (lucky level one) in having parents or grandparents who also had this ability, a genetic type of good luck. But there are so many other elements that make someone successful.

The point is this; it is no good blaming your misfortune on bad luck, true you may not be as "smart" as someone else but you can still do well, you just have to work harder or in a different way.

Talent is cheaper than table salt. What separates the talented individual from the successful one is a lot of hard work.

Stephen King

If you do believe in luck (and it's fine if you do) all I would say is, if something doesn't quite go to plan or if something blocks your way and stops you from getting what you want, don't be too ready to blame your bad luck.

I am a lucky person trick

There is a simple trick that a friend of mine, who does believe in luck, uses. If something happens that appears to be bad luck, he remains convinced that it will turn out to be lucky in some way because he believes he is a "lucky person". He just doesn't know how it will turn out lucky at the time. But, sure enough, at some point in the future, he will come back and say, "Remember that day when I had that problem? Well, if I hadn't had that problem, X then Y would not have happened and that opportunity would never have come my way. See? I told you I was lucky."

The other problem I have with the concept of bad luck is that it has an element of inevitability about it: whatever you do, it does not matter because this thing called bad luck will conspire to ensure that, in some shape or form, the event will turn out badly. This is a very unhelpful mindset that can sometimes cause you to make things turn out for the worse, simply because you are willing it to happen.

Think about it...

Do you really believe that someone or something is deliberately making every event turn out badly just for you? Maybe it's just the way you are looking at it?

No, I don't believe in that type of bad luck; I think it's just the way you frame the event. And for things to begin to work in your favour, you need to stop using the inevitability aspect of bad luck as a justification to not motivating yourself to solve the problem.

Shallow men believe in luck. Strong men believe in cause and effect.

Ralph Waldo Emerson

Luck does play a part in exam success; there are events outside your control both good and bad that can impact upon you performance. Just don't be too ready to blame your misfortune on something as simple as bad luck; it may have more to do with you than you think!

Motivation – Start with what you want

So you do need some luck to pass exams, but perhaps not as much as you once thought. There is, however, another very important element to exam success: motivation. How is it that some people appear to be driven, able to concentrate despite distractions and remain on track with their studies when others cannot? Is this luck, or is it more to do with their motivation?

The ability to remain focused and motivated is equally important during the learning/ tuition part of studying and the revision phase. There is a simple rule: the more you do something the better you get. It's called practice. And so, if you spend more time practising questions, you will get good at questions. Conclusion: you need to be motivated so as to help you practise as many questions as possible.

Much has been written about motivation, and, as I write this book, I have to question my own motivation from time to time. Why don't I start at 6.00 every morning and work until midnight? Why don't I wake up every morning with one single burning desire to write to the detriment of everything else? Some days I do, but certainly not every day.

Motivational direction – towards

Motivation can be thought of as the wants, needs and beliefs that drive an individual towards a particular goal or perceived outcome. It will generally affect a person's behaviour: they will do something as a result.

Jenny Curran: Do you ever dream, Forrest, about who you're gonna be?
Forrest Gump: Who I'm gonna be?
Jenny Curran: Yeah.
Forrest Gump: Aren't-aren't I going to be me?

Forrest Gump, movie

Types of motivation

If motivation is about being driven towards a particular goal, then, to be motivated, you must set a goal or outcome in such a way that it invades your thoughts and affects your actions. In principle, motivation is about goal-setting. You cannot be motivated if you don't want something. To be motivational, wants should be positive and, in this context, the word positive means that your wants should move you forward. Positive is often misunderstood and is thought to mean that you look at everything in an optimistic, rose-coloured and sometimes unrealistic way.

This concept of *moving forward* needs some explanation. There are, in fact, two ways in which you can move towards something and still be positive. Firstly, you can be pulled towards something, very much as a magnet pulls when it attracts, and secondly, although still moving forward you are being pushed away, as when a magnet repels. When setting objectives and outcomes to motivate, we are talking about the *pull towards* type of positive, we need it to be attractive; you must want something as opposed to not wanting something e.g. you should want to pass your exam as a opposed to not wanting to fail, your goals should be positive.

Moving away or being pushed away from a problem is still motivational, as it is considered positive because it is going forward; however where you end up is not always certain. More about away from motivation later.

Positive motivation is both pushing and pulling

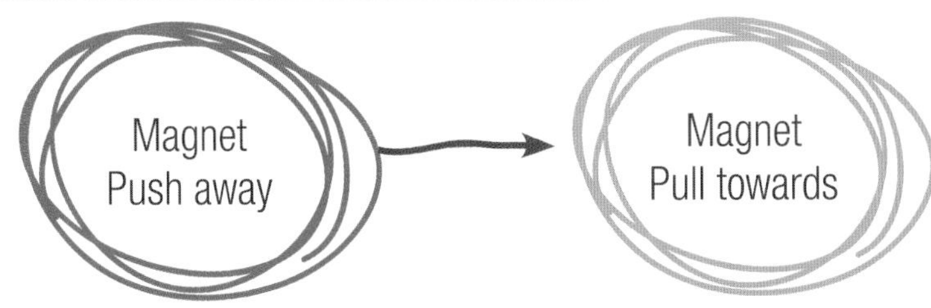

A quick question, clear your mind… good. Under no circumstances do I want you to think about a creamy, cool, refreshing, tasty ice cream. I mean that: DON'T think about that ice cream!

Did you think about the ice cream?

The reason for setting positive goals is because the brain struggles with the concept of negatives. For example, one of the most common reassuring statements people make that achieves exactly the opposite is, "Don't worry". The brain fails to recognize the word don't and so the word worry is brought into your conscious thoughts when in fact it may not even have crossed your mind. This is why "your want" should be a positive outcome. If it isn't, it would be far less likely that your brain, and therefore you, would act on it.

Don't worry if that doesn't make sense right now; it will later – whoops!

The other interesting aspect about motivation is that it is self-induced. It is your motivation, not someone else's. True, other people can motivate or inspire, but what they are doing is empowering you and inspiring you to believe in yourself to the extent that you can achieve anything you want. Motivational experts remove your self-doubts and instil a sense of inner confidence, so you believe that what you want you can have.

What you want can be thought of as the target, what you are aiming for. The energy and direction is really your motivation. So, to be motivated you need two things: firstly, you must want something and secondly, you must have sufficient energy and direction to get it.

The distinction between needs and wants

Wants and needs can at times seem almost impossible to separate and you could argue that we don't need to. But as most people pursue goals driven by wants, as is the case in wanting to pass an exam rather than needing to pass, i.e. it is a necessity, it is vital to your very survival, I will attempt to add some clarification in this section.

To need something implies it is a necessity, and so we can think of food, water and even love as necessities. Some of these needs are biological, as with water, or emotional, as with love. Steven Pinker, in his book *How The Mind Works* (published 1997), argues that we have emotions in order to help us make choices. "An animal cannot pursue all its goals at once and so evolution has created emotions in order to help it decide what to do."

In the fable of the indecisive ass, donkey if you prefer, who stood at an equal distance from the berry bush from which he could eat and the lake from where he could drink, he chose neither and died, simply because he was unable to make up his mind. The ass would have certainly benefited from the emotion of feeling thirst before hunger, in order to help make his decision.

Pinker goes on to suggest that emotions are mechanisms that set the brain's highest-

level goals, which, once triggered, lead to a series of sub-goals, that we call thinking and acting. So maybe our emotions are the main determinants of our needs.

Our wants, on the other hand, are probably created more by the environment, the people and objects we have close to us. These wants are not necessarily time sensitive, they do not have to be current, and thus some wants could go back to your childhood. The results of experiences stored in your unconscious that suddenly come out in later life.

If you are surrounded by people who all send their children to private school and the expectation is that these same children will go to university and you believe that this is the right thing to do, then this may well create a want or desire for you to send your child to private school and, ultimately, university. If, of course, you don't think private school is right then it could motivate you to do the opposite. Whether you do or don't will depend on how strong your motivation is.

The strength is determined by how much you believe sending your child to private school is the very best thing you can do. And one of the things that has a significant impact on beliefs is how powerfully you can see the image of your future and these events happening. Can you see the event in your mind's eye? Is it in colour or black and white, how many people are there? The more vivid the thoughts, the stronger the emotional context, the more motivational energy you will have, the more likely you are to achieve your objective.

Wants, which I suggested above as being created by your environment, could of course become needs, things that are essential, necessities, if you add an emotional element. This would be the situation if you were afraid (an emotion) of the consequences of your child not going to private school. This idea, that a want can suddenly feel like a necessity, is one of the reasons it is sometimes difficult to separate the two.

To summarise, wants are not things that you have to have, your life does not depend on having them, despite your emotions sometimes making it feel that you do! Needs, on the other hand, are essential to your very existence, you cannot live without them. On the whole, people do not suffer motivational problems with needs. If you had no food you would not have to go through the process described in the next section to help you feel more motivated, you would be motivated enough....

It is for this reason that we will talk more about wants from this point forward.

Identify what you want

So the first step towards motivation is to identify exactly what you want. Then, create powerful future events relating to that want in as much detail as possible. People who are driven and achieve their goals sometimes against great odds do this naturally; other people may need a little help.

If you don't have a clear direction or focused-on want, then, as the Cat in Alice in Wonderland put it, it doesn't matter which way you go.

"Would you tell me please which way I ought to go from here?"

"That depends a good deal on where you want to get to," said the cat.

"I don't much care where..." said Alice."

"Then it doesn't matter which way you go," said the cat.

Alice in Wonderland by Lewis Carroll

Without a clear view of what you want, it does not matter what you do or in which direction you go.

The other interesting element of this is that, if you have no purpose, then you arguably will never know whether you achieved what you wanted. This will mean that you will not experience the emotions associated with success. Success, in this context, is internal, for example how you personally define success, rather than other people's definitions (external success), which may include money and status. Internal success can only be achieved if you get something you really wanted.

True internal success can only be achieved if you get what you want. External success is generally the "things or objects" other people think successful people have.

What's your motivation?

Think about something that you have achieved or made happen in the past. This might be as simple as having booked a holiday. Why did you do it? What did you want from the holiday? Why did you put time aside and spend your hard-earned cash on that holiday? Did you have a purpose? Did you think that you deserved the break?

Let's explore the process you went through before you booked the holiday. Sit back for a second and identify your motivation.

What was the purpose or objective in going on the holiday?

Perhaps the purpose was to relax, and, as you think about that holiday, are you seeing pictures or hearing sounds or maybe both? Are you on the beach, relaxing on a sun lounger, the sun beating down, a cold glass of orange juice (or something stronger) in your hand? The sea is glistening, and all you can hear is the gentle sound of waves as they break upon the golden sands. And, as you look at the sea and smell the salt in the air, you breathe in slowly and sink back, feeling more relaxed than you could ever imagine...

Think about how powerful those images, sounds and smells of the holiday were. Do you really want to go on that holiday? Will you wake up tomorrow excited with a burning desire to book the holiday as soon as you possibly can?

If so, you are indeed motivated. It must of course be within your control to be truly motivational: this means that you must be able to actually book the holiday yourself, or influence others to the point that they will do it. But, in essence, that's all you have to do. If the process works for booking a holiday, it should work for any other objective or outcome you want to achieve.

The point is: if you want to achieve something, you need to "feel" motivated enough that your next step is to take action and do something about it.

Of course this is easier to do with something like a holiday, where the sensory experience is very vivid and powerful. But what about the motivation necessary to pass an exam, what do you see, hear and touch then? Visualising yourself sitting another exam, which may well be the reward for passing the one you are currently attempting does not seem very exciting or motivational. To make passing exams motivational you have to think more about what you will get as a result of passing and visualize that, rather than the experience of working towards the next exam. What will you gain, will it be a better job, respect from your peers? Will it be more money, what will you do with that money? Create a vision of those experiences, not the exam room.

In summary, you need a positive objective, something you want as opposed to something you don't want. You then need a very clear picture of what the outcome will be if you achieve that objective. Not only should you be able to see it and hear it, but you should also smell it and, if possible, taste it.

Improve your motivation by goal setting

This next section contains specific questions that will help in clarifying objectives and, in so doing, will make them motivational. The process of asking, answering and refining the questions will establish a very clear positive outcome in your mind. If it is you that needs motivating, then get a friend or colleague to ask the questions. I appreciate that this process may not be fully understood and can seem strange the first time you go through the questions but stick with it, it does work.

Motivation questions

1. **What do I want?** - State the goal in positive terms

- Ask - What do you want, then write it down....

Guidance
This needs to be something you want, so, when asked, "What do you want?" you say, "I don't want to fail my exams." Reframe this by asking, "What do you want instead of not failing?" Or simply say "This needs to be something you want as opposed to what you want to avoid."

SPS: What do you want?
Student: I want to pass my exams

2. **What will I accept as evidence that I have achieved my outcome?** - Make it real

- Ask - How will you know that you have this outcome? What will you see, what will you hear, how will you feel? or
- Ask - If we made a video of this outcome, what would we see and hear and how would it make us feel?
- Ask - When exactly do you want this, when will it end, how will you know?

Guidance
The purpose of this question is to create a powerful sensory-based experience. The more powerful the experience, the greater the motivation. You need to press them on this to ensure the goal is clear in their mind.

SPS: How will you know when you have passed your exams?
Student: I will have the certificate on my wall in my office and mail will be addressed to me with my professional body's designatory letters after my name. I will hear my parents saying that they knew I could do it and I will feel proud of myself.

3. **Is achieving this outcome within my control?** - Must not depend on others

- Ask - Is this within your control?
- Ask - Is this something which you can achieve? Or does it require OTHER people to behave in a certain way?
- Ask - What resources do you need to be able to achieve this?

Guidance
The outcome cannot be dependent upon the performance of others. This is important, many people set goals that depend on events or individuals over which they have no control. Although you can influence both people and events, you cannot make them happen. You need to concentrate on what you can do to influence them and make those your outcomes.

For example, if the answer to what do you want was, "To pass my exams," then, when you get to this point it will become clear that this outcome is not achievable by you. To pass the exam, you need the examiner to consider your script worthy of a pass. So the outcome needs to be refined to smaller outcomes that can be achieved by you. Like, "I want to practise more questions." This is within your control.

Asking these questions will also help identify the steps that you have to take to get to your goal. Separating it in this way facilitates its passage and completion, often within shorter time frames than expected.

SPS: *Is this something which you can achieve on your own, is it within your control?*
Student: *No not really I need the examiner or marker to give me a high score*
SPS: *What is it that you can do to help get the marker to give you a high score?*
Student: *I can produce an answer that they think is good enough to pass*
SPS: *And what is it that you can do to help get a sufficiently high mark?*
Student: *I could work harder and practise more questions*
SPS: *Oh okay, so you want to be more motivated to practise more exams questions, this is one of your goals, is there anything else? Etc. etc*

4. **Are the costs and consequences of obtaining this outcome acceptable?** – What do you gain and lose as a result of achieving your outcome?

- Ask - What are the advantages of making this change?
- Ask - What are the disadvantages of making this change?
- Ask - What will achieving this lose you?
- AND finally, ask - If you could have it now, would you take it?

Guidance

These questions are deliberately difficult to answer, they will make you think and as a result you will have to re-read them several times. They will identify if what you want (your outcome) is really best for you and the balance of your life? If you achieve your outcome, how will your life be affected? The speed of response to the last question will give you some idea as to how clear the outcome is and the strength of the desire.

SPS *What are the disadvantages of making this change?*
Student: *Disadvantages of practising more questions? I suppose I might not have a social life?*
SPS: *Are you willing to give up some of your social life, because if not this could be one of the things that is holding you back. Don't forget it is not forever, it is only for about 4 weeks and that's not very long at all.*
Student: *Now you have put it like that I don't think that should stop me*
SPS: *Great so if you could have your goal of practising more exam questions now, would you take it?*
Student: *without hesitating – yes*

Write them down

The final stage of the outcome-setting process and, arguably the most important, is to write down your outcomes, don't just think about writing them down; WRITE THEM DOWN NOW!

NEWS A study of the 1953 graduates of Yale University clearly demonstrates the importance of committing goals to paper. The graduates were interviewed and asked if they had a clear, specific set of goals written down along with a plan for achieving those goals. Only three percent had such written goals.

Twenty years later, in 1973, the researchers went back and interviewed the class of 53 again. They discovered that the three percent with specific, written goals were worth more in financial terms than the entire other 97 percent combined!

Now have a go

1. What do I want?

2. What will I accept as evidence that I have achieved my outcome? What will I see, hear and feel?

3. Is achieving this outcome within my control? If not, redefine the outcome.

4. Are the costs and consequences of obtaining this outcome acceptable?

Motivation – Make your goals positive and write them down...simple.

Motivational direction – away from

Now, much of the above is based around the logic of setting positive goals so that they will act as a beacon and draw the individual towards them. This is an example of what we call motivational direction; perhaps unsurprisingly, this is specifically referred to as towards motivation. Some people, on the other hand, can be motivated not towards something but away from something (away from motivation). They are motivated away from what they don't want.

Jenny Curran: Can I have a ride?
Pickup-Truck Driver: Where are you going?
Jenny Curran: I don't care.

Forrest Gump, movie

This, of course, like so many other things, is not new; motivating people with a reward as opposed to a threat of something nasty has been around since the beginning of time. You will generally be motivated towards your goals but away from your fears.

Threats are away from (sticks); rewards and bribes are towards (carrots)

However one of the problems with away from motivation is that, although you are moving away from the stick (pain), there is no guarantee you will end up with the carrot (pleasure). You might end up with something very different. This is why the towards direction is the preferred method.

Going away from does not guarantee where you end up.

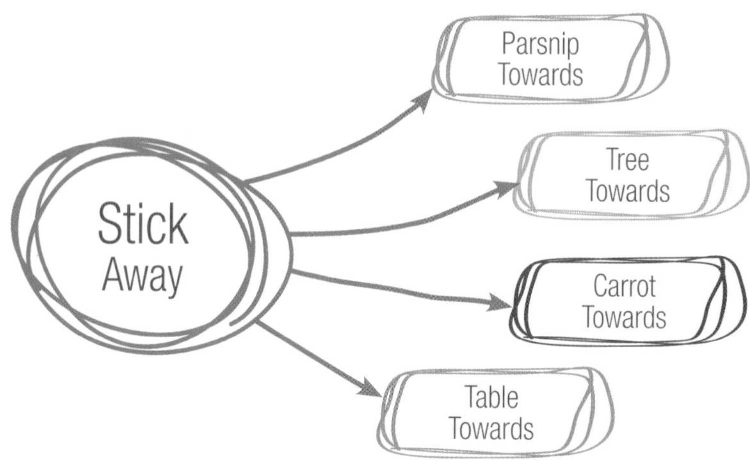

This type of away from motivation can be effective for certain people in certain contexts. I do find that lots of students are motivated away from failure. So sometimes it may be more effective to motivate students with the suggestion that working hard will reduce their chances of failure rather than increase their chances of success. In fact, if I think back to when I was a student, I think I worked hard because I was more afraid of failing than I was attracted to the opportunities of passing. Also, with hindsight, passing the exam was not my ultimate goal or outcome; it was only one outcome on the way to achieving another much greater one. It was just, at that time, the biggest one in my field of vision.

The important point is this: it is preferable to set targets so that you have something to aim for, this in turn will create a positive force. But don't limit yourself to the positive methods of motivation. The threats can be equally motivational, although arguably not as effective. They do motivate and so move you forward it's just not so clear where you may end up. And that is not always a good thing.

I have spent a lot of time explaining why and how setting targets works, in order to inspire you to have a go. And if, initially, it seems a little confusing, that's okay. The important thing is that you set an objective and that you write it down; the rest is very much a refinement that will hone those objectives and, in so doing, make them more likely to be achieved.

Inspiring tales and inspiring people - Topping up the motivation

Having a strong and clear outcome or objective is only one of the tools that can help with your motivation and ultimate exam success. Everyone needs to be inspired to keep their motivation as high as possible. It's almost as if it needs to be topped up from time to time like the oil in a car. We should perhaps, at this point, clarify the difference between motivation and inspiration.

As discussed above, motivation is a process of moving from what you have to what you want to have, powered by a force that is partly created by the strength of your beliefs.

Inspiration is more to do with something that arouses feelings to do well. It is generally created by a person you relate to, who demonstrates attributes that you admire and, to a certain extent, may be envious of. It doesn't have to be an actual person; it could in fact be a story about a fictional person.

One of the best ways to create feelings to do well, and a technique used by motivational trainers, is to tell stories of people's achievements, often against great odds. The story then acts as a metaphor for you. The more you relate and associate with the characters (be they spiders or people), the more inspired you become. One of the most famous is the story of Robert the Bruce and the spider.

Robert the Bruce

Robert the Bruce, King of Scotland, after being defeated in battle, escaped and found a hideout in a cave. Hiding in a cave for three months, Bruce was at the lowest point of his life. He thought about leaving the country and never coming back.

While waiting, he watched a spider building a web in the cave's entrance. The spider fell down time after time, but finally he succeeded with his web. So Bruce decided also to retry his fight and told his men: "If at first you don't succeed, try, try and try again."

Origin - Old legend.

This story has a simple message and one that you can read over and over again perhaps when you have met with failure. What if you have not been successful in an exam? What story would you tell yourself. How about the one about the student who failed an exam which proved beyond any shadow of a doubt that he was not very good at that subject and clearly not very clever? The student should realise his limitations and not have ideas above his station. You see, the interesting thing about people is they tell themselves stories all the time. So why not tell yourself stories that help you achieve your goals rather than stories that don't?

Only tell yourself and others stories that are helpful.

This reminds me of the time I was working in the accounts profession and one of the partners said to me that he thought it was important that you know your limitations. I am not sure if he was talking to me or himself, as he did have the habit of doing this. He probably had no idea the impact his statement had on me. Neither do I think he would remember this event as it was a conversation in the middle of a very ordinary day, over twenty years ago. What I do remember thinking at the time was, "What?! You should never know your limitations! You should never put limits on what you can achieve, never!"

And years later, having had time to reflect on what he said, I still feel the same. What I would add, however, is that, although you should not create an artificial ceiling for your dreams and ambitions, you should be aware of the limitations you might have with regard to your skills and abilities, because it is these skills that you will need in order to achieve your dreams.

There is little point in having a dream to become a great swimmer if you are very poor at swimming. Yes, you can improve on your current performance, but you are never going to be world-class. This, in itself, can be hugely disappointing. What you can do, though, is redefine your outcome and, rather than being a great swimmer, perhaps you could become a great swimming coach. Your skills may lie elsewhere: you may be a good communicator someone able to inspire others to achieve their dreams. This may be your strength, and you should build on your strengths in order to achieve your dreams.

Don't create artificial ceilings for your dreams and ambitions but be aware of your skills and abilities as this is where limitations actually lie.

Sir Steve Redgrave

Stories can be from many years ago as with Robert the Bruce or, in fact, taken from the modern world. Sir Steve Redgrave, five times gold medallist, is an inspiration in many ways, but what I find most impressive is that he remained motivated for twenty years and that, after every Olympics, he had to wait another four years before he could achieve his ambition.

A perhaps unlikely hero for a book about examinations, however Quintuple Olympic Gold Medallist Rower Sir Steve Redgrave has proved himself the greatest Olympian Britain has ever produced. His Olympic successes began in 1984, when he won the gold medal in the coxed fours and ended in Sydney in 2000. He became the only UK athlete ever to have won Gold Medals at five consecutive Olympic Games. Sir Steve was 38 when he won that final gold and he managed to motivate himself to stay at the top for all that time, but what is his secret?

In the many talks that Sir Steve delivers in his capacity as a sports personality, we can get an insight into his thoughts on motivation.

"Sometimes your dreams and goals may seem impossible and so it may prove necessary to break them down into small manageable chunks."

Sir Steve tells the story of a swimmer, who realised that, if he was to have a chance of winning the 100 metre back-stroke event at the Olympic Games in four years' time, he would need to cut 4 seconds off his time. A tough task at this level. But the swimmer then broke that into smaller goals: cutting the time back by 1 second per year, or 1/12 second per month, and the goal started to look achievable - and the swimmer won his medal.

However, *"You can have your dreams, your goals and your strategy but it's all for nothing without the hard work. And that discipline isn't just setting the alarm clock for your early morning training session - but also getting up when it goes off!"*

Steve also stresses the importance of *believing in yourself and your "game plan", and, having established that, to have the confidence to focus on the "winning" rather than the "how much"*.

One other thing that I have always found interesting about Sir Steve Redgrave is that I would have assumed that someone who has committed such a large part of their life to one single objective would naturally enjoy the process. The training and practice required over all of those years would have consumed his days and so when asked if he missed training, his reply was simple but astonishing:

"No. I hated training. It was a means to an end. To keep fit now I have to motivate myself with a goal, the London Marathon or another sporting event."

Lessons

From this we can gain some very useful tips.

Firstly, when setting goals, make them challenging but achievable. Make them inspirational, but not so big that they appear daunting. This is achieved by setting small goals that can be achieved, each one a stepping stone towards your ultimate objective or dream.

Secondly, there are dreams, which, if you think about it, are probably powerful images and future episodes that you have created in your imagination. There are goals which are the short-term smaller targets that you set yourself. And there is your strategy, which is the plan of how your goals when achieved will contribute to your dreams. But they all mean nothing without the hard work. The day-to-day practice and repetition may be both painful and boring, but is essential if you are to develop the skills that are needed to be ultimately successful.

And finally, Steve teaches us that, if your dreams are sufficiently powerful, they can overcome the pain you feel when going through the process.

Break your goals into smaller more achievable targets, but never lose sight of the dream.

The man on the plane – one final story

One of the things I find strange in the UK is the attitude some people have towards the value of education. There seems to be a general sense that they are being forced to learn as opposed to being privileged to learn. Whilst I appreciate that school is not for everyone (that does not mean that learning isn't) and some of the reasons for people's dislike of

school or education is probably down to bad experiences from school, I cannot always understand this perspective. I believe that we are learning animals and that is one of the attributes that has made us, as a species, successful.

At this stage, it might also be useful to separate learning from school. Learning is what you do; school is the place where you go to do it. Also, learning in this context does not mean learning maths but is the process of acquiring a skill or knowledge; this applies equally to playing football as algebra. What we do need to do is learn things that are useful. So, here is a tale of a man that I met on a plane. I found it a humbling story and one that I use sometimes to remind and inspire myself as to how fortunate we are.

It was on a night flight, returning from Kuala Lumpur, that I had the good fortune to sit next to a 55-year-old Malaysian man. As with long flights, we fell into conversation and I asked what the purpose of his flight to the UK was. "I am coming to the UK to study engineering," he said. "I have three children and have been saving up for five years. Such is the cost and expense of my journey that I can only afford one return trip in that time and so I will miss my family dreadfully."

"So you are paying for yourself"? I asked.

"Yes, in fact I have given up work to study, and when I return I hope to get a better job, but my main motivation is that I have always wanted a degree and I am willing to make some sacrifices to get it."

That's what I call motivation and, for me, when people are complaining about a course or school I always think of that man and his personal ambition to learn.... Just great.

I am not the smartest or most talented person in the world, but I succeeded because I keep going, and going, and going.

Sylvester Stallone

Perhaps an unlikely person to include in a book about exams, but if you want to find out about motivation put 'Sylvester Stallone, motivation' into Google and read his personal story and how the first Rocky film was made.

Choose your attitude

So, motivation is about setting and achieving goals. Attitude on the other hand is a frame of mind, affecting one's thoughts and behaviours. They are not completely unrelated, but, in order to create some clarity, I will treat them as if they were.

Positive and negative

There are several frames of mind that people can have, but, once again, for simplicity, I will consider just three: positive, negative and indifferent. Of the three, the best one to adopt for exam success is positive. Positive was defined earlier as moving towards something; here we are talking about a positive attitude, not a direction. To have a positive attitude, you are looking at a situation with the purpose of getting a useful and helpful meaning out of the circumstance, event, relationship… etc.

So, in many ways, it still means moving towards, but you must be moving towards something useful and helpful. There is also an implication that it is a perspective, a way of looking at something. This suggests that the event, whatever it is, can be looked at in many ways and so, to take a positive view, you are looking at it in such a way that you can gain something rather than lose something.

Contrast this with a negative attitude. If positive means you are looking at a situation or event with a view to gaining something useful or meaningful, then a negative attitude implies you are looking at the situation in a way that you are losing something and so not gaining anything meaningful. This cannot be useful; one of the things you might lose with a negative attitude is your confidence.

Being negative is not the same as being realistic. A realist is someone who sees it as it is, the interesting thing is that there is probably no such thing as "how it is": it's just a perspective. There is, however, an implied element of practicality about being realistic. That means, after looking at the problem, you then test it to see if it will work. Now this can be useful.

On the whole, there is little use for negative thinking when it comes to passing exams and as for being indifferent, it is a nice concept, but, on a practical level, probably not possible. To be indifferent seems to imply that you have no attitude or see nothing positive or negative in an event. It is hard to be indifferent about something that has such an important impact upon you as passing an exam.

Impact upon the ageing process

The University of Texas found people with an upbeat view of life were less likely than pessimists to show signs of frailty. The researchers say their findings suggest psychosocial factors - as well as genes and physical health - play a role in how quickly we age.

Journal Psychology and Ageing

Dealing with setbacks

Now, a word of warning, positive thinking should not be confused with the Vicar from chapter three. He thought that everything would work out in the end. He believed in divine intervention: "What will be will be." A kind of destiny, independent of how much effort or not you put in as an individual. The Vicar is not a positive thinker; he is naive and, to a certain extent, lazy. He uses his attitude to avoid hard work and not feel bad about it. To a certain extent, the Vicar lacks motivation: his vision is not sufficiently strong and his outcomes not well-formed so he simply treats his failures as being acceptable.

The positive thinker has objectives and well-formed outcomes and thus is motivated. He will treat his failures as exactly that: failures. Yet, rather than feeling negative, an emotion that may create self-doubt and so halt progress towards his goal, he will draw on his positive attitude and so move forward, having learned something useful for the future. You might say that he has gained experience.

"I didn't fail the test; I just found 100 ways to do it wrong"

Benjamin Franklin

Now that's positive thinking…

Read the next statement: "Positive thinking is for people who live their life not seeing it *how it is*. They have a Pollyanna view of the world, afraid to face the truth."

Can you see that this statement is no more than a perspective? There is no such thing as "the truth", only the event. What you really want is a perspective that gives you more choices and possible solutions in order for you to continue towards your goal. The fact is that you are more likely to come up with great ideas and solutions when thinking positively than when you are thinking negatively. This is not about right and wrong; it is about which perception is the most useful to you in getting what you want.

Perception

If the event is exam failure and, with your "how it is" hat on, you may perceive that you are not very good at exams, what happens next depends on your objective. If you want to become a doctor, then the fact is you need to pass the examinations. So, if you conclude that you are not very good at exams, the reality is you will never become a doctor. I would guess that passing an exam is an important element in being a good doctor – but probably not the most important one. Now, this may be something you have to face up to. It may be, as I suggested earlier, that you need to recognise the limitations of your skills and abilities, never your dreams and ambitions. And so change the direction of your dream towards something that your skills are better suited to. However, this is rare; you are unlikely to have to do this more than two or three times in a lifetime.

Positive and negative thinking – which one is right

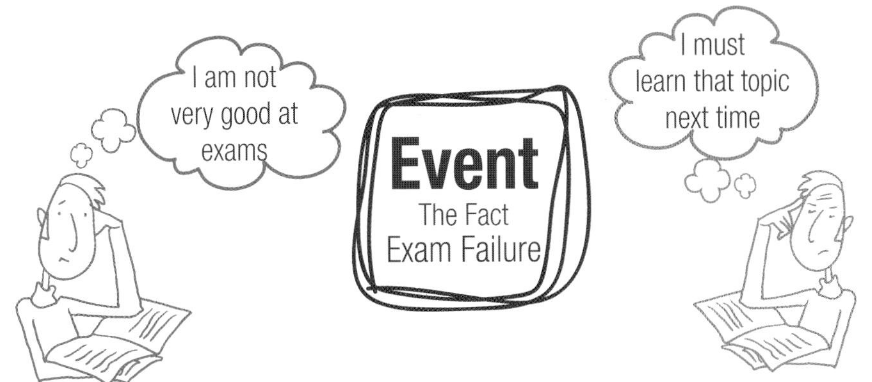

This is more likely just a minor setback. This is something you need to overcome, not something you need to give into and completely change direction. If every time you had a barrier placed in your way you decided that you need to change direction, then arguably you would spend more time changing direction than achieving your dream.

When sitting exams, there are lots of times when a positive attitude would be useful. What happens if when practising an exam question you get something wrong? The fact is that you got the answer wrong, there is no denying that. The next step is to ask yourself what your objective is: let's assume it's to pass this exam". If so, is it helpful to look at this event from the perspective that getting it wrong means that you don't understand this subject and never will? You might even go further and tell yourself that you are in fact not very clever and that you have been fooling yourself for far too long.

Looking at the problem from this perspective will not help you to pass the exam. All that will happen is you will stop studying and go and do something else. The truth is that, to pass this exam, you need to master this topic. If we took a more positive view, you might tell yourself that It was fortunate that you have discovered the problem with this topic now rather than later when you might not have had time to go back and study it in more detail.

Which one of these approaches is more likely to result in your passing the exam? And that is what it is all about: how can you look at the fact or event from a perspective that is helpful?

Pessimists are more likely to be right

In a study of insurance sales agents conducted by psychologist Martin Seiligman, optimists outsold pessimists by 57%. However, when asked to estimate the chances of getting customers to buy their products, the optimists generally got it wrong, they thought it was far higher than it actually was.

Changing perception – negative to positive

The first part of the process of changing perspective is to recognise that you are applying a perspective in the first place. You need to catch yourself looking at the event from a negative point of view. This is not always easy, so try asking yourself, "Is the way I am feeling right now helpful? Am I coming up with solutions or simply going back over the event."

If so, take a break and come back and write down all the positive aspects to the situation. Don't judge them, just write them down, even the silly ones. Put on some music that makes you feel happier. Look in the mirror and smile, force it. Read an inspiring story or quote. Phone up a positive person and ask them how they would look at it. Why not pretend to be that person and see how it feels? Take stock of all the things you have learned; this is probably only one thing in many that you can't do.

The key point to all of this remains the same. If feeling negative is not helpful in achieving what you want, then use some of the ideas above to move you into a more positive frame of mind.

If you are not moving forward, check your attitude. Ask, "Is the way I am feeling right now helpful?" If the answer is no, then change.

But can you choose - Yes, you can

But do you have control over your attitude in the first place? Do you have control over your frame of mind? Well, think about it: if you don't, who does? The statement choose your **attitude** is very self-empowering, it implies that you have a choice…

I first came across this in a book called *Fish* (Stephen Lundin, Harry Paul, John Christensen) and, although set against the background of improving customer service, it has as one of its values the fact that you can choose the way you feel, and thus the frame of mind you have. Some people believe that the way you feel and thus your attitude is directly caused by outside influences, such as unpleasant experiences or negative people. But, while external pressures may trigger our feelings, they are our feelings. We can either be subservient to external events, few of which we have any control over, or we can take charge of our own response.

By saying that you should "choose your attitude", I am not suggesting that you are always upbeat and positive, only that that you make your own choices and not try to pass them off on something or someone else. Once you accept that you are the only one who is choosing your attitude at this moment, you can decide whether to keep it or not. You control your attitude, not the other way round.

Exam nerves and exam stress

As individuals, we all move through what we call states or moods, during the day. A state can be thought of as a temporary way of feeling, although most people have what we call a baseline state, which is the one with which they feel most comfortable. When people get themselves into a confusing and unhelpful frame of mind, it is often referred to as being in a right state, although paradoxically we probably mean a "wrong state".

Exam nerves are a good example of a state. Although they can be useful, most of the time they don't help when it comes to passing exams. They can, in fact, result in well-prepared students failing, which, in my simplistic view of the world, is simply not fair. Years ago, people used to suffer with their "nerves", now it is more common to hear the expression that they are suffering from stress. And so, exam stress and exam nerves can be considered very much the same thing.

Three way relationship

A good way to think of stress is as a three-way relationship between demands on a person, that person's feelings about those demands, and their ability to cope with those demands. Stress is often more debilitating when the individual feels that they don't have the ability to cope with the demands placed upon them.

Stress is a three way relationship

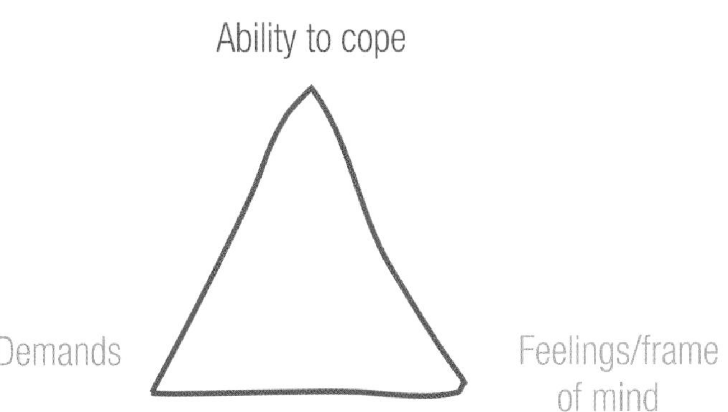

The demands are simply external events that we face every day. This could be a test submission deadline, new topics or subjects that you have to learn, family or social commitments. In themselves they are neither good nor bad; they are simply events that require us to devote some time and energy, in short we have to do something.

They only become problems or stressful events if we don't feel we can deal with them. Do you have the ability or time needed to handle this demand? If the answer is no, then it starts to become stressful. The level of stress you experience is amplified by the way you feel, your frame of mind or mood. In the right mood you may look at the event and feel as if you can cope, in the wrong mood it can look like a mountain that you are unable to climb.

Stress is perfectly normal

Whilst you can choose an attitude, be it positive or negative, there is an element to stress that can feel beyond your control. Stress does have elements that are more biological in origin. In fact, stress is a very natural, and in many ways an essential, reaction.

Let us go back in time about one and half million years: imagine you are out hunting for food. You have wondered into a part of the forest where you have never been before, the foliage is dense and the canopy above covers the sky. There is damp smell and all around you can hear the noises of the forest. The bush to your left moves and you think you hear footsteps, but, when you turn, there is nothing there. You continue until you find a clearing, but by this time you are exhausted and beginning to see danger around every corner. You are sweating and your heart is beating faster than normal; you feel that something is not right. Then suddenly, as if from nowhere, a sabre-toothed tiger leaps from a tree above, snarling and biting. Its fangs sink deep into your back but you manage to throw it to the ground. Its back legs are bent, it is ready to pounce and for one brief moment you stare straight into its eyes, what do you do? Stay and fight or run…?

You decide to run; your heart begins to beat even faster as it pumps blood around your body, your brain releases huge amounts of adrenaline and your skin's glands release sweat in order to cool down your hot muscles as they power you away from the tiger and hopefully to safety.

In 1929, Walter Cannon first described this series of physical reactions and suggested it was a perfectly normal process that the body goes through when faced with a situation that the individual feels they do not have the resources to win. So there is, in fact, good reason for this sequence of events. The difference is, however, that in a modern world the exam has replaced the sabre-toothed tiger; it is something that you look at and face, unsure as to whether you are going to stay or run. Of course, it is not just the exam but the whole process of learning that can become the challenge. It is just that, when learning, there is always an exit, there is always the opportunity to say, "I will leave that and come back to it later." But in the exam room this is not an option and so the level of stress is higher.

RESEARCH

In 1971, a survey by Jenkins, Ayzanski and Rosenman, originally formulated to detect behaviours which lead to heart attacks, identified two personality types, type A and type B. Type A personality generally refers to hard workers who are often preoccupied with schedules and the speed of their performance. Type B personalities may be more creative, imaginative, and philosophical. Jenkins et al concluded that people with the type A personality were more likely to suffer from stress which in turn leads to heart problems.

I think we need to be careful with the conclusions from this. I am certainly not qualified to comment on the accuracy of this research but, in principle, I am always wary of any analysis that concludes that people can be fitted into boxes. In my experience, people are always more complicated than the frame you attempt to put around them. However, the extremes can be useful in creating a spectrum that we can use as a form of self-analysis.

Levels of stress

Below are characteristics and behaviours exhibited by people with different attitudes to stress. Take a look and ask yourself how close your behaviour is to both Type A and Type B.

The Type A personality generally lives at a higher stress level and is driven by

- Achievement of goals, and constantly working hard to achieve them. ( )
- Finding it difficult to stop, even when they have achieved goals. ( )
- Feeling the pressure of time, constantly working flat out. ( )
- Being highly competitive and, if necessary, creating competition. ( )
- Hating failure and working hard to avoid it. ( )

The Type B personality generally lives at a lower stress level and typically

- Works steadily, towards goals but doesn't become stressed when not achieved. ( )
- Avoids competition as they prefer to direct their energies elsewhere. ( )
- Does not mind losing and either enjoys the game or may back down from the challenge. ( )
- May be creative and enjoy exploring ideas and concepts. ( )
- Is often reflective, able to think about events, separating their impact into what affects them and what does not. ( )

Try not to think of these as good or bad; in one sense it would be good to have a type A profile, because many of the attributes described are probably associated with success and achievement. However, they are also the attributes of an individual who is highly-strung and so unable to cope. Think of it like this, the type B personality would probably not react sufficiently quickly to the threat created by the sabre-toothed tiger and the type A would be so stressed they would either not move or drop dead of a heart attack in the process.

All this type of analysis does is make you aware that, as an individual, you are different and so you may react in a different way to the same stimulus. It also means that we need different coping strategies for different people.

Strategies to help with stress

Let us assume that you are predisposed to feel more stressed than others. This may be as a result of your upbringing and environment or, as some of the most current research suggests, be related to your time in the womb. In many ways, the reason does not matter.

Let's consider ways of coping with stress regardless of your own sensitivity to it. What we actually want is the right amount of stress. Tests have shown that people perform badly in exams when they are under too little stress, just as when they have too much stress. They operate best with a medium level. So that is our objective: you need the right amount of stress for the circumstance and for your personality type enough to ensure you react but not too much that you cannot think.

It is also important to remember that despite your predisposition to stress, the level is not constant, it changes. For example, after the exam you don't feel stressed at all. Unless of course you have decided to find something else to stress about, what the result would be perhaps.

So, we are looking for strategies that will help channel these temporary feelings so that they are helpful and not problematic.

Exercise

One of the reasons exercise is so good for stress is explained by our sabre-toothed tiger example. During the confrontation, the person would either run away or fight; either way the body would be involved in a large amount of physical exertion. If you experience stress, one of the best ways to relieve it is to exercise. The symptoms of stress - increased heartbeat, sweat, and adrenaline – are all useful when you are exercising, but can be damaging if you don't release the tension in some way.

Diet

Make sure your diet contains the necessary vitamins: plenty of fruit, vegetables and oily fish for those omega threes. Lots and lots of water, avoid coffee, tea and fizzy drinks. One of the ways of detecting stress is that people actually stop eating properly.

Mental

Exercise and diet are important and they will certainly help with reducing your stress levels. They are however probably not as powerful as the mental strategies. Remember, stress is largely self-created as a means of helping in a crisis situation, and is necessary from time to time to motivate. It is a temporary way of feeling that will pass. There are a number of ways in which you can deal with stress using mental strategies. Below are a number of situations, specific contexts, with some ideas as to what you might do that might help.

Imagine the following situations:

Context - Trying to study before the exam, you keep getting the wrong answer. What you begin to do is tell yourself that if you can't get this right, you will almost certainly fail. You begin to get hot and start thinking of how bad things will be when you do fail.

Action – First, recognise the situation. You are talking to yourself in unhelpful language that is stopping your work. Take a five-minute break, walk around, have a drink (preferably water), put on some music. Then think back to a time when you were in exactly the same situation, maybe six months ago when studying a different subject. You felt the same then and you passed. Tell yourself this is just the normal "good exam nerves" phase that you go through to motivate you to work harder.

Context – In that period before the exam, you keep getting lower grades than anyone else. This problem may be exacerbated by confident students telling you how easy things are.

Action – Don't keep measuring your performance against that of others. Simply recognise your own improvements. Do you feel that you are learning things and improving? True, it might not be as quickly as it is for others, but their progress might slow down on the next topic. Measure your own improvements, not comparisons. Consider your strengths, not your weaknesses. The Japanese have a saying called Kaizen, which means continuous or step-by-step improvement. What a great mantra, "all I do every day is get a little better".

Action - There is another solution to the confident student problem. Spend time with people who think like you, who also find it difficult. There is nothing worse than feeling you do not belong and that everyone is better than you.

Context – For whatever reason, in the exam room you begin to panic. This is possibly triggered by something you can't do. You are wasting time and this is making things worse.

Action – First, recognise the situation. Then, take several deep breaths. In through the nose, hold for five seconds, and then out through the mouth. Do this until the feeling passes. As you do this, keep telling yourself that "you can do it."

Action – First, recognise the situation. Why not tell yourself that you have almost certainly failed? And although this might initially sound a very negative strategy, it will release the tension. You may as well just carry on and finish the exam, after all in your mind you know that you have failed, so what do you have to lose. You can now move on to the next question without the pressure hanging over you as to what will happen if you fail.

Action – This next one involves a bit of preparation. When you are studying and you feel that things are going really well and you understand something or have overcome a real problem, when in fact your confidence is at its highest, suck on a particular mint or sweet, the stronger the flavour the better. So when you are in the exam faced with a situation where you cannot think, take some time out and suck on that sweet. It will bring back those feelings of confidence. If you are not allowed sweets in the exam room then a strong scent on the back of your hand can be just as effective.

Action – Imagine your teacher/lecturer is next to you. What would they tell you to do? Think of what the best person in the class would do at this point.

Action –Tell yourself that you have worked hard and you knew it would not be easy. If you are finding it difficult, then just imagine how hard it must be for all the other poor students.

Action – Put it in perspective. Add up how much of the paper you have already completed. You are probably already halfway through the paper and this is only a very small part of the exam.

These are just a few of the strategies that can be used. The sweet one is really effective. The important thing is to recognize that these are coping strategies. They will not turn you into a genius, but they can put you back on track mentally so that you can continue with your studies or answer another question. Exams are passed by what is on the page, not what is in your head, so the more you write, the better your chances get.

In conclusion

This chapter was all about the right mental approach for both studying and answering questions in the exam. In my view, being motivated, choosing the right mental attitude and using exam nerves to your advantage are key elements in exam success.

I think that there is a tendency to suggest that passing exams involves no luck at all, and it's all down to hard work. Although the saying "Luck is what happens when preparation meets opportunity", it would be wrong to suggest that random luck (lucky level one) does not exist. It's just that you can't rely on it or even plan for it. And yes, bad luck can strike, but it's not something that is conspiring to make sure you don't pass. It is a random misfortune that may, in fact, turn out to be exactly the opposite; it's just that you can't see how at the moment.

Maybe the Spice Girls got it right. "So tell me what you want, what you really, really want." They weren't interested in what you don't want. To pass exams, you need to be motivated and motivation works best when you know what you want and are moving towards that objective or outcome. The simple rule is to set objectives and outcomes and write them down. But don't forget the "stick"; at times everyone would probably benefit from a "kick up the backside."

If motivation is about goals and outcomes, then attitude is about recognising that there is a choice how you look at something; a positive that is helpful and a negative which is probably not. It is not about fooling yourself with an artificial "rosy" view of events, but finding the best way to view the situation in order to move forward towards your goal. It is a "simple choice"...

And, lastly in this chapter, we looked at exam nerves, or, as it is probably more appropriately called, exam stress. It's no good saying to people, "Don't get stressed." It's not something they consciously choose to do. The important thing here is to recognise that stress is a perfectly natural way of motivating yourself. There is, in fact, good stress and bad stress. We think of something as being bad stress when it stops you moving forwards. This happens in exams when you start to panic and cannot recall anything that will help answer a particular question. On the other hand, that same panic may energise you into answering a question more quickly and so finishing the exam on time. Have a look at the tips for combating stress and give them a go. Stress is not your enemy but it does need keeping under control and I hope that some of the ideas given above help.

Oh, so what exactly did the Spice Girls want? "I wanna really really really wanna zigazig ahh..." I wonder if they got it?

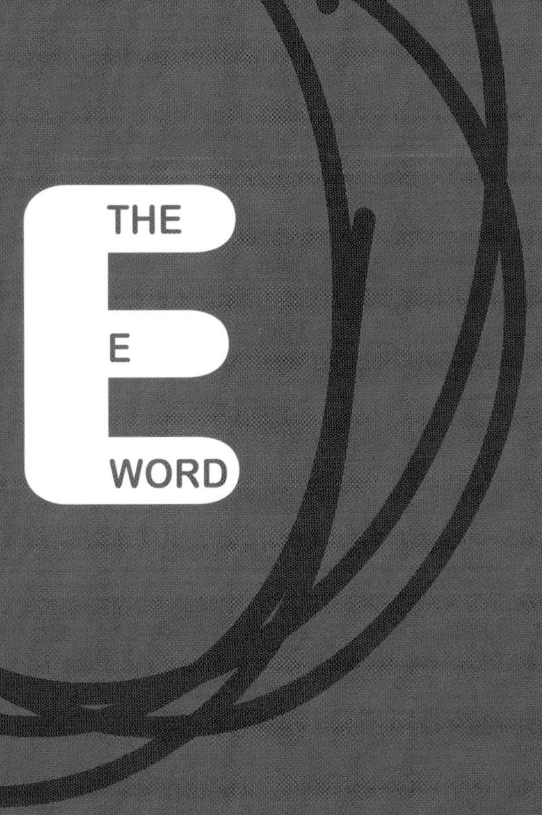

chapter 5
Learning

Learning is the **continuous process** by which experience or practice results in positive changes in behaviour

About this chapter

It would be remiss in a book about passing exams not to include something about how you can improve your ability to get the information into your head in the first place. That's not the same as saying how do you keep it in your head, for that you need the chapter on memory. No this chapter is all about the process of learning, how we learn and by understanding this perhaps being able to learn more easily. It might of course be a very simple process; intelligent people learn things and less intelligent people don't. For this reason I start off with a discussion of intelligence.

It is important to state early on that I do not consider myself an educational expert, and that this chapter is in many ways a collection of current views on learning interspersed with my own personal and practical observations gained over many years in the classroom. The world of learning is a complex one, with new concepts and ideas being developed on a regular basis. But what sense do they make and do they hold any practical help for us as individuals and learners.

The chapter is broken down into four main areas, one what is intelligence and does it matter, two a brief explanation how the brain takes in information, three is there such a thing as an individual learning style and if so is it helpful and lastly can what you believe about yourself make a difference.

Intelligence, can you blame your parents?

I am keen that this chapter does not become an academic discussion of learning and so although I will draw upon the thoughts and views of several leading authorities on education and learning, my intention is to inspire first and inform second. For me the question of intelligence is actually about avoiding the pigeon holing and labelling that people use in order to position others. In many ways it is an expansion of the views expressed in chapter 2 when we talked about the impact of league tables. There are occasions where a label or title gives a sense of identity to the individual. For example if someone picks you for the football team because you are the best striker in the school, this is a positive label and therefore helpful. However if someone puts you into the "rubbish team" this label will probably achieve the opposite and so would probably be considered unhelpful. The problem is this, when you label people they begin to behave in accordance with that label. They begin to believe they are the label.

The result of this so called "labelling" has a significant impact on peoples' behaviour. In the world of entertainment star performers are often told that they are "the best". This is because in order to perform it is necessary for some to draw on this belief so that they are able to deliver a confident and memorable performance. It can however get out of hand when the belief is taken to apply to everything they do. Yes, they may be fantastic singers, but that does not make them fantastic at everything. Having a large ego is a relatively

common trait in the world of entertainment; it has almost certainly developed as a result of this type of excessive praise.

And so to my problem with intelligence, it is also a label, a label that can be used to help or hinder. People who are considered or should I say labelled as intelligent will almost certainly have more opportunities, will probably be more confident and on the whole feel more valued by others, whilst those who are considered less intelligent, feel and experience the opposite. It is another example of the league table mentality. I am of course not suggesting that we should think less of those considered intelligent. No what I want to avoid is people thinking that because they are less "intelligent" this in some way frames everything they do and so limits their ambitions and destroys their confidence.

What is intelligence?

But what does it mean to be intelligent? Although most people have a good working knowledge of what they think intelligence is, when pushed to define it they will often describe it in terms of people being smart, the ability to pick up facts easily, finding school work easy etc. And although most of these descriptions are examples of what so called intelligent people can do they lack clarity.

There are several definitions of intelligence:

"Judgment, otherwise called good sense, practical sense, initiative, the faculty of adapting one's self to circumstances".

Alfred Binet

"To my mind, a human intellectual competence must entail a set of skills of problem solving, enabling the individual to resolve genuine problems or difficulties that he or she encounters".

Howard Gardner

So intelligence could be thought of as the ability to solve problems and in so doing learning from those experiences. If we follow this definition everyone is intelligent. The only question is "how intelligent" and for that we need a uniform test so that comparisons can be drawn.

The Intelligence Quotient (IQ)

In 1905, the French psychologist Alfred Binet published the first modern intelligence test. Ironically his principle goal was to identify students who needed special help in coping with the school curriculum not to create a system for measuring high achievers like Mensa does. Interestingly Mensa actually means table in Latin.....

This work by Binet was the origins of the IQ test.

The IQ range

Classification	IQ Limits	% Included
Very Superior	128 and over	2.2
Superior	120-127	6.7
Bright Normal	111-119	16.1
Average	91-110	50
Dull Normal	80-90	16.1
Borderline	66-79	6.7
Defective	65 and below	2.2

David Wechsler (1896-1981) Psychologist

Mrs. Gump: Remember what I told you, Forrest. You're no different than anybody else is. Did you hear what I said, Forrest? You're the same as everybody else. You are no different.
Principal: Your boy's... different, Miz Gump. His IQ's 75.
Mrs. Gump: Well, we're all different, Mr. Hancock.

Forrest Gump, movie

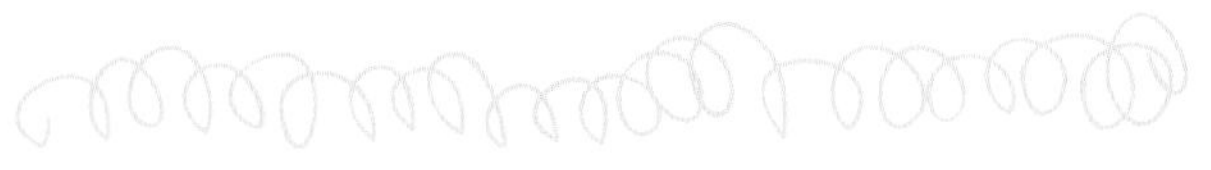

Once the league table is created the ranking will begin. Measuring has some value and can be useful in an empirical sense. For example we can look at people that have become successful in their field and check out their IQ

- Bill Gates (160) CEO, Microsoft
- Stephen W. Hawking (160+) Physicist
- Bobby Fischer (187) Former World Champion in Chess
- Christopher Michael Langan (195+) smartest man in America!

But how clever do you have to be?

To be in Mensa you have to be in the top 2% of the population. However you don't have to be in the genius category to come up with genius ideas. The famous Nobel Prize Winner Francis Crick who found the structure for DNA had only an IQ of 115!

In his book *Outliers* Malcolm Gladwell makes some very interesting observations about IQ. The book is in principle about success but has a section on IQ. In it Gladwell argues, very convincingly that to be successful you don't need to have the highest IQ, you just need "enough" IQ. In effect, it does not follow that the greater you're IQ the better you will do. Some people score significantly on the IQ scale but achieve very little, don't pass the important exams, don't hold down jobs, have problems with relationships etc. If we assume that you have an average IQ (remember 50 percent of the population falls into this category!), then to some extent we can ignore intelligence and move on.

You only need to be intelligent enough!

So who is the smartest person in the world? Well according to the *Guinness Book of Records* (1989 last recorded for this category) this accolade belongs to Marilyn vos Savant an American magazine columnist, author, lecturer, and playwright who has an IQ of 228. Interestingly Marilyn herself thinks IQ tests are measurements of a variety of mental abilities, but believes that intelligence itself involves so many factors that "attempts to measure it are useless".

Drill Sergeant: Gump! What's your sole purpose in this army?
Forrest Gump: To do whatever you tell me, drill sergeant!
Drill Sergeant: God damn it, Gump! You're a god damn genius! This is the most outstanding answer I have ever heard. You must have a goddamn I.Q. of 160. You are goddamn gifted.

Forrest Gump - movie

Nature or nurture

So can you blame your parents? Is intelligence genetic, like the colour of your hair or the size of your feet? Does it change? Is it hard wired? Can you get cleverer? Or do you simply have to accept your lot.......

This takes us into the debate about nature or nurture. Are you genetically programmed with intelligence and if so is there any point in trying harder, a bit like the vicar in chapter 3. This nature, nurture argument is a complicated one and having read widely on the issue I am not sure what the answer is or strangely enough whether it matters.

However here are some of the facts:

- There is a large body of evidence to suggest that intelligence is genetic. This has been proven by taking identical twins and measuring their IQs which shows in many cases that the IQ is the same.
- There is also evidence to suggest that your father's profession, social group, diet, number of years at school, TV viewing and many other environmental factors have an impact. One other very convincing argument in favour of nurture is the so called "Flynn effect". James Flynn noticed that IQ was increasing in all countries all the time, at an average rate of about 3 points per decade, predominantly due to environmental effects.
- If you trace intelligence back to its genetic origin the genes themselves, there is evidence to show that genes evolve and change with their environment, such that the question might be, "when does the nature end and the nurture begin?" And so the womb is considered a place where intelligence can develop and evolve.

So, there are arguments both ways, some authors have concluded that nature accounts for 48% of intelligence and others have shown it could be as high as 80%. Rather than investigating this further which I don't think will be conclusive, let's assume the genetic part of your intelligence is say 60%. This leaves us 40% to play with and I think that should be enough.

Mrs. Gump: You have to do the best with what God gave you.

Forrest Gump, movie

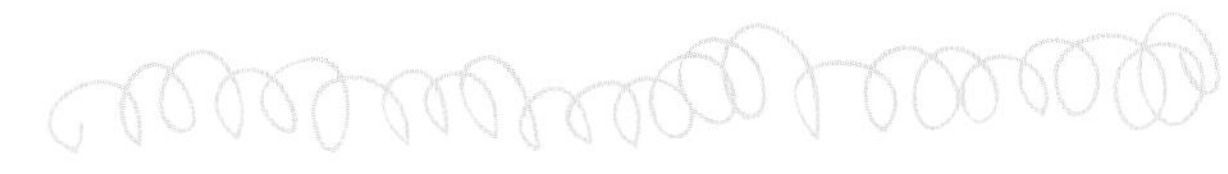

Suzuki school of music

A brief word in support of the nurture argument and one that I cannot ignore is the amazing results achieved at the Suzuki school of music.

Originally founded by Dr. Shinichi Suzuki in Japan in the 1940s, the Suzuki approach has spread worldwide and is recognized as a major force in music education today. The approach focuses on developing the whole child through music. The aim is to nurture creativity, sensitivity and self-esteem and to help children *"become better human beings and create a better world." Dr. Suzuki has said, "The potential of every child is unlimited" and "any child who is properly trained can develop musical ability just as all children develop the ability to speak their mother tongue."*

The Suzuki school of music

I love some of these words, "developing the whole child" – "potential of every child is unlimited".

Children trained in the Suzuki method learn to play in the same way that they learn to speak, by hearing a sound and then reproducing it. This is what Suzuki calls the mother-tongue method. The pupils imitate not only their teachers but also their peers, and find confidence in the common enterprise. Parents are essential to the success of the training and are involved directly as home teachers. Parental participation is inversely proportional to the age of the child - the younger the child, the greater the parental involvement.

With these techniques the Suzuki school has consistently produced concert standard musicians by the age of 11 or 12. This is a very powerful argument in favour of nurturing.

Below is the ten point plan known as the Suzuki method.

1. Expectation of Success - All children can learn to play music.
2. Early Beginning - Begin to play music when they are between 3-5 years old.
3. Listening - Listen every day to recordings of the repertoire, many months before they begin study.
4. Nurturing - Parents always encourage their children's musical effort.
5. Social Environment - Play music in weekly private lessons and regular group classes.

6. Parent Teacher - Parents become 'home teachers.' They help the child during their daily practice.

7. Repetition - Students repeat new skills many times until they master them.

8. Performance - Students perform a lot in group lessons and recitals.

9. Review - Students continue to play their early pieces, using them as the foundation for technical studies and to advance through the repertoire.

10. Natural Reading - Students learn to read music around 6 years old when they have learned to "play by ear".

This is not a bad ten point plan as to how to study. The key points for me are, the **expectation** of success, this confirms what we said in chapter 4 about setting a positive outcome. Next, **repetition**, the need to go over things until you have mastered them. **Performance**, in an exam context the performance would be to practise past exams and lastly, **review**, go back over past exam questions that contain the core principles even when you have attempted them before and arguably understand the principles, so as to cement the basics.

What Suzuki has proven is that you can take "ordinary" children and educate them to the same very high standard. It is a very powerful argument that you can learn anything and one that supports the view that nurture works.

Multiple intelligence theory (MIT)

And finally on the topic of intelligence I want to bring to your attention the work of Howard Gardner, Professor of Cognition and Education at the Harvard Graduate School of Education. He has written many books on education but his most famous remains *Frames of Mind* (1983). In this he makes reference to something he calls ***multiple intelligence theory*** (MIT) and suggests that there are probably eight intelligences not one as we might at first assume. This in many ways changes our somewhat narrow view of intelligence from the idea that someone is or isn't intelligent to recognizing that there are many different fields in which you can be intelligent.

The intelligences he identified are below.

Clever with Words

Linguistic intelligence involves sensitivity to spoken and written language, the ability to learn languages, and the capacity to use language to accomplish certain goals. Writers, poets, lawyers and speakers would perhaps be among those that would have high linguistic intelligence.

Preferred learning style would be to listen to words or write them down.

Clever with Logic and Numbers

Logical-mathematical intelligence consists of the capacity to analyse problems logically, carry out mathematical operations, and investigate issues scientifically. This intelligence is most often associated with scientific and mathematical thinking.

Preferred learning style would be to produce calculations, responding to logic and structure.

Clever Musically

Musical intelligence involves skill in the performance, composition, and appreciation of musical patterns. It encompasses the capacity to recognise and compose musical pitches, tones, and rhythms. This area is clearly associated with composers and musicians.

Preferred learning style would be to listen to music and peoples voices, being more interested in how they sound.

Clever Physically

Bodily-kinaesthetic intelligence entails the potential of using one's whole body or parts of the body to solve problems. It is the ability to use mental abilities to coordinate bodily movements. Howard Gardner sees mental and physical activity as related. Footballers, athletes, dancers and bricklayers would be considered kinaesthetically intelligent.

Preferred learning style would be doing, touching, feeling and tasting.

Clever with Pictures and Space

Spatial intelligence involves the potential to recognise and use the patterns of wide space and more confined areas. People who are spatially intelligent often "think in pictures". Spatial intelligence is highly developed in artists, architects, designers and sculptors.

Preferred learning style would be to look at pictures and images.

Clever with People

Interpersonal intelligence is concerned with the capacity to understand the intentions, motivations and desires of other people. It allows people to work effectively with others. Educators, salespeople, religious and political leaders and counsellors all need a well-developed sense of others.

Preferred learning style would be to talk, listen and have contact with people. Likes teamwork and working with others.

Clever in Self understanding

Intrapersonal intelligence entails the capacity to understand oneself, to appreciate one's feelings, fears and motivations. In Howard Gardner's view it involves having an effective working model of ourselves, and to be able to use such information to regulate our lives. Being self aware or emotionally intelligent, would suit novelists who are writing about the inner self, Gardner chose Virginia Woolf as his role model.

Preferred learning style would be self reflection. The ability to reflect back on one's performance during the learning process is clearly very important.

Gardner has come up with an "eighth intelligence. The **naturalist intelligence** refers to the ability to recognize and classify plants, minerals, and animals, including rocks and grass and all variety of flora and fauna. This intelligence was clearly of value in our evolutionary past as hunters, gatherers, and farmers; it continues to be central in such roles as botanist or chefs.

Incidentally, Gardner went on to suggest that examinations only really tested linguistic and logical, mathematical forms of intelligence and so favoured people that were good at these. He considered it a failing in the education system. This bias probably still exists although it could be argued that there are many more vocational training courses about today and opportunities for non-mathematical and non-linguistics intelligent individuals. I am thinking here about footballers, musicians and even chefs.

Another piece of the jigsaw

When I first came across this a lot of things fell into place. Why could some people think through complicated mathematical problems and yet not even be aware of their inability to communicate with others? If they were "clever", surely they could see the benefit of good communication and so simply use their intelligence to become good at this as well? How could someone be a talented footballer, able to spot opportunities to pass a ball way ahead of others, then pass the ball with pin point precision, yet struggle to find the words to express what they were thinking or explain how they did it? People would say that they "led by example" or let their own performance "do the talking".

The very idea that some people are genetically gifted with some intelligences, but not others seems to make a lot of sense and does perhaps explain why some people seem to grasp certain subjects with ease whilst finding others far more difficult.

My momma always said, "Life was like a box of chocolates. You never know what you're gonna get."

Forrest Gump, movie

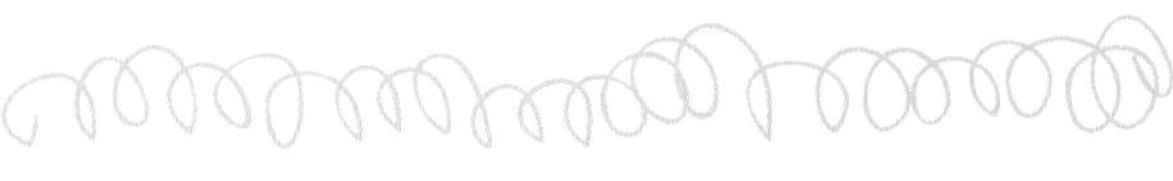

Although Gardner's ideas are far from perfect and he has his critics, he does give us a potential framework from which we can begin to understand a little more about the raw material from which we begin our learning process.

In Howard Gardner's book *Five Minds for the Future*, the five minds are disciplined, synthesising, creating, respectful, and ethical. It differs from multiple intelligences in suggesting that intelligence is more synergistic i.e. these five types of intelligence work together, as opposed to how they appear separate in MIT. These are the five minds that Gardner thinks we should develop in the modern world, both for the individual and society at large. I wonder if the ideas put forward in this new book will have as much impact as his first.

So why do I think you need to know this?

The reason I think it is important to discuss intelligence is because it can become a huge hang up. It can be used as an excuse as to why you are not performing or why you can never be successful. You may begin to think that you are less able to achieve and so destined to be below others.

Understanding intelligence will help you avoid the trap of using it as an excuse for not performing.

Comparison is not always helpful

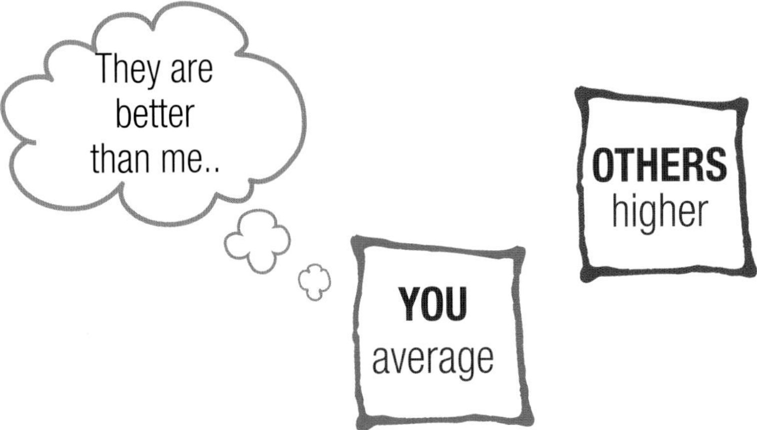

Now this is not an argument to suggest that you can become a maths professor at Oxford regardless of your mathematical intelligence. This is about not allowing this "intelligence thing" or the "intelligence trap" as I like to call it to get in your way. The bottom line is that you cannot do anything about your genetic intelligence anyway. Let us accept the idea that 60% of your intelligence is actually beyond your control. What you must do is work to improve the 40% that you can influence. Think of it as a moving forward rather than comparison with others.

Who cares how well others are doing?

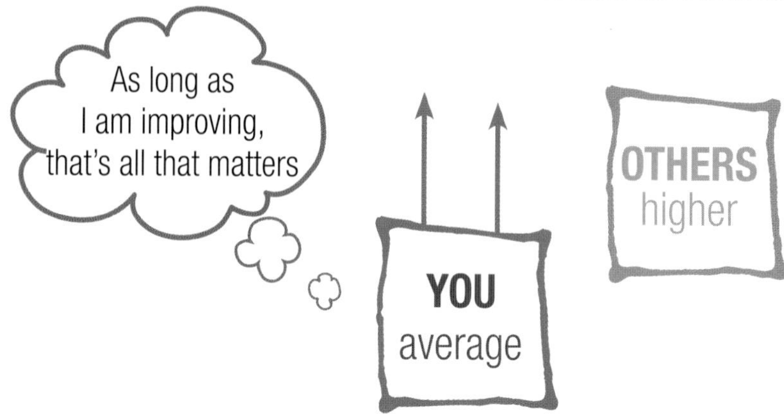

You may consider this a form of burying your head in the sand or fooling yourself. Yet we are always doing this to a certain extent from the day we go to school. You might be the best in the school and as a result feel confident and a sense of achievement. But when you move to senior school you realise you are not the best. Were you fooling yourself before? Not really you just did not know brighter people existed, partly because you didn't look. The question to ask is did you move forward?

If you became cocky and complacent then you may not have improved. And if this is the case you should compare yourself with others and so rise to the challenge that the competition can bring. If on the other hand you are moving forward but when you look at others they seem to be doing better than you and this makes you think "who am I fooling? I can never do this!" then simply stop looking at them.

The reason for this is that it is important that you continue to study and improve. The exam will be the ultimate leveller. You will be compared with the more intelligent student on the day of the exam; there is no getting away from that. But there is little point beating yourself up over something you cannot change. Remember there are many elements to exam success, and how easy you find it to learn is only one of them. Passing is what is important, how easy it was to pass really doesn't matter.

"I once took an IQ test where the questions seemed absurd. I couldn't focus on any of the mathematical problems, and I think that I scored about zero. I worry about all the people who have been classified as stupid by these kind of IQ tests. Little do these people know that often these IQ tests have been dreamed up by academicians who are absolutely useless at dealing with practicalities of the outside world.

Richard Branson's Losing My Virginity

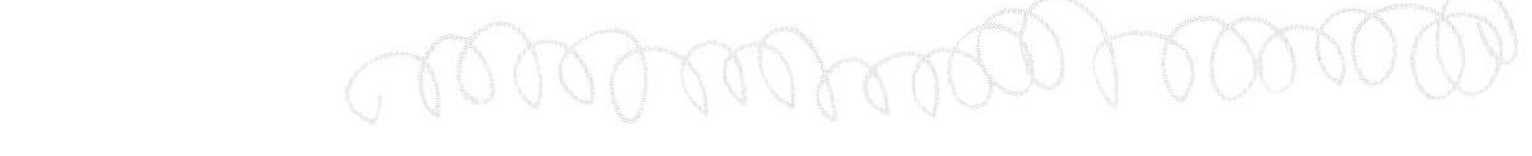

This quote from Richard Branson gives you some idea as to what he tells himself in order to get around the intelligence trap. It seems to work. Incidentally in 1993, Richard Branson received an honorary degree of Doctor of Technology from Loughborough University, maybe he does have a high IQ after all........

How do you learn?

In keeping with my opening statement in this chapter with regard to "not making it too academic", I feel that I should clarify my objectives in this section. My purpose is to explore the learning process by the use of metaphor rather than scientific fact. In my research into learning, I have discovered many facts, but these on their own do not constitute "answers", just perspectives that can be looked at and interpreted in many different ways. I want you to be able to understand the process sufficiently that it will help you learn, not explain the current thoughts on exactly what is happening. This is because you are more likely to remember a metaphor about how the brain works than the detailed explanation as to exactly what is happening. And so if you are sitting comfortably then I will begin.

The brain – makes learning possible

I have been fascinated by the brain for over twenty years. I think the interest first developed when I began studying and was able to detach myself from the problem of studying and look at the process involved in getting the information into my head. From that point on I wanted to know if there was a better way of learning.

The brain looking down and forward

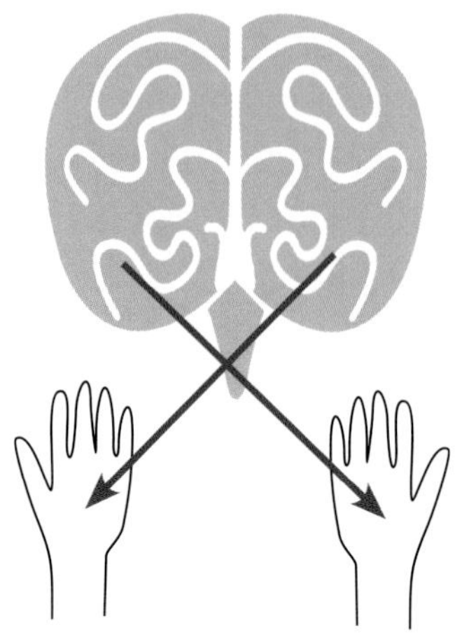

Some brain facts

- Represents about 2% of total body weight
- Uses 20% of all the oxygen we breathe
- Connected by 100 billion neurons
- 30,000 neurons can fit on the head of a pin
- About 75% of the brain is water
- Most senses are opposite, right ear sends messages to the left hand side of the brain

It did not take me long to figure out that I was not a genius partly because I was not and had never been top of the class in any of my subjects, and so would have to work hard if I was going to be successful. I have always thought of myself as a late developer but at the age of 24, time was running out. And so I began not only to study the subjects I needed to pass but also exploring how I could get the information into my head in a way that best suited me. Understanding the mechanics involved in learning put things in perspective and removed the mystery.

There are 100 billion neurons in the brain

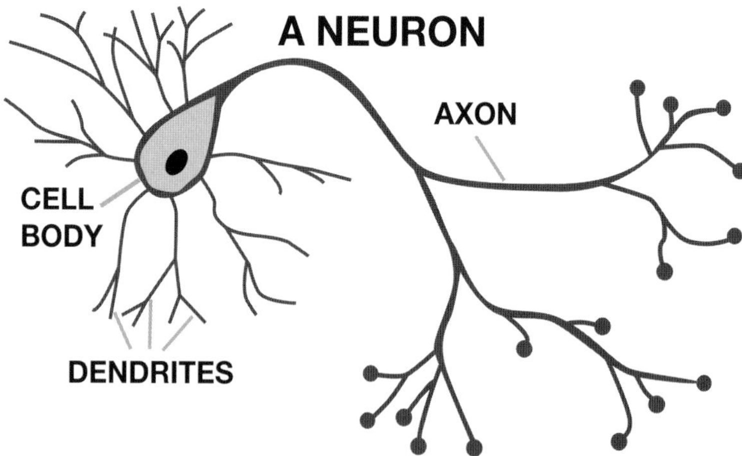

When I read that the brains ability to absorb information was limitless, I thought *Wow! What is my problem? It must be the way I am trying to learn*. The statement has a lot to do with the sheer volume of neurons that exist. When a dendrite connects with an axon (see below) from another neuron a thought or memory is created. There is a small gap between each neuron called a synapse and this is bridged by a small electrical impulse that is created by you when the learning process begins. If you try to learn something once the connection may not be made and so you have to repeat the exercise again over and over again. This is one of the reasons that repetition is essential when it comes to learning.

When two neurons connects a thought or memory is created

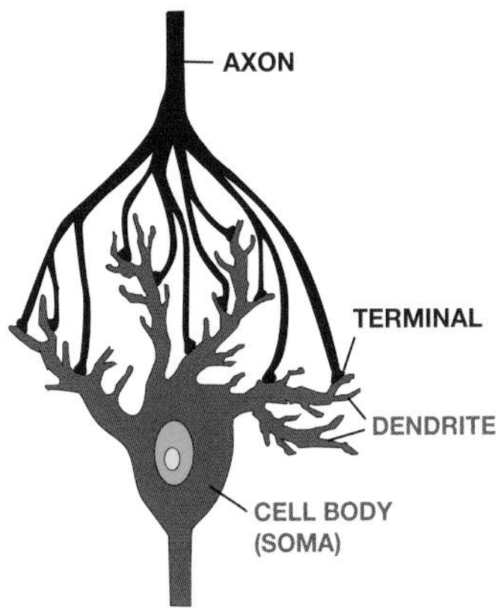

So when you are going over something in order to get it into your head, visualise the neurons trying to connect. Imagine, that every time you repeat the exercise the connection is getting stronger and stronger. This will give reason to your action and help understand why repetition is so useful.

The main thing to take away from all this is that the brain's capacity to learn is immense so all we have to do is find the best way of using it. One other thing that needs stating at this point is that without the ability to memorise learning would be pointless. How can you learn if you can't recall what it was that you learned? Memory is a sufficiently large subject that we will deal with it in chapter 7.

Right and left brain

Although most scientists will tell you that the idea of a rigid divide is a popular myth, they even have a word for the public's enthusiasm for the subject *"dichotomania".* Brain imaging studies confirm that the right and left hemisphere do have quite specific functions.

The main theme to emerge... is that there appear to be two modes of thinking, verbal and non-verbal, represented rather separately in left and right hemispheres respectively and that our education system, as well as science in general, tends to neglect the non-verbal form of intellect. What it comes down to is that modern society discriminates against the right hemisphere. **Roger Sperry (1973)**

The right side of the brain is the more creative or as Roger Sperry said non verbal. From the right hand side of the brain comes our ability to appreciate colours and hear music. The left hand side of the brain on the other hand is more logical or verbal. The left hand side of the brain gives us the ability to construct and understand language, in black and white.

NEWS Italian researchers found people were better at processing information when requests were made to the right ear than the left. Commenting on the story Professor Sophie Scott, of the Institute of Cognitive Neuroscience at University College London, agreed. "Most people process speech and language on the left-hand side of the brain and while it is not cut-and-dry a lot of what goes in our right ear will be dealt with by the left-side of the brain. The findings are reported in the journal Naturwissenschaften.

Roger Sperry was of the opinion that our education system tends to neglect the more right sided individuals. I understand the point that Sperry was making and to a certain extent Howard Gardner came up with the same conclusion. If you remember Gardner said examinations favoured people who were clever with words or clever with numbers. But although I understand the point the reason I mention it is because this chapter is about how we learn and I think it is important that you begin to notice things about yourself and how you might learn. Perhaps you find math's more difficult than art; perhaps you can learn dance steps easier than statistics or algebra. We are back to our intelligence argument, you are just intelligent in different ways. However the Gardner and Sperry point is still probably right, academic examinations, the ones *that matter*, the ones that show *how intelligent you are*, do have a bias towards numbers, words and the left brain. Sperry made his point in 1973 and little has changed, in fact you could argue with the discovery of the league table, it has probably got worse. So what can you do if you are a right brained, non wordy non mathsy person?

Well the first thing is to recognize that this bias exists and so it might be more of an uphill struggle. Secondly use learning techniques that are more suited to the way you think and learn, mind maps, images, music perhaps. And lastly, although this book is about exams and how you pass them, after the exam and after you have passed, the skills that you have may well be far more useful in the workplace than the mathematical linguistic skills that were required in the exam room. So take heart, with effective learning techniques and great examination skills you can get through the exams and then it's just up to you, the playing field is level, let's play!

Conscious and unconscious

Along with our rudimentary understanding of the brain I think we should include something on the actual process of thinking, as thinking plays a key part in the process of learning, you could argue the key part. So for this reason I want to introduce two different ways in which we think, consciously and unconsciously.

Take a second and think about your first day at school...... what do you see, what can you hear, who is with you, think about who took you there and even perhaps what you did.

Chances are you are probably using your conscious mind to do this. You are aware of what you are doing and feel to some extent that you are in control. Conscious thought is often associated with a little voice in your head; something called your "internal dialogue". Now this little voice can play a very import part in how you feel and how effective you are when solving problems and learning. As ever I am not trying to define consciousness that would certainly be outside the scope of this book, I just want to give something that we can work with, a practical understanding if you like.

Now think about how you drive a car. You get in the car, put on your seatbelt, check that the car is not in gear, start the engine, move away from the curb, put on the radio and drive at 70mph whilst listening to the radio and moving the pedals without even looking where your feet are.....

How many of those procedures do you really think about or to be precise are consciously aware of? Most of what you do when driving a car is what we call unconscious, you don't think about it, you just do it. Now from a learning point of view this is great, something that you don't have to think about, you can just do!

We can further examine this unconscious, conscious learning process by looking at the four levels of learning

Four levels of learning

Unconscious Incompetence	We don't know what we don't know
Conscious Incompetence	We know what we don't know
Conscious Competence	We know what we know
Unconscious Competence	We don't know what we know

Level one is where we don't know that we can or can't do something, we have never even thought about it. Level two, we know that we can't do something, perhaps you know that you are poor at spelling. Level three, we can do something but we really have to concentrate, we are using all our conscious thought. This is probably the level most people get to when they sit exams, you can do something but it does not come easy, all the way through the exam you really have to concentrate so as not to make a mistake. And lastly level four, we are at this great place, we can just do something and we don't have to think. Just like driving the car.

Now for the bad news, the best way of getting from level one to level four is..... repetition. The reason you can drive a car without "thinking" is because you have taken your brain through the same procedure over and over again. The reason that this is bad news is because once more we are going to have to work hard to learn. There is no easy way. It does however add further weight to the argument that someone who might be described as intelligent may just have practised a lot. The other interesting thing is, if you asked them how they seem to be able to do something making it look very easy, they would probably say that they don't know, it just comes naturally or even that they are a genius.

Learning styles

The term 'learning styles' has many definitions often being used interchangeably with terms such as 'thinking styles', 'cognitive styles' and 'learning modalities'. However, a number of researchers have attempted to break down the concepts and processes that underlie the term into what is widely recognised as three inter-related elements:

- **How you process Information** – How you perceive, store and organise information, for example, visually, auditory etc
- **The environment in which you learn** – Your preference towards learning in a certain way, perhaps with others or on your own or in a certain setting or at a particular time of day.
- **Learning Strategies** – Your use of differing methods to learn specific subject matter in a particular way. For example making notes or using mind maps rather than in a linear format.

Because we will look at learning strategies in the next chapter and mention how you should study and the environment in which you study in passing throughout the book, for the purposes of this section I would like to take learning styles to mean how you process information.

It might also be useful to look at learning through the eyes of Peter Honey and Alan Mumford who saw the whole process of learning as a never-ending spiral.

Learning is a never ending spiral

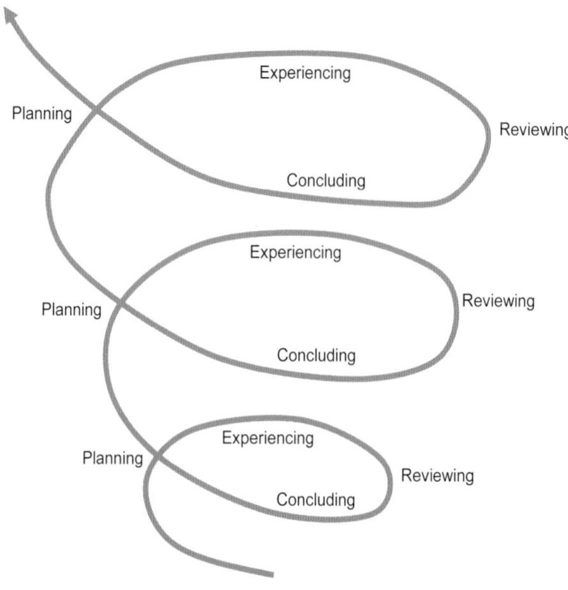

Although it is not possible to have a diagram that reflects everything that takes place in the process of learning, the Honey, Mumford spiral does provide us with a simple and easy to understand model. The model also links learning styles to stages in what the researcher, David Kolb, first referred to as a 'learning cycle. For example, the preferred method of learning for the Activist would be having the **experience**, for the Reflector it would be **reviewing** the experience, for the Theorist it would be **concluding** from the experience and for the Pragmatist **planning** the next steps. More on these learning styles over the page. None of the stages are fully effective as a learning approach on their own and each stage plays an equally important part in the total process, though the time spent on each one may vary considerably. Honey and Mumford maintain that the four stages Planning, Experiencing, Reviewing and Concluding, are mutually supportive.

Firstly planning, it is a good idea to sit down and plan what you want to learn and when you will learn it. Chapter 8 looks at the use of timetables as a means of helping with revision. Secondly, you then experience the event using your senses, this is where you find the content, the substance of what you want to learn, perhaps by reading, writing or attending a lecture. Thirdly, at some point you need to think back, review and reflect on what you have learned. This might be very structured as is the case when you go back over your notes in the revision phase of your studies or less formally when you let your mind wander whilst doing something else like walking or listening to music. And lastly concluding, this could be included as part of reviewing but is probably too important. This is where you consider what it is that you have learned. This final stage in some ways cements the knowledge, think have you learned what you wanted to learn, if not then start the whole process again.

How you process information

In this section I want to look at two different approaches to learning styles, or to put it another way two different ways in which we might process information and so learn. Firstly the approach developed by Peter Honey and Alan Mumford and secondly an approach that looks at processing information via our senses, VAK, Visual, Auditory and Kinaesthetic.

Honey and Mumford

One of the most popular ways of looking at learning styles was developed by Peter Honey and Alan Mumford. The Honey Mumford Learning Styles Questionnaire (LSQ) is not a psychometric instrument, but rather "a checklist that invites people to begin to take stock of how they learn". The four suggested learning styles (Activist, Reflector, Theorist and Pragmatist), are intuitive and easy to remember. Below is a brief outline of each style, although you could complete the LSQ to identify your style and you will get a reasonably good idea just by reading the headings.

Activists

Activists involve themselves fully and without bias in new experiences. They enjoy the here and now and are happy to be dominated by immediate experiences.

- Strengths: Seize opportunities. Open to changes and novelty. Enthusiastic.
- Weaknesses: Action without thinking. Risk taker 'over-doer'. Little attention span.

Reflectors

Reflectors like to stand back to ponder experiences and observe them from many different perspectives. They collect data, both first-hand and from others, and prefer to think about it thoroughly before coming to any conclusion.

- Strengths: Cautious. Thorough thinker. Methodical.
- Weaknesses: Reserved. Worried about taking risks. Lack assertiveness.

Theorists

Theorists adapt and integrate observations into complex, but logically sound, theories. They think problems through in a vertical, step-by-step way.

- Strengths: Think logically. Rational and objective. Good at questioning in a methodological way.
- Weaknesses: Single-minded. Uncomfortable with intuition and subjectivity. Rigid thinking.

Pragmatists

Pragmatists are keen on trying out ideas, theories and techniques to see if they work in practice. They positively search out new ideas and take the first opportunity to experiment with applications.

- Strengths: Practical and realistic. Get straight to the point. Technique oriented.
- Weaknesses: Not very interested in theory or basic principles. Go for the most obvious solution but not necessarily the best one. Very task, more than people, oriented.

There of course will not be one single learning style that exactly fits the way you learn, individuals are far too complex for that, but you may find one that seems to be closest to how you think and this can help you tackle learning problems in the future. For example if you are struggling to understand something it might be because it has been presented by way of a theory and you may be more of a pragmatist, keen to try the idea out yet restricted to attempt to understand it simply by reading and thinking. This may not be a bad discipline, but not useful if you begin to think that it is your ability that is lacking rather than simply the way in which the problem has been presented.

As with the VAK system (see below) we do have to be very careful, these are preferences not labels. Just because you exhibit some of the characteristics does not make you a pragmatist no more than you are visual. You will exhibit all learning styles and, if you are finding it difficult to understand something, change the learning style and it might then make sense.

Just because you show a visual preference does not mean that listening to an audio recording would not be helpful or, in fact, make it easier to understand.

VAK, Visual, Auditory and Kinaesthetic

Take a second and look around the room, what do you hear? What do you see? What can you touch? What can you smell? What can you taste?

The argument is simple: everything you have learned at some point has come to you through your senses, but have you got a preference, is there one method that you as an individual are more receptive to than another? Once again I need to stress this is not who you are, it is not your only method of learning, it is just one that you seem to find the most effective. Now although there is much merit in thinking about how we could enrich the learning experience by including your sense of smell (olfactory) and your sense of taste (gustatory), from a more practical point of view we are going to include these under the heading kinaesthetic. This leaves us with a slightly easier way of linking our senses with the methods of learning that are best matched.

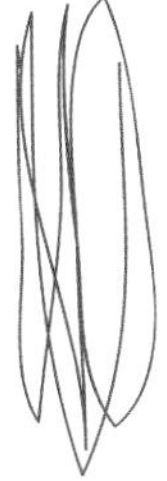

Learning style	How we learn
Visual	seeing and reading
Auditory	listening and speaking
Kinaesthetic	touching and doing

If you are now curious about what your preference might be there are several tests you can do to find out. Most of them are simply questionnaires asking you to think about what you do and linking these behaviours to your preference.

"I hear and I forget. I see and I remember. I do and I understand."

Chinese proverb

This is just such a great quote, simple yet profound. The amount of times when looking around a lecture room I have thought, how many words will you remember tomorrow from this lecture, how many words said will simply disappear, yet when thinking back will you remember the face of the person next to you, the diagram on page X, the picture showing the smiling face of the athlete who has just won a gold medal. Yet if you are asked to look at a question read the requirements and then answer that question, not only will you be able to remember it, you are also more likely to understand it!

If you don't want to complete one of the questionnaires that can help to identify your learning style you will get a reasonable idea just by reading some of the observations below. As you do however also be inspired by the many different ways you can learn.

Visual learners prefer to learn through seeing (65% of the population are visual)

- Are you good at spelling
- Prefer to be quiet when studying
- Are you interested in art, colours & fashion
- Do you find yourself doodling or drawing pictures
- Do you like looking at landscapes, horizons and vistas
- Use expressions like "I can see what you mean"

Learning strategies

- Use mind maps
- Copy and make notes using colours
- Ask for information presented in a picture or diagram
- Watch videos
- Use flashcards
- Use highlighters, circle words, underline

Auditory learners prefer to learn by hearing (20% of the population are auditory)

- Do you like to read out loud and are good at explaining to others
- Are you sensitive to sounds, background noise etc and enjoy music
- Prefer to read slowly
- Follows spoken directions well
- Find it hard to keep quiet for long periods
- Use expressions like "sounds good to me"

Learning strategies

- Use word association to remember facts
- Record lectures and notes and listen again
- Repeat facts out loud with eyes closed
- Participate in group discussions listening carefully to others

Kinaesthetic learners prefer to learn by doing (15% of the population are kinaesthetic)

- Are you easily bored by theory
- Are you good with your hands
- Prefer to get going, impatient with details
- Perhaps believe you are not academic, because until you do something it doesn't make sense
- Remember things by going back over the process in your mind or by rehearsing the movements
- Use expressions like "that feels great" or "I have a gut instinct this will work"

Learning strategies

- Make notes on small cards and rearrange them
- Work through exam questions sooner rather than latter
- Rewrite notes several times
- Walk around when reading
- Visualise how it would work in your mind's eye, see yourself doing it

You will almost certainly exhibit some from all of the above categories, don't make this too scientific, and go with the ones that are just most like you. Also remember you learn best when you deploy a wide variety of techniques that use many of your senses not just one. William Glasser the educational psychiatrist put it like this:

"We Learn....10% of what we read, 20% of what we hear, 30% of what we see, 50% of what we see and hear, 70% of what we discuss, 80% of what we experience and 95% of what we teach others."

William Glasser

But do learning styles work?

There is much debate about whether learning styles are important when it comes to how the information is processed and so how useful they are in learning. The very idea that one person is more visual and so should learn by seeing or any other single method has been much criticised.

"There has been an utter failure to find that assessing children's learning styles and matching to instructional methods has any effect on their learning."

S.A. Stahl (2002)

Susan Greenfield, Professor of Pharmacology at Lincoln College, Oxford University and former Director of the Royal Institution has even been brought into the debate.

Writing in the Times Educational Supplement Magazine (29th July 2007), Susan Greenfield said that, "from a neuroscientific point of view (the learning style approach to teaching) is nonsense".

"Humans evolved to build a picture of the world through our senses working in unison , exploiting the immense interconnectivity that exists in the brain, It is when the senses are activated together that brain cells fire more strongly than when the stimuli are received apart." Abridged

So, given this lack of consensus amongst researchers, why bother to consider learning styles at all? The reason I would suggest that knowing about learning styles is helpful towards our goal of exam success is not so that you can label yourself an "auditory learner", "theoretical learner" etc. This can narrow your ability to learn and even provide an excuse for poor performance, "I did not do very well at that because I am not that theoretical". No it is to broaden your horizons and give you alternative ways of learning should you get stuck when trying to understand something.

Understanding more about how you ***(might)*** learn can really help. Imagine you are sitting there at night reading and re-reading a chapter in a book, clearly getting nowhere, becoming more frustrated at your own abilities. What if you stopped reading to yourself and begin reading out loud, thus changing a visual internal auditory style to a visual external auditory one. Susan Greenfield is right, we learn best when we stimulate the brain with all our senses and not just one of them. Understanding about learning styles is about creating more choice and flexibility; if one method isn't working then change to another.

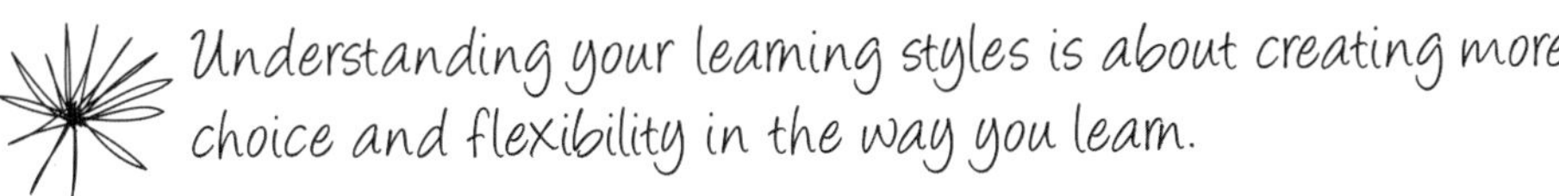
Understanding your learning styles is about creating more choice and flexibility in the way you learn.

Beliefs – why they matter

"Whether you believe you can or you can't, you are right."

Henry Ford

What you believe plays a very important part in the how effectiveness you are not only in learning but remaining motivated and focused on the task in hand. Beliefs are things that you believe to be true but may not be true. I like to think of them as emotionally held views. Our beliefs strongly influence our behaviour, what you do. It is difficult to learn anything without believing it will in some way benefit us, be that benefit a reward or the avoidance of punishment.

We all share some basic beliefs about the physical world. We believe in the laws of nature and as a result we do not walk off the tops of buildings, or need to prove more than once, that a hot stove will burn. We also have many beliefs about ourselves and the sort of world we live in that are not so clearly defined.

THE
E
WORD

The belief behaviour link suggests that if you believe something to be true you are more likely to behave in a way that fulfils that belief.

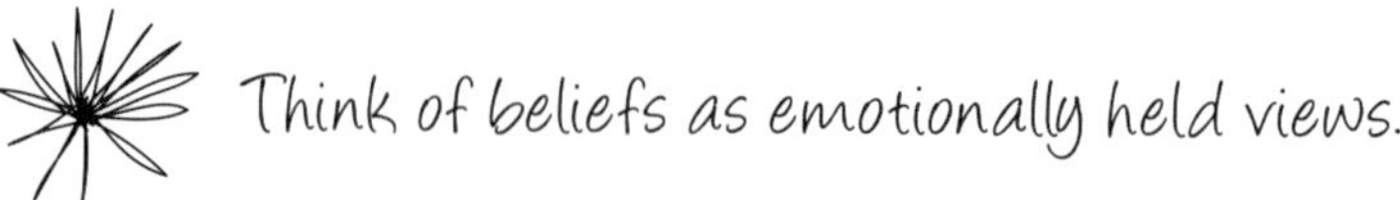
Think of beliefs as emotionally held views.

There are several very important points in the above paragraph and until now you may never have thought about them. One that what you believe **may not be true** and secondly that once you have a belief, be it true or not, you **behave** as if it is.

To gain a better understanding perhaps we should consider where beliefs come from.

Beliefs are learned

If we accept that you are not born with beliefs, let's leave aside the god gene for the moment, then all of your beliefs must come from your experiences of the world. What people, parents, relatives, teachers etc have told you and things you have experienced for yourself. What people have told you of course may not be true, although they may have believed it at the time. The world being flat was "true" at some point in history? And some of the things that you have personally experienced may also not be true, like the belief you had that you were a good driver until you had a couple of accidents and then perhaps questioned where that belief came from in the first place.

In *Awaken the Giant Within*, a book written by Anthony Robbins, one of the most famous motivational speakers in the world, Anthony uses a clever metaphor to explain how a belief is structured. The metaphor is that of a table top with legs. The table top is our belief, and the supporting legs are our sensory evidence we use to support that belief. The sensory evidence referred to are your experiences of the world. For example, when you were young like many children you probably believed in Father Christmas, sorry! The reason you did this was because your parents told you he existed, one leg, you read books that told you of his existence, two legs, your school mates told you he was real, three legs and then the final leg, the presents appear on Christmas day, magic. Now think did your behaviour change because of that belief, were you so excited you could not sleep; beliefs affect behaviour.

The reason for exploring beliefs is not to make you question all of your beliefs, some of them are useful and in many ways define the person you are and how you live your life. What we need to look at are the belief that may not be useful. These beliefs may be holding you back and blocking your ability to learn something.

The physiologist Albert Bandura argues that one of the reasons effective and decisive people are effective and decisive is because they believe they are effective and decisive.

RESEARCH

Limiting beliefs

Limiting beliefs are those beliefs that are not helpful in you achieving what you want. For example if you want to pass a maths exam, having a belief that you will never pass or are not very good/bright is not helpful. Where does that belief come from? Is it the fact you have never passed a maths exam before? That does not prove that you will never pass one in the future. It is just a game you are playing. So ask yourself this question "does the belief that I have help me or hinder me in passing this exam?" If it is not helpful, then choose a belief that is. I know this is very easy to say, but on the basis that the belief you have is probably not true why not have one that may also not be true, but at least helpful and you will need to reinforce this belief with suitable "supporting table legs". And again here is the link, what you believe effects how you behave, so if you don't think you will ever pass a maths test do you think that will affect how hard you study, will it affect your confidence and how good you feel about studying. And If you don't feel good about studying how likely are you to do it. Forget looking for this true belief and accept those that are helpful, the truth is vastly overrated.

Give up that search for the truth, its vastly overrated.

Belief is not ability

A word of warning, do not confuse beliefs with ability. To pass the maths exam you need more than just the belief that you will pass, you need knowledge, skills, ability and many other things. I may believe that I will play football for England. Now although this is an excellent belief for someone who wants to play football for England, I face certain barriers. I am too old, not fit enough, I have no experience and frankly, lack the skills. The belief alone will not make this happen, but what it will do is help harness my resources so that I can focus all of my energy on doing my very best. You could think of this as a way of forcing you to try hard, very, very hard in fact. Holding the belief or not holding a negative one will simply modify your behaviour such that you will begin to do things that will make it more likely that you will be more successful in getting what you want.

As well as recognizing limiting beliefs and changing them there are some beliefs that you might want to adopt because they are helpful or useful. Notice that these are not specific beliefs, they are general ones that should help you deal more easily with many of the barriers to exam success like exam failure, "there is no failure only feedback", maintaining yourself self esteem, "We are all intelligent in different ways", and problem solving , "there are many solutions to this problem".

Useful beliefs

- Everything is possible with time, practice and hard work
- We are all intelligent in different ways
- Don't compare with others, look only for improvement in yourself
- You are not destined to fail nor succeed, the future is not written
- There is no failure only feedback, learn ways to improve, even when success is distant
- Learning makes you better at your job and more employable
- There are many solutions to this problem
- There are no unresourceful people only unresourceful states or moods
- Learning is a privilege, not a right, so make the most of it
- Anything can be learned with time, motivation and attitude

Now you could think of these as sayings or internal chants that you will repeat to yourself when you come across a problem. But please turn down that doubting voice in your head that keeps saying "but everything isn't possible ….." remember we are not after facts or predictions just ways of creating behaviours that are helpful.

I will leave the Queen from Alice in wonderland with the final say on beliefs.

"I can't believe that!" said Alice. "Can't you?" the Queen said in a pitying tone. "Try again: draw a long breath, and shut your eyes." Alice laughed. "There's no use trying," she said. "One can't believe impossible things."

"I dare say you haven't had much practice," said the Queen. "When I was your age, I always did it for half an hour a day. Why, sometimes I've believed as many as six impossible things before breakfast."

Alice Through the Looking Glass, Lewis Carroll

In conclusion

This chapter is much larger than some of the earlier ones, partly due to the complexity of the subject but also because the process of learning is vital to our ultimate goal of exam success. I hope that the section on intelligence gives you some direction and clarity as to what is important, focus on things you can change like beliefs, attitudes and pay less attention to the much overrated subject of intelligence and how clever you may or may not be.

The way in which a neuron links with another to create a thought or a memory makes a very compelling argument as to why revising and going over and over content is so important. The idea put forward by Roger Sperry that we have both a left and right side of the brain is meant to open up your mind to some of the learning techniques put forward in the next chapter. Some of these techniques require the use of your imagination and creativity, these you will find on the right side of your brain. Logic is only one part of the tool kit you have available to learn, only when you use both sides of the brain does the learning process truly get easier.

Think about how you learn, but don't get caught by labelling yourself as a visual learner or an auditory one. The section on learning style should be taken as further evidence that we learn in different ways visually, auditory, theorist or pragmatist. Recognise the differences but use them all.

I hope the last section on beliefs has left your really useful beliefs in place, but has perhaps made you think about some of the things you believe that may be limiting your behaviour and so are not particularly useful. If not then get some that are.

The E Word Interviews.

A Teacher

Q Could you introduce yourself and tell us about your interest/involvement in the exam process?

I am currently teaching religious studies at GCSE, A/S and A2 at a local comprehensive.

Q Do you think some people are more naturally talented, are they able to pick things up easily, what do you look for or spot in people?

I think that some youngsters do pick things up much quicker than others. However from my point of view it's more their interest in the subject and their belief as to whether they can do it or not that is more important.

Q How would you define intelligence?

In the book you said intelligence was difficult to define and I have got to say that yes it is. But then I came down on the side of this idea of multiple intelligences. I do think that some youngsters are good at being able to write an essay and others can go to their science lessons where they are required to do very short answers and get one hundred percent, but they won't do that in religious studies where they are required to do an essay.

Q Do you think the exam system rewards people who are mathematical/logical?

I don't think so, simply because of the other subjects on the curriculum - the artistic can equally gain a GCSE the As's, the A2's. Although I would acknowledge that Maths and English are seen to be the keys to the next step, you have to get your maths and your sciences probably before you can go onto the others.

Q Ever come across anybody who you think was brilliant?

Actually this year I have come across someone. I have a year seven boy who has produced work that is fantastic, it is his use of language that is impressive. What I don't know is if he is good at other subjects. It is a problem with the system because you are only involved in your own subject; you get very few opportunities to observe students in a different setting. On the odd occasions when I have, on what we call enrichment days, it has been very interesting. Sometimes when you give people a different environment to work in you can get a different impression as to their abilities. When I do role play, I will often find that a youngster will shine who might not do so in a normal classroom setting.

Q Do you know your IQ and if not how would you define your own intelligence?

No I don't but I would say I am very much of an average intelligence. This view is probably based on my own performance in the exam room which was pretty average. Which is interesting, because I am defining my own intelligence by my exam performance, all those years ago.

Q Did you find anything particularly interesting in the book about how we learn?

Yes, it was the section where you talked about how the two neurons connect in order for learning to take place. This bought home to me the importance of revision in the exam process. I had just finished writing reports where I had constantly said that children need to carefully revise i.e. go back over what they had learned. What the book said about learning by duplicating activities just backs this up.

Q Is there anything from your experiences as a teacher that helps with learning?

I don't know whether this is jumping the gun a little bit, but it would be the benefits of understanding learning styles. I have come across learning styles before, it's part of our vocabulary as school teachers. We might be observed in a classroom environment and one of the things they would be looking for would be that I set activities that enable all learners to do something that best suits them. It might be, design a piece of work that shows the life of Mohammed. You can do this as a role play, you can write it as a script or you can do a poster. So you try to accommodate all different learning styles.

Before I came across learning styles I may have simply set questions for them all to answer rather than the way I explained I would do it now.

Q When they get to the exam though, is this not a set of questions?

Yes and that has been our argument as teachers, that it is all very well doing all these different activities but actually when it comes to the exam they have had to write, for GCSE two short essays. However they have adapted the RST exam recently, where you now have three shorter questions to start, so those students who probably have the knowledge but can't express themselves very well can at least gain some marks.

Q Mind mapping, is this something you do at school, do you like it?

Again people have introduced this, in fact we had someone come and speak to the youngsters about doing mind maps. They put a mind map on the board and encouraged the children to respond and they were all able to do this more easily by looking at the map as opposed to large chunks of text.

And only in a session this week I was asking a youngster revise a particular topic, and he said just a minute I am just thinking of my mind map. It is obviously something that works for

some people. I tend to use mind maps as a revision tool for students but perhaps would not use them for my own learning.

Q Have you come across people who could do better, who have limiting beliefs and so don't perhaps belief in themselves?

In my experience the actual ranking of ability in secondary school and primary school does limit belief. For example when my daughter was at primary school they had different coloured tables and it became known which table was the top table and which was at the bottom. This had an effect on her that had lasted until she went to college, where she has now been given other opportunities that have effectively changed her beliefs.

Q What beliefs do you have as a teacher?

I left college and got the first job that I applied for which gave me confidence and self belief. However over the years I feel that some of that confidence has been eroded by the need to be good at things other than teaching. I am more than happy walking into class and teaching students I suppose because fundamentally I believe I am a good teacher.

Q What do you believe about your students?

I believe that they all have value. In some departments I think staff find it difficult to believe that certain students have value if they are not very good at their subject. Whereas I believe every student has some value and that they can achieve something, if not in my subject then in others.

Q Do you think beliefs are learned and do you have any useful beliefs

Yes I do I think they are learned, it is about a self fulfilling prophecy.

I believe that all students can gain something from school. If it's not the magic grade A to C then hopefully given the nature of my subject I will have given them something else to think about.

Q Is there anything you would like to add that we haven't really discussed?

I have really enjoyed this reflection that nothing in my professional developments has enabled me to do this, to analyse what I do, so thank you.

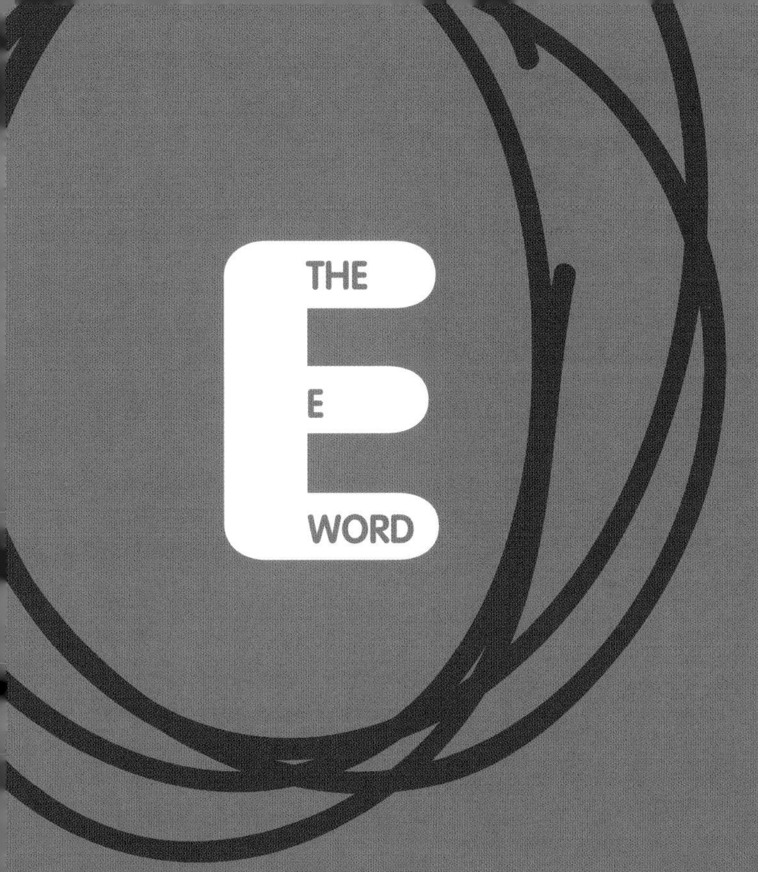

chapter 6

Learn smarter - techniques to improve how you learn

About this chapter

If we are going to learn techniques that will improve the way in which we get knowledge into our heads, then we should take some time to understand what it is we are trying to learn. Obviously it's not possible to deal with the specific content of the subject, but we can explore some ideas as to what knowledge is, how it might be structured and why perhaps sometimes it won't go in.

This chapter is split into two parts: one, what is knowledge? and two, what specific techniques can we use that will help with the process of learning? For example, what is the most effective way of making notes? What can you do when you are faced with too much to learn? What is the best frame of mind to have or be in when learning? How can a habit make learning easier?

This chapter cannot contain all of the things you can do to learn. In fact, I hope that some of the examples and principles will not only inform but also inspire you to develop your own techniques. It should not be read in isolation. Some of the topics discussed in the previous chapter, ***learning,*** could also be considered to be ways in which you can improve your ability to learn. For example, musically intelligent people with an auditory bias may find it easier to revise if they make an audio recording of their notes with some classical music in the background.

What is knowledge?

There are several definitions of knowledge. From the Oxford English Dictionary we have: "**expertise, and skills acquired** by a person through experience or education; the theoretical or practical **understanding of a subject**." For a more philosophical definition we should seek the wisdom of Plato, who thought that knowledge was a "justified true belief." I like that, as it suggests that knowledge is not really facts but simply something you believe at a point in time and can prove to be true - yet this proof is only as reliable as the concepts and ideologies of that generation, or an earlier one.

Knowledge has no boundaries

As I have done in other chapters, I want to explore knowledge using visual representation rather than relying on a literal black-and-white definition. This, I hope, will enable you to manipulate what I am saying in your own mind, so as to give a more practical framework from which you can learn.

Imagine a cube and, on the front of the cube a central image. Radiating from that central image, four related topics all connected by a line. If you're finding it hard to imagine, then look at the diagram below, *knowledge is three dimensional*. Any one of those lines could in turn then connect with another or in fact with another cube.

Now think what happens when you learn something. You start with a topic, let's say Finance. This becomes the central theme as shown in the diagram below. Now there are several different aspects to Finance that could relate to it, but I have chosen Money, you could argue that Finance is simply about Money. Next link Money to something that relates more to Money than Finance. In this example I have chosen Borrowing and Debt. If you don't have money then you will have to borrow it. This is shown in another box, but notice it is behind the Money box, this is where the three dimensional element comes in, it could of course be in front, this is just an example, use your visual imagination, do what it does best.

Accounting is another aspect of Finance and it would also have links going off into a three dimensional world. Of course, this is just a picture, but it does show one way to think about learning.

When you first learn something it's all you know, it is simple and you cannot discuss or think about it in depth. But, as you learn more, your knowledge expands from this central theme. You are aware of more than Finance; there are other disciplines, Law, Science, etc. At some point though, your brain will make the link to something that, on the face of it, may be unrelated, such that Finance is less scientific and more artistic and creative then you first imagined. This type of association or realization is what gaining a greater understanding is all about.

Why are you able to link art with accounting, well thank you fantastic brain for that, we are hard wired to learn and this is just one of the ways we do it.

Knowledge is three dimensional

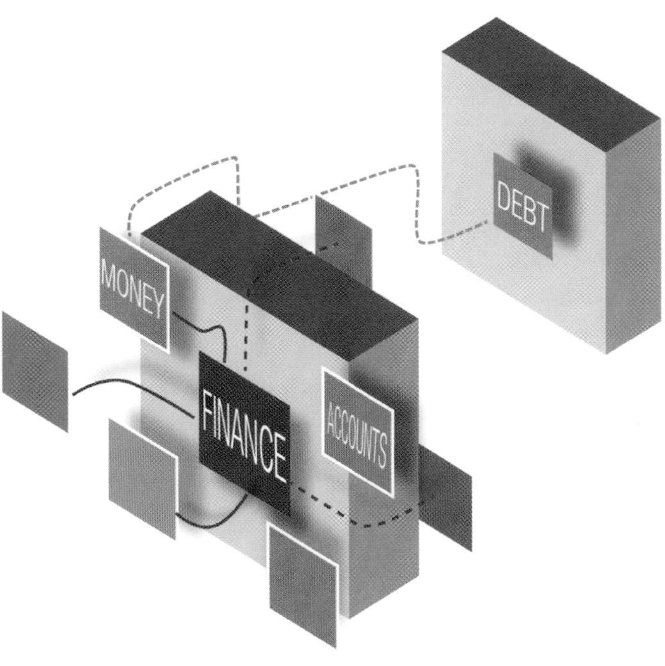

The reason I want to explain this is because I think it will help with your understanding of what happens when you learn, and so will encourage you to use mind maps and record information in a way that is "brain-friendly". There is more about this in the section on note-making. It also shows why, when you are first learning, you perhaps think that someone is "intelligent" or "bright": as they seem to be able to move effortlessly from one topic to another. Their depth of knowledge is considerable. All they are doing is linking things that they know. Bottom line, the more you learn, the better you get at learning. The more you know, the more you have to link, thus the greater your depth of knowledge.

Imagination is more important than knowledge. For while knowledge defines all we currently know and understand, imagination points to all we might yet discover and create.

Albert Einstein

Knowledge blocks

Building on what we have discussed above, I want to talk about what I call "knowledge blocks". A knowledge block is something that you need to know that may be relatively trivial, yet when learned will open up a whole world of understanding that was somehow already there but hidden from you.

Look again at the diagram above. What if you could not remember that Money is related to Finance or, worse, could not understand why. This might stop you making the link to Debt and in a much less logical way stop you seeing the bigger picture that ultimately leads you to the conclusion that finance is more about art than science. This block of a relatively simple fact or piece of information is a knowledge block. But when someone reminds you that Money is related to Finance, it opens up the link and the entire subject then seems to make sense, and it will happen in a split second, a eureka moment if you like.

This is one of the reasons you need to work at understanding and not be afraid to ask what might at times seem trivial questions: one simple piece of information might be key to grasping a fundamental principle.

Levels of knowledge

Although the definition of knowledge is somewhat vague, we can gain a better understanding of what it is by looking at different levels of knowledge and how they are examined. These levels, in one sense, represent different levels in understanding. You require a greater depth of understanding to pass an opinion than if you are simply regurgitating facts. You start with the basic facts, ***the content***, move on to the justification for why you think something, ***justified understanding***, then you learn why something might not be correct and so are able to argue both sides, what is good and what is bad, ***debate***, and finally end up with what you think, ***justified opinion.*** The reason for clarifying these different levels is so that you can change the way you study, depending on what you are being asked.

Although we start with content, there is a danger that you assume that this is the most basic level and so easier, but it is not. In many subjects, learning content is the hardest thing. Also, if you think about it, it is not possible to have an opinion or, to be precise, have a *justified* opinion, if you don't have any facts on which to base that opinion in the first place.

1. Content (facts or skills)

   For my purposes I am going to define content as two things: something that you ***know***, a fact perhaps, or something you ***can do***. This is the detail of the subject that you are studying. In order to find out if you have learned the content of your chosen subject, you would be set a test. Typical questions to test whether you know the facts would be: ***do you know who is considered to be the first Prime Minister of the United Kingdom?*** Or, for a skill: ***what do you get if you add 2 + 2 together?***

   What I am most interested in is this: what is the most effective way of learning content? Well for fact based content, having a good memory would be a start, or, to be precise, being good at memorising. This means you could improve your chances by using some of the memory techniques outlined in chapter 7. Also, why not take an exam focused approach, looking at past exam questions and working through the answers.

   For skill based content the above will not be as effective. Here it would be better to learn using a more iterative,"building block" approach. Start with a very simple example and then build it up to a more complicated one. What is important here is, practice. Go over and over the same question until you can do it, then move onto the next more difficult one. You can learn many skills simply by rote learning and cramming can be very effective.

   I don't hold the view that cramming is a bad thing. Most of the people I have spoken to about exams have all admitted to cramming at some point. I would define cramming as studying very close to the exam and using the proximity of the exam to motivate. All I would say is that you can't leave everything to the last minute and so can't cram the whole subject.

   Notice when you are being tested on facts and skills; you don't necessarily need to understand much about France or why 2 + 2 = 4. When it comes to examinations, examiners are not simply looking to examine content. They don't simply want to find out if you know something; they want to find out if you understand how that content came about. This requires a greater depth of understanding and leads us onto the next level of knowledge.

2. Justified understanding (***why*** something is something)

   So, if we accept that content is the facts or skills, to have a justified understanding you will need to know why do we have a Prime Minister if the Queen is the Head of State? This is a very different type of question. But, once again, memory can help and so can the exam focused approach. Looking at answers as to why something is something can be rote-learned. It may be that it looks as if you have an understanding because you correctly answer the question but that understanding has not come from first principle, i.e. ***I personally know this because I have thought about it***; it is instead coming from the recollection of having read somewhere that this is the right answer.

   So these questions can be answered using memory techniques and by practising questions set on this subject in the past.

Some exams require you to learn content, where there is more application you need to learn process.

3. Debate (Ability to argue both sides)

   These questions are now beginning to get harder or, should I say, different. We are able to rely less on rote and memory and perhaps need to start understanding what we are doing. For debate-style knowledge, we are more interested in your ability to recognise that there are often different solutions to questions: a particular answer is only correct in certain circumstances but not in all. There is a higher level of application: can you apply what you know to this situation? You should be able to see other ways in which something might be done, to spot the weakness in the technique and not simply accept something as being correct. The type of question you get here would be: ***can you discuss the importance of both the Prime Minister and the Queen?*** I am assuming ***discuss*** implies that you need advantages and disadvantages of the argument.

   It is becoming difficult to answer this type of question simply from memory and looking at past questions, although it is always helpful to see how someone else answered this or a similar question in the past. In order to do these questions we need to learn **structure and process**. Most questions that involve debate are easier to answer if you put yourself in the situation being described and visualise the circumstances in the question. Imagine you are being asked to support the point being made and then imagine you need to criticise the point being made. Here, when you see the word ***discuss,*** can you imagine headings in your answer headed ***advantages*** and ***disadvantages***, or ***pros*** and ***cons*** - the good points and bad points. The process is to put yourself in the situation and visualise.

Can you discuss the design of this chair?

What is GOOD about the chair?

Pros, advantages

What is BAD about the chair?

Cons, disadvantages

Debate!

4. Justified opinion (What do you think and why?)

   Taking into account all of the content (facts) you know, all of the advantages and disadvantages of the possible solutions, what is your answer? What would you do? Why? This final level is called *justified opinion*.

   This is not just ***what*** you think; in exams we want to know ***why*** you think it. This is to ensure that your opinion is based on a sound rationale and is supported by content. A typical question here might be: *Should the United Kingdom have a single elected Head of State. Can you give your opinion together with justification as to why you hold that view?*

   In theory, this question may never have been set before. It relies on your having learned everything that has gone before: content, understanding and debate. Looking at past questions will, however, still help as you will be able to gauge the style of question and the depth of answer required, but the approach has to be more about structure and process. Practising this type of question will help you but you will need a good structure and thinking process to do really well.

The other interesting thing about all this is that your opinion may change if you subsequently learn more content. Imagine if you were of the opinion that there is no such thing as a black swan as in Nassim Nicholas Taleb's book of the same name. This is not a random thought, but is justified by the facts that genetically it is not possible to have a black swan. Then you come across the fact (content) that one exists: you see it with your own eyes. You will, as a result, change your opinion, although you will have to go back and check your earlier facts as to why this was not possible. This learning process is continuous.

Levels of knowledge are continuous

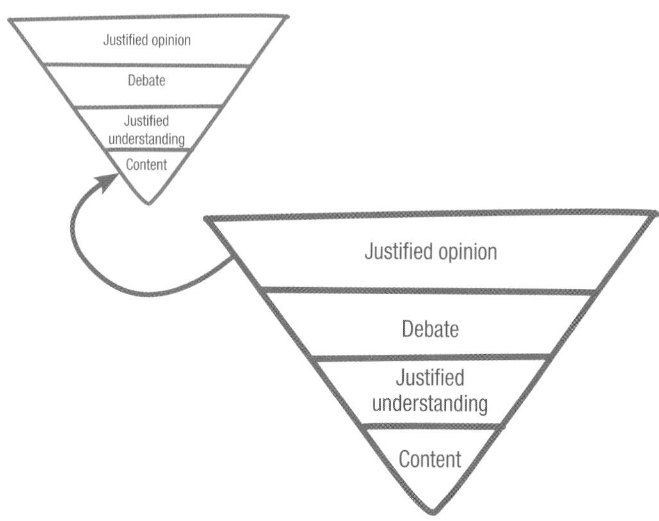

The Knowing Doing gap

This section takes for its inspiration the K*nowing Doing gap* by Jeffrey Pfeffer and Robert I. Sutton They put forward the argument that, despite there being no shortage of information about how to improve business, businesses aren't improving as much as you would expect if mere knowledge were everything. Somehow, there is an important discontinuity between knowledge and implementation.

I think there is a message in this as to how we learn. I have come across many students who know things and yet don't or can't do them. Imagine that you have just read something in a textbook, everything seems to make sense and you feel that you have understood the point being made. If asked, you can remember exactly what has been written and can repeat it if need be. And yet, if something slightly different is asked, you are unable to answer the question. This is an example of knowing yet not being able to do. The truth is what you do know are facts, your depth of knowledge is lacking, you have not understood the topic sufficiently that you can apply the knowledge.

You only have a one-dimensional understanding of the problem and so, when asked something related yet not the same, you are unable to make that mental leap. This is yet another reason why you should practise what you have learned by looking at questions, and past exam questions will always be best. Question practice closes the knowing-doing gap: it takes knowledge and gets you to explore several different ways in which that knowledge can be applied. Reading the answer will help but, at some point, you really need to practise the question. By doing this you are learning how the knowledge is applied and so are improving your depth of understanding. The good news is that, in any particular exam, there are not that many ways in which something can be applied. So for every question you do, the odds of getting it right on the day increase.

This first section has been all about knowledge, what it is and the different ways in which you might think about it. I want you to be able to explore knowledge in a much more creative and dynamic way and as a result develop a greater understanding of how you take in information that will make it seem easier.

The next section contains some very specific and practical techniques as to how you might continue the process of getting knowledge into your head.

Useful techniques to improve learning

Effective note-taking

Whatever subject you are studying, at some point you will need to write something down. This may be simply to record what you have learned so that you can refer to it later, as would be the case if you had attended a lecture. However, making notes serves a far more important purpose than simply recording what is said. The very process of making notes facilitates learning and aids your ability to recall. In order to understand why, think back to the VAK learning styles example in the previous chapter. If everything you have learned has come to you via your senses, the more senses you can engage, the more easily you can learn. So, when you are making notes, you are listening (auditory) writing (kinaesthetic) and perhaps reading back (visual) after you have finished. So, regardless of the way in which you make notes, the fact that you are making them will help.

Copying

Don't underestimate the benefit of copying when making notes. Teachers often criticise students for not making their own notes, yet copying is still better than just reading. Looking at answers and then copying out those answers can be beneficial. What is often associated with copying is lack of thought and it is thought that makes copying more valuable. So, if you do copy notes from a text or even another student's work, do it with some thought.

Purpose of notes

Although notes help with the process of learning, people make them for a reason and most of them begin with R...

- **To record** things that are said in a lecture that may be lost if not written down. When doing this, try to write what is being said in your own words but be careful not to lose the meaning. It is important that these notes are as neat as possible and are reasonably structured with headings so they can be followed later.
- If you are reading a textbook, making notes is often helpful in **checking your**

understanding. Once again writing something out more concisely in your own words will consolidate the content.

- They provide you with something that you can **Reflect, Rearrange, Rewrite** and **Reorder**. This constant process of changing notes so that they "make more sense to you" is vital in creating understanding and in transferring the knowledge into long term memory.

- And, finally, notes will provide you with a hard copy from which you can **Review and Revise**.

In order to explain the different ways in which you can make notes, I have included an extract from a textbook to use by way of example.

Equity share capital

Types of company

If a group of individuals wish to work together with the objective of carrying on a trade or business to make a profit or earn a living, the two forms of association open to them are either a partnership or a company limited by shares. One of the attractive features about being a company limited by shares is that the owners' liability for the debts and actions of the company is limited in amount to a predetermined share, the nominal value of the shares they own. Some of the other characteristics that distinguish a limited liability company from a partnership form of business are as follows,

1. The limited company has an autonomous legal identity. Both ownership of the assets and responsibility for the liabilities lie with the company itself, not with its members (shareholders). With a partnership there is not a separate legal identity; the members can be sued as individuals for the actions of the partnership. A partner can be sued for all the debts of the partnership.

2. The members of a company are not, in their personal capacity, agents of the company or of one another. The directors are the company's agents for the management of its affairs; members only participate in the management by voting at meetings. In a partnership, in the absence of agreement to the contrary, each partner is entitled to share in the management.

3. The business in which a company can legally engage is limited. It can act only within the powers conferred upon it by its memorandum of association. A partnership can carry on any business that the partners may wish.

4. For a company there are statutory provisions regarding its meetings, its accounts and its audit arrangements. A certain amount of information has to be made available to the public. There are fewer requirements on a partnership.

5. A company enjoys 'perpetual succession'. It does not come to an end with the death or bankruptcy of its individual members. A partnership comes to an end with the death of any partner. If the remaining partners wish to continue in an association a new partnership can be formed.

Linear notes

Of the many ways in which you can make notes, this is probably the most common. It is so-called because they are made in a straight line, normally going from left to right. There are a couple of ways that you could do this: firstly, read the narrative and rewrite in your own words; or, secondly, read the text and copy out short paragraphs. Copying out the paragraphs is easier, but not as effective as writing up the notes in your own words, largely because it involves more thought.

Think about how the section you are making notes on will fit with the subject as a whole: in the extract above, the main heading is dealing with equity share capital, which is a source of finance. This extract is looking specifically at what type of organisation would need equity share capital, a limited company, and what about this differentiates it from a partnership.

Taking the example above, this is what copied notes might look like.

Equity share capital - Types of company

Objective of carrying on a trade or business is to make a profit. The two forms of association are either a partnership or a company limited by shares. Debts and actions of the company are limited to a predetermined share, the nominal value of the shares they own.

Characteristics - Limited Liability Company verses partnership

1. Ownership and liability lie with the company - Partners are personally liable.
   Ownership of the assets and responsibility for the liabilities lie with the company itself.

2. The members of a company are not agents of the company or of one another - Partners are agents.
   The directors are the company's agents.

3. The business in which a company can legally engage is limited – Partnership can carry on any business the partners so wish. It can act only within the powers conferred.

4. There are statutory provisions regarding its meetings its accounts and its audit – Partnerships carry fewer provisions.
   Some information has to be made available to the public.

5. A company enjoys 'perpetual succession' – Partnership comes to an end on the death of any partner.
   It does not come to an end with the death or bankruptcy of its individual members.

This is obviously an improvement, as some of the detail has been removed although you always run the risk of missing a vitally important point. Of course if you have some knowledge of what has been examined in the past or of specific past exam questions, your choice will be more informed. Headings and white space have made it easier to read. As mentioned above, if you had read the extract several times and then written the notes in your own words, the repetition involved in re-reading and the mental process of having to think what you were going to say would help even more.

Bullet points and key word notes

I consider bullet points to be notes reduced to keywords and lists, with the bullet point making it easier to read and providing some degree of structure. As with other forms of note-making they should be kept short. Bullet point notes are even more effective if you give some thought to the key word itself. The key words should capture the main point, the very essence of what is being described in the narrative.

Once again, using the example above, the notes would be:

Equity share capital – Types of company
Two forms of association

- Partnership
- Company limited by shares
- Limited Company V Partnership
- Asset/liability are company's V Partners liable
- Members not agents V Partners are agents
- Limited engagement V Partners decide engagement
- Statutory provisions V Partnerships much less
- Perpetual succession V Partnership death ends

Of course these notes will not read well if you have never read the original text, and they are not meant to. The key words act as a link to that original text, a reminder. However, now the notes are in a shorter format, we can begin to think about ways in which we can remember them; the less content you have, the easier it is to use some of the memory techniques outlined in chapter 7.

Mind maps

Although mind maps have many uses, in this chapter I want to concentrate on how they can be used to make notes. In chapter 7, we will discuss more about why they are so effective in helping memorise information.

But what are mind maps? Tony Buzan, who was certainly responsible for bringing the idea of mind mapping to a larger audience (there is much debate as to whether or not he invented them) said that they are an expression of radiant thinking and a natural function of the human mind, a powerful graphical technique which provides a universal key to unlocking the potential of the brain.

I hope that's clear. No, I don't understand it either.

In the context of making notes, I would define a mind map as a way of recording key words that, unlike linear notes, start with a central theme that is often an image, and have content that radiates out from this central theme like branches from a tree. They should be colourful and the note maker should use their imagination in drawing the map, bringing in images and showing connections in any way they wish.

Mind map – making notes

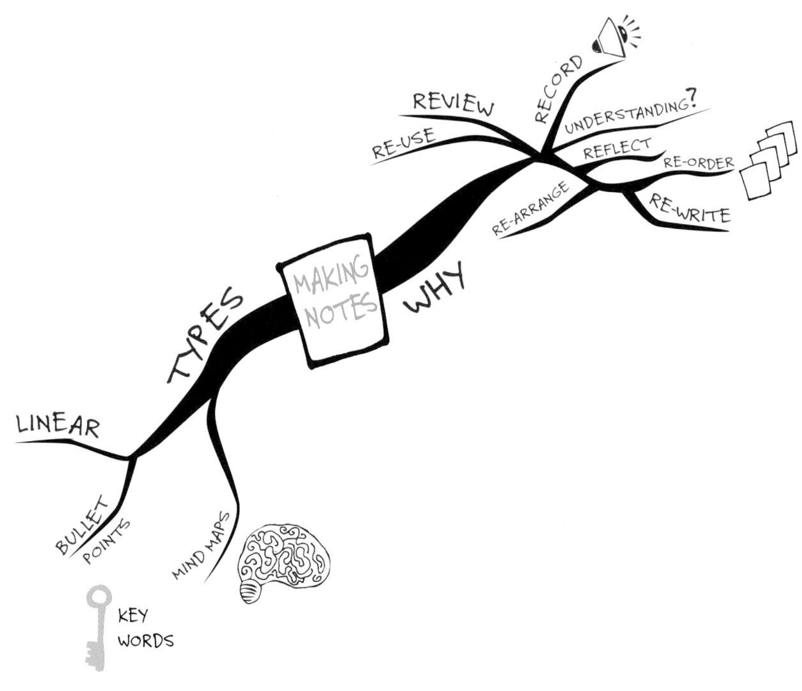

How to draw a mind map

There are and should be few rules to mind mapping as the individual should bring as much of him or herself to the process as possible. But there are some guidelines.

1. In the centre of your paper, draw a square, a circle, or an image that will help you focus on the core issue of the mind map. Inside it, write the name of the subject or topic you are studying. It is probably best to have the paper in landscape rather than portrait. Don't necessarily restrict yourself to A4 paper. Why not use A3 or even bigger?

2. What are the main points or substantial topics that relate to your central theme? Draw branches from the circle, like branches from a tree, to these sub topics. Print the key words on these branches, use block capitals if your writing is not so neat. You can also use geometric shapes for these new areas, or sketch a small picture. Why not do both?

3. The structure will broadly follow the key words that you highlighted from the text. You may, however, find that some of the topics or key words lead you to make connections that at first you did not see. Make the associations and don't be afraid to re-draw the mind map if it gets a little messy.

4. Begin branching off into smaller but related topics. Think fast! Your mind may work best in 5-7 minute intense periods. Using different coloured pens to show the relationship between separate yet related topics can be very powerful. You can use symbols as well as pictures if that seems to come more naturally.

5. Mind maps work to a great degree because of your choice of keywords and the fact that they are short and to the point. Don't feel that you have to expand on these; you don't.

6. Let your thoughts and imagination go wild when it comes to the images. Although a mind map is logical and so requires you to use the left side of your brain, it also requires the use of colours and images, both of which involve large amounts of right side brain activity. Don't worry about how good at drawing you are. You don't need to be particularly good at art; it just needs to be legible and only to you.

Mind map – Equity share capital

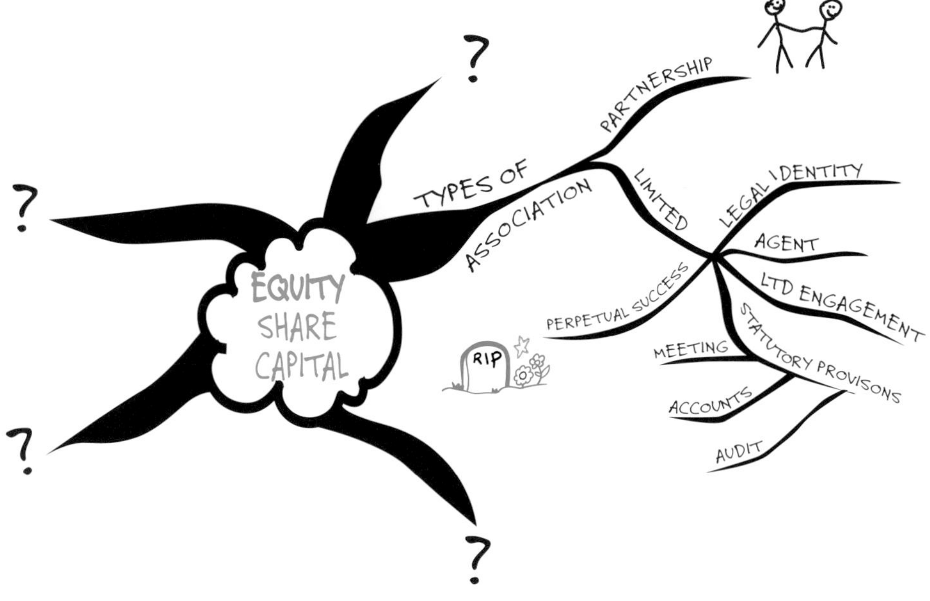

I personally find mind maps one of the most effective learning tools I have ever come across. A map is much more than a simple note taking technique used to record content. It presents that content in such a way that aids learning. You will recognise how topics inter-relate and so begin to ***understand*** the subject, not just ***remember*** it. It is also, as the name suggests, a map: it shows you the whole subject, not just one part of it, so that you can see where you need to go next. And, like a map, you can take many different routes to get to your destination and, in so doing, learn more about the subject. It is also ideal for revision and is much easier to review than traditional notes largely because of the pictures, associations and colours used in its construction.

I would recommend that you draw mind maps for each topic or contents of each chapter. So, if you have ten chapters, you would have ten individual chapter mind maps. In order to see how these all fit together you will require one big overview mind map that covers every chapter or topic, a mind map contents page if you like.

Knowledge is a mind map

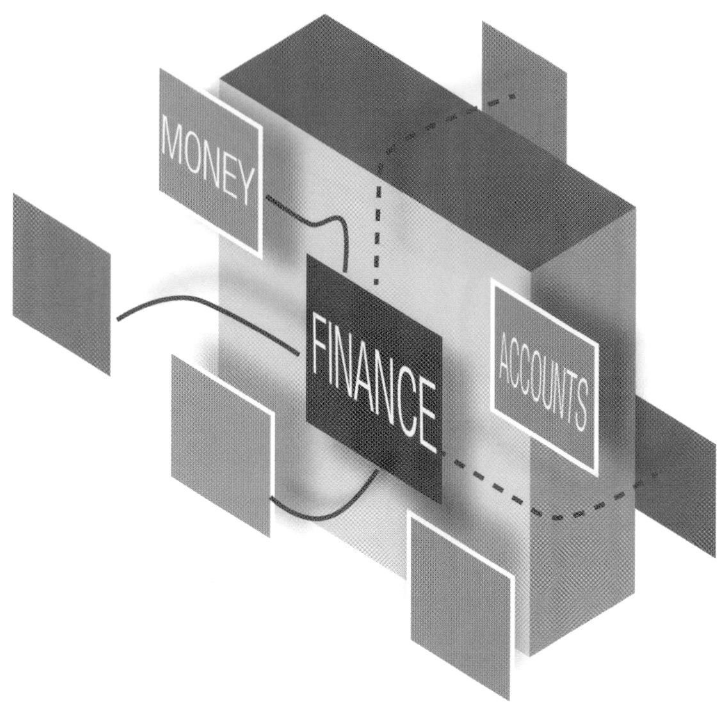

Remember this diagram in the section on knowledge earlier in this chapter. This is drawn as a mind map because that's one of the best ways of explaining how knowledge can grow and links together. It was just a three-dimensional version.

Each topic is expanded in smaller mind maps

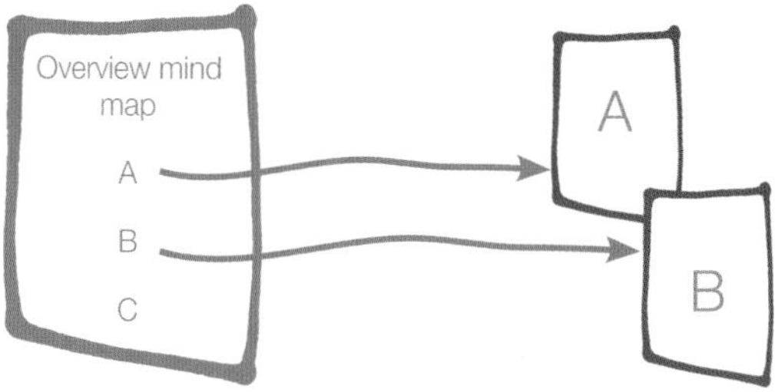

Spider diagrams and Concept maps

Many people do something they call mind maps but are probably best described as spider diagrams, bubbles linked by a single line. These really aren't mind maps as they don't use images, have little linking narrative and are often drawn in black and white. They might be best described as relational diagrams. They are great for showing the links or relationships between different ideas or facts.

Spider diagram

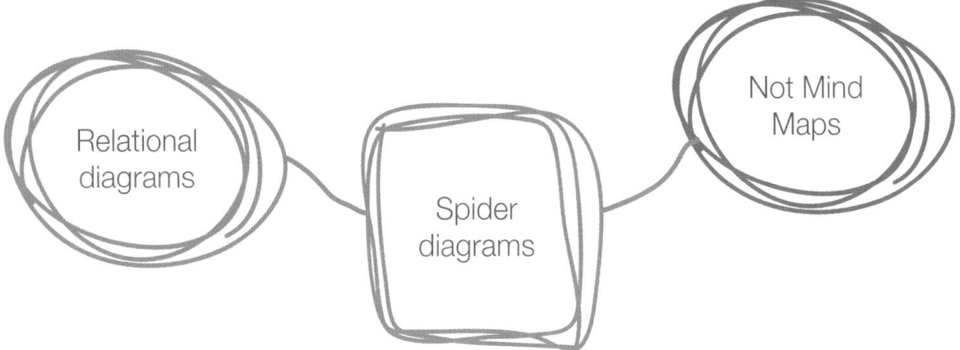

Alternatively, you might want to make notes using a concept map. These consist of two things: concepts and the relationships between them. Concepts are usually represented as labelled circles or boxes, which are called "nodes", relationships as lines or arrows connecting the concepts. Lines are usually labelled with verbs in order to specify the relationships between concepts, while arrows are used to show the direction of the relationship. There is an example on the next page.

Sleep helps with learning

NEWS Researcher Professor Michael Stryker said: "The study suggests that if you reviewed your notes thoroughly until you were tired and then slept, you'd achieve as much 'learning,' in the brain as if you'd pulled an all-nighter repeating your review of the material."

I would just like to expand on the point made above about how sleep helps with learning. One problem many people experience following a period of intense study is getting to sleep straight afterwards. The reason for this is that studying requires a high level of concentration and your brain is constantly being asked to stay awake. So I would suggest that you always do something that you personally find relaxing after putting your books away. For some this may be to read a novel, others may prefer to watch some mindless TV.

Concept map

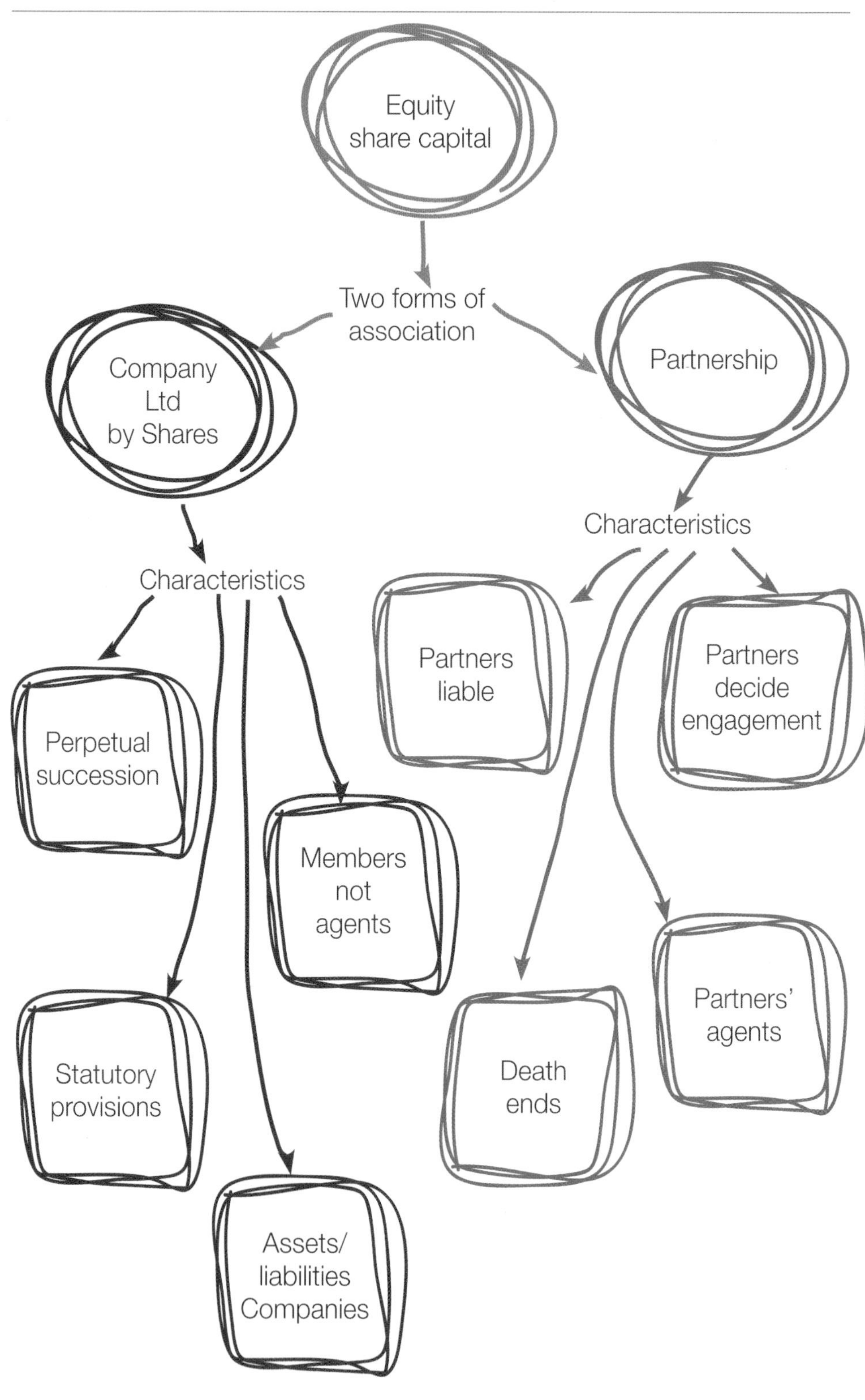
Equity
share capital
Two forms of
association
Company
Ltd
by Shares
Partnership
Characteristics
Characteristics
Perpetual
succession
Members
not
agents
Statutory
provisions
Assets/
liabilities
Companies
Partners
liable
Partners
decide
engagement
Death
ends
Partners'
agents

Putting notes on cards

Although putting notes on cards is not really a different way of making notes, it is a different format for notes. Specifically for our kinaesthetic learners, it enables you to organise your notes and so your thoughts. You can sort the cards, perhaps putting the more difficult topics at the top as a reminder that you need to spend more time on these areas. The notes are very mobile and so can be taken on the train or to work. And why not write on the cards relating to these topics the key exam questions that you need to practise.

State – what is the best mood to learn

Although not really a learning technique, getting into the right state before you learn is probably one of the most useful things you can do to make the techniques you are using more effective.

A state or mood is the way that you feel right now. Take a second and ask yourself: how do you feel? What mood are you in? Do you feel happy, sad, interested, not interested? Biologically, your state is partly created by the neurotransmitters that connect those axons and dendrites in your brain. They are the chemicals that help make those neurological connections. Rita Carter, in her book "Mapping the mind", refers to these chemicals as *rivers of the mind*. How you feel directly affects the quality of those connections and in turn the effectiveness of what you can learn.

Many people believe that their mood is to do with events not under their control. One thing that should be recognised early on is that it is your mood, it is your frame of mind and you are in control of it. This is very empowering as it means that you cannot be in a state or mood that is not helpful for very long.

You are in control; it is your state.

Just think about it for a second: what is it that upsets you or puts you in a bad mood? The most common response to this is probably people, "things" and, of course, the weather. Let me just repeat that list again, people, "things" and the weather. Can a person walk into a room, say nothing and change your mood ***without your permission***, as if they have some magical power? If they can, what is it they have? What is it they are doing?

You are in control

The point I want to make is that, although you do feel angry, upset or frustrated, it is not anything they are doing but instead what you are doing to yourself. The reason this is important is that if you don't recognise that you have at least some control over your mood and the way you feel, then getting into a state for learning will not seem possible.

The best states for learning are those that make learning easier or at least seem easier. Curiosity is a great state of mind if you want to learn more. Children seem to get into this state naturally. They do it by asking why and looking at the world as if they have never seen it before. *Why are dogs noses wet? Why are manhole covers round? Why are some people left handed?

If you are reading a textbook with a sense of curiosity and have lots of questions you want to know the answers to, you will feel excited, turn over the pages with interest, wanting to learn, reading with an expectation that you will find the answers in the next paragraph. And when you find those answers you will perhaps feel satisfied or even more curious as this answer only leads you to think of other questions. With that frame of mind, learning will become more effective, easier, more fun and you will learn more.

Curiosity is a great state of mind for learning – just ask why?

If you can accept that your state is, to some extent, under your control, then all you have to do is get into that state before you start learning.

How do you get into a useful state?

We are all said to have a baseline state, a state or frame of mind that you feel most comfortable with and probably stay in more than others. This, of course, may not be the best frame of mind in which to learn and so needs changing if only temporarily.

There are lots of things that can help you move from one state to another. Most of them work on the basis of a fixed association, called an ***anchor***. Take photos, for example; when you look at a photo, you will often experience a state change. As you look at the image, it will remind you of the events of that day, the people that were there, the smells, the sounds, and you will also begin to experience the feelings you had on that day. What your brain has done is to anchor the emotions you had then to the image and so, by looking at the image again, those emotions flood back. This is one of the reasons we so prize photos, because they are really our route into experiences and emotions that we have otherwise forgotten.

So, if you want to change your state into one that is conducive to learning it is a good idea to have a room or object that you can look at or touch and the moment you touch it, your brain says, "It's time to learn". This will probably be your study, but it could be a particular pen, desk, computer, or anything really. Your internal dialogue will also play its part in how you feel and the state you are in: if you keep telling yourself that something is hard, then your state may well change into one of frustration as to why you find things so difficult. So be aware of your internal dialogue and keep checking that it is conducive to the state you want to be in.

Music can be a great state changer; once again, it acts as an anchor and can induce feelings of relaxation, reflection, thoughtfulness, excitement etc. It is possible to study with music on in the background but I would suggest that this is restricted to instrumentals, as words can often distract, particularly if you are an auditory learner.

People can influence your state, so surround yourself with people who are positive (see chapter 4 on what *positive* is). You are more likely to solve a problem, perhaps something you are trying to learn, if you have people around you sympathising and getting you to appreciate that you have felt like this before, so giving you the confidence to say that you *can* do it.

Being in a confident frame of mind is another very important state. If you think you can learn something and you are confident you *will* be able to learn it, then you are more likely to be able to learn it. How can you create that feeling of confidence? Think about a time when you were in a similar situation, i.e. when you were unable to understand something. Acknowledge that you have felt like this before but that it all worked out fine in the end. This helps your brain recognise that it is not an impossible position and that, although you may not know what you did, you are resourceful enough to be able to solve it. Your mood then changes from one of despair and frustration to one of confidence, confidence that you can do it. The key point, of course, is this, you are more likely to solve the problem in this confident frame of mind than the frustrated one, so just change your mood. After all it is your frame of mind, it is your mood, and it is in your control.

** Manhole covers are round so that they don't fall down the hole. The others you will have to find out for yourself!*

The law of boxes – too much information

It was Aristotle who came up with the idea that we think in boxes. He argued that when we think, we structure our thoughts in such a way that you could imagine each idea is filed away in a box. To a certain extent, this is very logical and yet a little strange that we are talking about an idea or thought as being in a box. Whether this is true or not, we can use this metaphor of thinking to our advantage. It is not a coincidence that we have the saying "think outside the box".

When you are studying, it is always a good idea to break each topic up into separate parts; in practical terms this is often best done by using file dividers. When we come to think about how a subject is structured, we can use this rule of boxes to help break the subject down into manageable chunks.

See the diagram below, it shows a subject or topic with parts that make up that topic. Now imagine this for everything you need to learn, every single topic broken down. It would be huge. You would probably think that you could never learn all of this and, to some extent, you would be right.

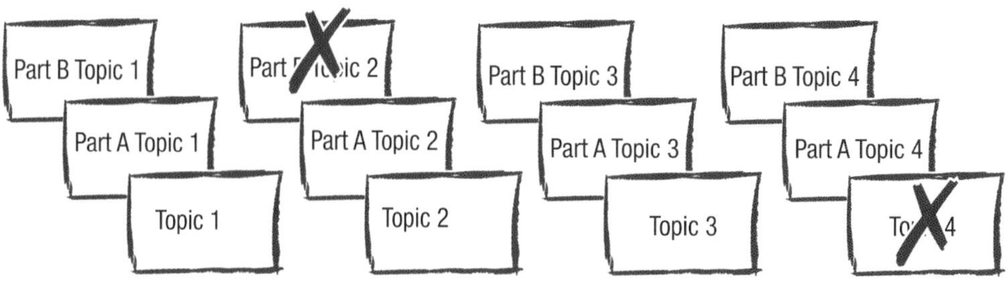

The good news is that if you follow the exam focused approach you don't have to learn everything: you only need to focus on the **key examinable topics**. But there is still a lot to learn, perhaps too much. So here are a couple of ideas. Take any of the 4 topics and ignore one of them, at least for the time being. Or ignore part A or B of say topic 2. Now can you learn what's left?

I know this sounds very basic, but mentally this process is important and, once again, it's about focus. Sometimes you get stuck, you become overwhelmed by the amount you need to study and, as a consequence, do nothing… and that's the worst thing you can do.

This is a visual process which not only helps with the learning experience (visual learners) it means we can do other things that can help. For example, don't just ignore the topic, make it look smaller in your mind's eye and perhaps move it to one side rather than ignoring it.

Make problems look smaller

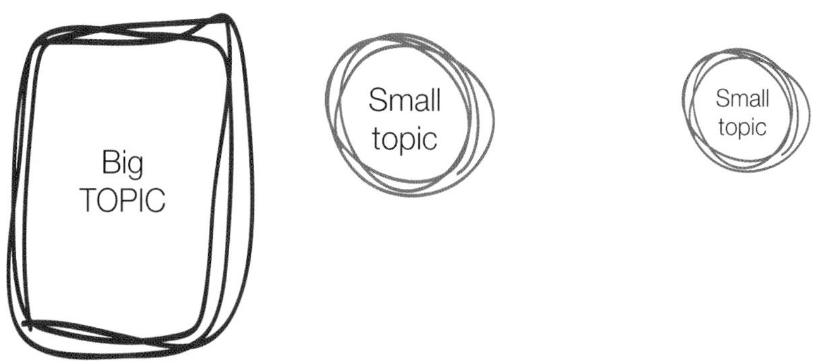

This is not so much about missing things out, but more to do with taking things away so that what you should do and the direction you should take becomes easier to see, a "wood from the trees"-type approach. Have you ever been in a situation where you have had too much work or too much on your mind? How much better does it feel if someone simply says, "Let me worry about that" or, "I will deal with the financials if you deal with the operational side"? Well, it's a bit like that. The mental relief you experience empowers you to go forward and solve your part of the problem.

If you don't have time to go back and study what you have missed, then you do run the risk that if that topic is examined you won't be able to answer the question. But, if you have followed the exam focused approach, then you will only be missing out the less examinable topics, so the odds of it being important from an exam point of view are less. And you have at least been learning something. Looking at everything you need to do and worrying how you can possibly learn everything and in so doing, learning nothing, is clearly a much worse strategy to follow.

Using the law of boxes in the exam

Not only can thinking in boxes help you learn more effectively, it can also help with problems on the day of the exam. Imagine you are in the exam and you have looked at a question, a 25-marker, broken down into 3 parts. Part one is 10 marks, part two 5 marks and part three 10 marks. Put each of these parts into a mental box. Let's assume that you find part one the hardest and so, like many problems, it will tend to look bigger. So, once it is in a box, make part one look smaller. Get on with answering the parts you can do and come back to the smaller part at the end. Of course the 10-mark part is important; it is worth 10 marks and so can't be ignored but by using the law of boxes you can put it in perspective, make it look less of a problem so that you can maximise your marks on the two other parts.

25 mark question

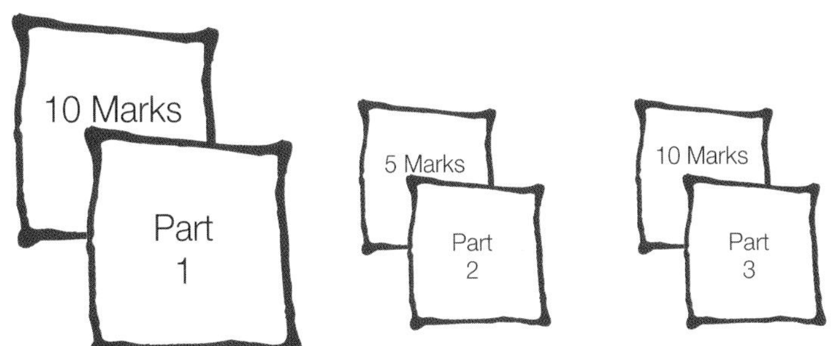

Make the difficult question look smaller

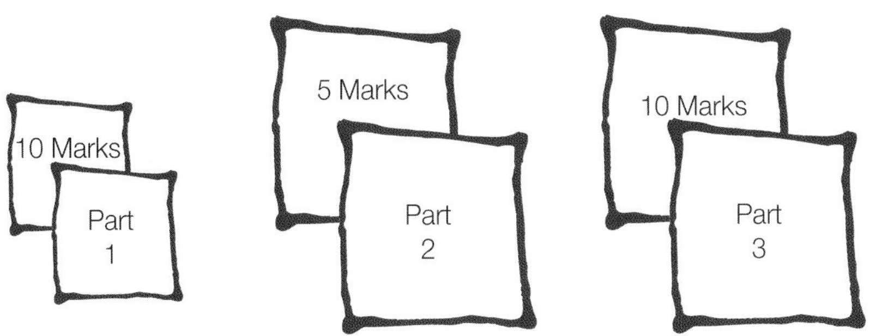

When you come back to part one, you will be amazed how much different it looks and so it will be easier to answer. We will look at more exam techniques in chapter 8.

Make learning easy – get a habit

Habits are routine behaviours that we tend to perform, largely without thinking. In 1989 Steven Covey, the well-known management guru, brought out his now-famous book, *The 7 habits of highly effective people*. In it, Covey argued that successful or effective people have very useful habits. Now, a habit can be both good and bad and is simply a behaviour we repeat mostly without thinking or, to be precise, without conscious thought. Habits are unconscious behaviours.

Here are Covey's 7 habits:

Habit 1: Be Proactive – This is about making personal choices: you can't blame everything on your parents, and you have to take personal responsibility for your actions. You are in charge...

Habit 2: Begin with the End in Mind – This is about having a Personal Vision. Visualise where you want to go and use the vision as a roadmap to get there.

Habit 3: Put First Things First - managing time and events according to the personal priorities established in Habit 2. This is about prioritisation...

Habit 4: Think Win/Win - Win-win means agreements or solutions that are mutually beneficial and satisfying to all.

Habit 5: Seek First to Understand, then to be Understood – This is more about communication and listening. Listening to what people say gives you a better chance of other people understanding you.

Habit 6: Synergize – This is the habit of creative cooperation. Two heads are better than one.

Habit 7: Sharpen the Saw – This means having a balanced program for self-renewal in the four areas of your life: physical, social/emotional, mental, and spiritual.

Now here is an interesting observation. I did not set out with Steven Covey's habits in my mind when I began to write this book, but it is interesting how many of these habits are incredibly useful if you want to improve your ability to learn and so pass exams.

Begin with the end in mind is a key thought in the exam focused approach. The vision of wanting to pass the exam, created the idea that practising and so learning from exam questions is more effective than learning the subject.

Sharpen the saw refers to the need to take time out, to do things that help in giving you energy or focus on a longer term objective. It always reminds me of the story of the Canadian and Norwegian log chopping championships...

Once upon a time, there was a very strong Woodcutter. He asked for a job from a timber merchant and he got it. The pay was really good and so were the work conditions. For that reason the Woodcutter was determined to do his best. His boss gave him an axe and showed him the area where he was supposed to work.

The first day, the woodcutter brought down 18 trees. The boss was very much impressed and said, "Congratulations, keep it up!" Very motivated by the words of the boss, the woodcutter tried harder the next day, but he only could bring down 15 trees.

The third day he tried even harder, but he only could bring down 10 trees. Day after day he was bringing down less and less trees. "I must be losing my strength," the woodcutter thought to himself. He went to the boss and apologised, saying that he could not understand what was going on.
"When was the last time you sharpened your axe?" the boss asked.

"Sharpen? I had no time to sharpen my axe. I have been very busy trying to cut trees."

But the main point here is not the specific habits that Covey came up with, although they are great. No, it is the fact that you need to develop habits, habits that are useful for you in whatever you want to achieve. Now if that is to pass an exam or improve your knowledge of a particular subject, what habits would be useful? Take a second and write down what those habits might be.

Develop habits that are useful for learning and so learn without thinking....

If a habit is an unconscious behaviour and the habit you develop is helpful in learning something then you can learn without thinking. Now that sounds a really easy way to learn. You may have come up with others but here are a few I think might be useful.

1. Always have a book that you need to read for your exams with you at all times. Then, when you get 5 minutes, waiting for the train or even waiting for a lift, get the book out and start reading. It does not matter for how long. The other benefit is you will get far less frustrated by long delays and queues.

2. Do something every day that helps with your goal. It does not have to be something big, sometimes very small things can make all the difference. And as before, it does not matter how long you do it for, just do something. It might be as simple as placing post-it notes with the key words you need to remember around your bathroom mirror. Read them out loud every day until you remember them, and then change them for the next lot.

3. Think positive! Find things that you *can do* to improve on, not things that you *can't do*. We have discussed positive thinking before. So the point here is more about making a habit of it. The more often you try to come up with ways of improving, the better you get at coming up with ways of improving. And guess what? This is so much better than the alternative. If you get something wrong, don't accept it. Look at what you got wrong, then come up with ways of not getting this wrong again. Learn from your mistakes but only learn things that will help you improve.

In conclusion

This is a practical chapter, meant to leave you with some ideas as to how you can improve your ability to learn. It was certainly ambitious by starting with “what is knowledge?” I think it would be a bold claim to suggest that in this section I have managed to answer this comprehensively.

What I did want was to provide a visual guide as to what it is you are doing when you learn. Most people tend to think that knowledge has defined boundaries; in exams this is partly true, due to the syllabus. Although the exam focused approach should have taught you that just because it is in the syllabus does not define how it will be examined - only the exam can do that.

You may sometimes hear people say, “I have learned that.” When, in fact, they may have learned only one aspect of it. No, I wanted to show that knowledge grows in many directions, forwards, backwards as well as left and right and that it has no boundaries. This was partly to pave the way for why mind maps are such an effective way of making notes.

In the section on levels of knowledge the key point for me is that, where different levels are being tested, you need different techniques. For content and justified understanding, memory techniques are invaluable. This is because all you are being asked is to regurgitate facts. For debate and justified opinion, however, you are more likely to need to learn processes rather than content. *What thought process do I follow?* rather than *what facts do I need to recall?* Of course, one thing that works regardless of the level of knowledge is practising past exam questions. That works at every level…

In the second part of this chapter, I looked at what techniques you should use to improve the way you learn. This, of course, is not comprehensive but I hope it has given you some ideas and broadened the tools in your armoury.

The sections included making effective notes. Please try mind mapping, if nothing else.

The best frame of mind or state for learning? It has to be curiosity.

What do you do if you have too much information to learn? Put a box around it.

And lastly, if you want to be more effective in the way you learn, follow Steven Covey’s advice and get a habit. Just make it a useful one.

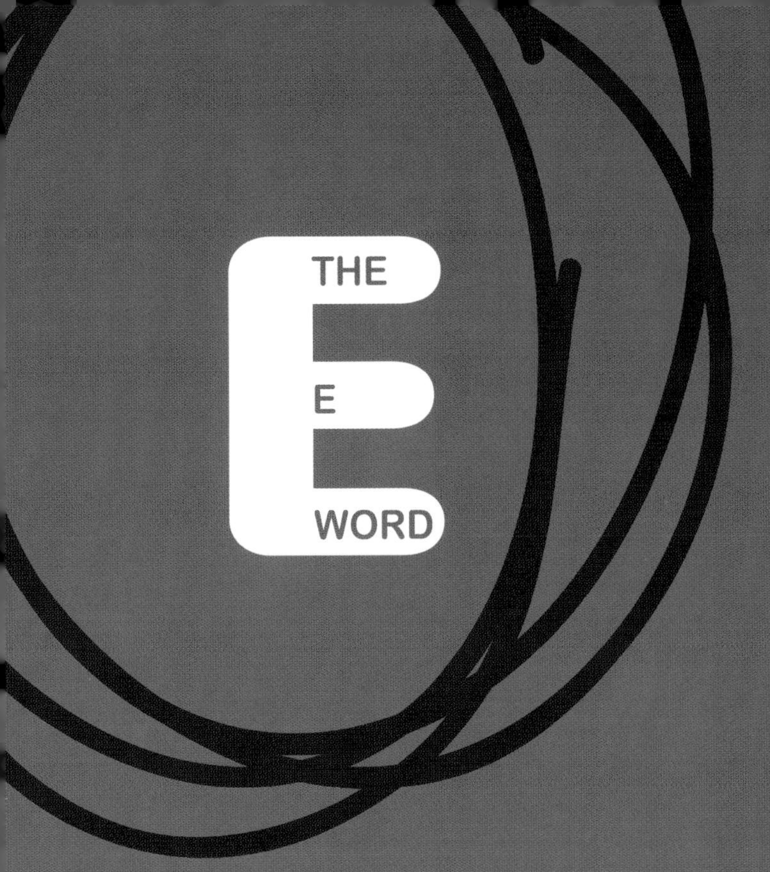

chapter 7
What's stopping you from passing?

About this chapter

One of the important things for me in this chapter is to separate the idea that there are people with good memories and people with bad ones. Research suggests that we all have pretty much the same capacity to memorise, yet some people are able to remember things so much more easily than others. I will argue that this is far more to do with the way they choose to take in the information than an inherited trait. I also want to explore the relationship between intelligence and memory, as there is often the misconception that memory is intelligence and, although there is a relationship at one level, they are not really the same.

To pass any exam you need a whole armoury of weapons; recalling what you have just learned is obviously key. The link between memory and learning is almost impossible to separate: how do you know you have learned something unless you can repeat it later? For the purposes of this chapter, I will assume that you can learn something and even understand how it works. The process of forgetting or not remembering is, therefore, the inability to be able to explain or demonstrate the answer at a later date.

This chapter explores memory from three perspectives. Firstly we look at what memory is, how it works and the different types and ways in which it can be viewed. Then we look at what I call the basic principles: they are the building blocks on which almost all memory techniques are based. And, lastly, we look at the specific memory techniques you can use to improve your ability to recall information at will. Some of these have already been introduced in previous chapters – for example, mind maps – others will be new, and some, on the face of it at least, will appear strange – and, from a memory perspective, the stranger the better. More on this later.

Memory defined

Memory is the ability to retain and recover information about previous experiences, facts or events. When we remember something, a process takes place in which our brains can access that event (or at least the memory of it) to provide us with a reconstruction of things we know or have done or learnt.

Memory is not located in one specific area of the brain, and there is much debate amongst the neuroscientists as to exactly how it works. But, in principle, you should think of the creation of a memory in very much the same way as we described thinking in chapter 5. A memory or thought is created when an electrical impulse is passed from one neuron to another, across the synaptic gap. It is helped in this process by those chemicals called neurotransmitters. These neurotransmitters change the way the information is inputted to the brain, helping cement and differentiate the experience by adding an emotional context.

Although it is not possible to be prescriptive as to one single location for memory (there is some evidence that muscles have memories for example), it is most likely to be found in the brain, specifically in the neocortex, the amygdala, and the hippocampus. The hippocampus is a major component of the brain and belongs to the limbic system. It plays an important role in long-term memory and spatial navigation. It is located inside the medial temporal lobe, beneath the cortical surface. The name is derived from the fact that early scientists thought its curved shape reminded them of a seahorse, and seahorses belong to the genus *hippocampus*. We have learned much about the brain and, in particular, memory from research into diseases such as Alzheimer's. Alzheimer's sufferers, for example, are known to experience a much greater reduction in the hippocampus than normal and this is one of the things doctors look for when coming to a diagnosis.

Remember - When two neurons connect, a thought or memory is created

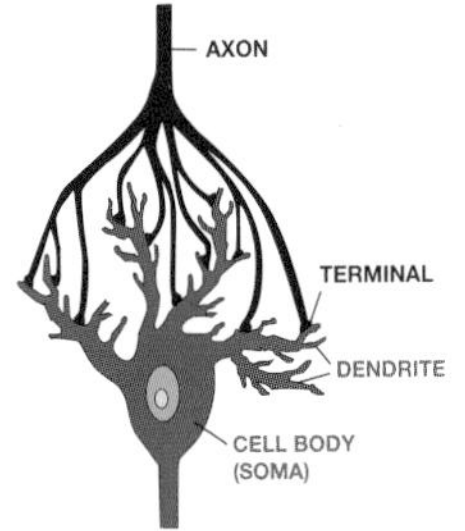

The reason for this brief medical lesson is to take away some of the mysteries and myths about how the brain works, as a way of preparing the ground for some techniques that we will look at later. At the moment, repetition is clearly important as this is the way we cement our thoughts and begin the process of remembering. The neurotransmitting chemicals that link the axon to the dendrite also play an important part in memory. How you feel about the event, the state you are in when you have the experience will affect the quality of the memory and so your ability to remember later.

We all have the same raw materials?

Our memories are fundamental to our sense of self, our personality, our history and the ability to navigate through our world. It's been said that memory is more about helping us predict the future than dwelling on the past. On almost every level of human activity, from communication and movement to problem solving and having relationships, our memories are called into action.

Could you imagine what it would be like if you could not remember anything for more than a few minutes? This was the recent tragic case of Cristina Malcolm from Durham, who was left with a 10 minute memory after medical staff failed to spot a brain haemorrhage that left her with permanent brain damage. So, although she can walk and talk and hold a conversation she simply can't hold the memory of that conversation for more than 10 minutes. And she is not alone. Probably the most famous case of this type of amnesia is Clive Wearing who, on March 29 1985, at the height of his career with BBC's Radio 3, contracted a virus that resulted in similar consequences.

The flip side to this is the fascinating case of Jill Price, whose scientific pseudonym was AJ and who has been studied by James McGaugh et al since June 2000. McGaugh is a University of California Irvine neuroscientist who specialises in learning and memory. Jill cannot forget anything and yet, when her brain was scanned more than two years ago, the results (yet to be published) don't appear to support the notion that she is different to anyone else. Her hippocampus and prefrontal cortex are reportedly normal. She can however recall with incredible clarity events such as what she'd done on every Easter since 1980. You could give her a date and she could even remember what she had had for lunch. So unique is her condition that it has been given a new name. They call it hyperthymestic syndrome, based on the Greek word thymesis for "remembering" and hyper, meaning "more than normal."

An average English speaker has a vocabulary of between 10000 to 20000 words.

Linguist Richard Lederer

Don't be envious of her condition though. She describes it as both a blessing and a curse; being able to forget is a very important part of the brain's function, you are meant to forget things. She can remember all events, happy and sad. For example, she can recall the very emotions she experienced when her husband died two years earlier, she simply cannot forget them. For her, the old saying that time heals is simply not true. And, as for her performance at school, it was very unremarkable; at the time of writing she is a clerical assistant, living with her parents in Los Angeles.

The team at University College London found that the master memorisers have neither higher IQs nor special brain structures to explain their talent. Instead, when debriefed after the memory tests, many admitted they always use an ancient Greek mnemonic technique known as "method of loci".

This involves visualising yourself walking along a well-known route, depositing images of to-be-remembered items at specific points, then retracing your steps during recall.

"What they basically confirmed is what people suspected - people with superior memories are superior because of their strategies," says Barry Gordon at Johns Hopkins University in Baltimore, US.

Reported in the New Scientist December 2002

Despite Jill Price being able to remember large amounts of information her brain is still hard wired very much the same as yours or mine. The research from University College London found that the master memorisers had neither higher IQs nor special brain functions. This tells us that, on the whole, we all start off pretty much with the same raw materials. Your memory is not better than mine nor mine yours and, apart from being unfortunate enough to suffer from an illness that may affect your ability to recall, memorising is more down to the way you choose to input the information in the first place and very little, if anything, to do with your genetic makeup.

We all have the same ability to remember.

Types of memory

It all starts off so simple: memory is the ability to recall something. But what exactly are you trying to recall? Is it a fact, like what is the capital of France? This is known as a semantic memory. Is it how to do something, like how to ride a bike, known as procedural memory? Could it be a past experience, going on holiday perhaps? This is an episodic memory. It might even be a memory of something you don't want to remember, the fear of flying or sharp needles. Before we look at how all these memories fit together, let's look at how memories are stored.

Sensory, short and long term memory

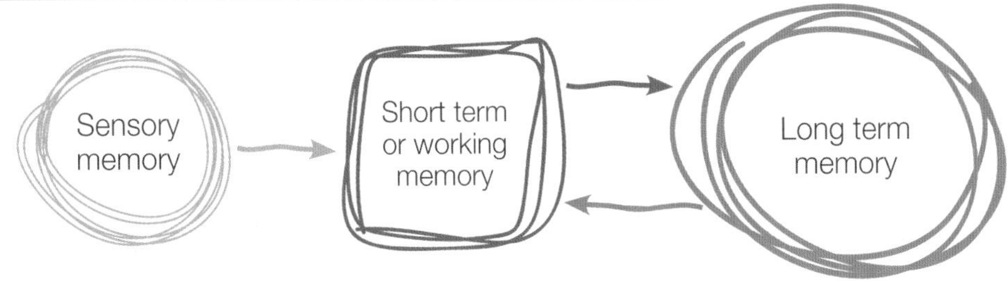

Sensory memory

Sensory memory refers to the initial recording of information in our sensory systems. It can be visual or *iconic*, as when an image is flashed before your eyes, or auditory or *echoic*, when you hear something. Smell, taste and touch complete the sensory memory possibilities. The key thing about sensory memory is that it only lasts around 4 seconds.

Short term and working memory

Having been recognised in the sensory memory, the event or experience moves into short-term, or working, memory. The key thing here is that the amount you can remember is limited to around seven pieces, or chunks, of information at any one time (see George Miller below).

Long-term memory

Long-term memory is memory that lasts for years. It contains everything we know about the world, including semantic, factual information, as well as episodic experiences. In general, long-term memory is organised so that it is easy to reach a stored item by a number of routes. By way of example as to how short-term and long-term memory work together, answer the following questions in your head:

Add 234 to 457 to 984.

Notice how you start to do this. Do you visualise the numbers very much as you would if you were writing them down on a piece of paper? If you are, then clearly you are using a visual sensory input and working on the problem in your short-term memory, drawing on your long-term (semantic) memory to understand the maths you are using to add the numbers together in the first place.

Next question: what is 2 x 2?

You probably shouted out 4. You just knew the answer and almost certainly did not use any visualisation at all. The reason is because many years ago, you rote learnt all of your times tables. This is an example of long-term memory: you may not even know how you know it, you just do.

How do they all fit together?

Now that we have some idea as to where and how memories are stored, let us revisit our list of memories. Episodic memory and semantic memory are a sub-set of what is called *declarative memory*, which is a term for information available to conscious recollection and verbal retrieval. *Procedural memory* is generally an unconscious process, i.e. you are not aware of how you can do something, you just can.

Declarative and non declarative memories

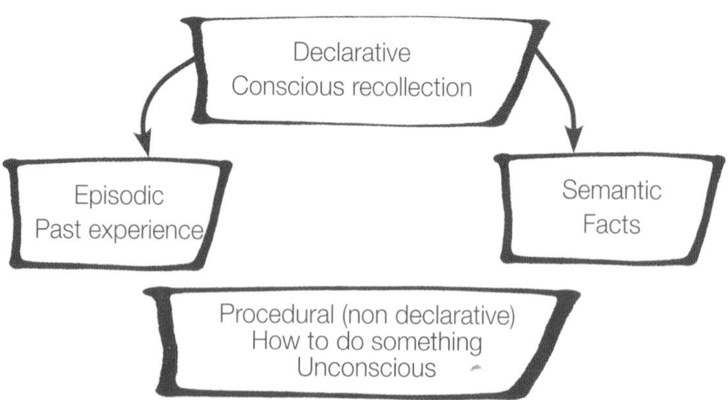

As for the memories that we retain of events or experiences we perhaps don't want to remember, like the fear of flying, these are a little more complicated. There is clearly a declarative/semantic memory of what an aeroplane is and knowledge that it might crash. You may even be aware of the statistics that flying is the safest form of transport. However, you probably have an unconscious memory of a past emotion that flying is dangerous and you should avoid it at all cost. This is probably a much more powerful memory system and will override your factual memory to stop you doing something that will endanger your life or, at least, something that your memory thinks will.

Interesting but so what?

If you want to pass an exam you have to be able to remember. I hope that understanding a little more about how your brain remembers and structures those memories will help you be less critical of yourself when you can't remember something. This inability is not, as you may think, a lack of intelligence and something you have to live with, but simply highlights an area that you need to pay attention to and learn some new techniques for coping with. If you still believe you have a bad memory, I want you to think about what type of bad memory do you have? Do you remember how to ride a bike? Can you still remember how to drive that car? Do you remember your last holiday? If so, you have no problem with your episodic and procedural memory. Chances are, it is your semantic memory that we need to work on and this is where the techniques we will discuss in the section below will help.

Being unable to remember is not a lack of intelligence, it simply highlights an area that you need to pay attention to and learn some new techniques for coping.

Incidentally one of those techniques is repetition, the need to do something over and over again. Imagine those neurons being linked together as you continue to fire the same information across the synaptic gap. This explains why practising past exam questions is so important. Not only can you learn by adding some new facts to your semantic memory but particularly for calculation- or computation-style questions, you are cementing those procedures, the *how* to do something in your mind. They are being added to your procedural memory.

Miller's Magic Number Seven

In 1956, George Miller's study identified that the amount of information which can be remembered on one exposure is between five and nine items, depending on the information. It has become known as the magic number seven. It is, in effect, the number of items that can be held in short-term memory at any one time.

Miller discovered that, if people were given a number of auditory tones varying only in pitch and were then asked to identify each tone relative to the others they had already heard by assigning it a number, after about five or six tones, subjects began to get confused, and their capacity for making further tone judgements broke down.

Of course people can and do remember more than seven things, but they do this by using a technique known as chunking. Think about your own telephone number. Chances are you will remember it by breaking it down into sections normally threes and fours.

Chunking

0121 373 1242

A Ukrainian neurosurgeon, Dr. Andriy Slyusarchuk, has set a world record in memorizing large volumes of data, reciting the value of Pi to its 30-millionth decimal place. Together with Ukrainian scientists he developed a unique system of memorizing information in large amounts, one that so far has no equals.

Russia Today 24 June, 2009

The idea that you can take large amounts of information and remember them more easily by breaking them into chunks could have been included as a principle of memory or a memory technique in its own right. In many ways, it is fundamental to the whole way we learn. You may need to learn the whole subject, but you will find it easier if you break it down into separate sections or chunks. And, in turn, those sections are further broken down into smaller sections, and so it continues. This process creates the metaphor that learning is like a series of building blocks: one brick or chunk building on another.

Break studying down by chunking:

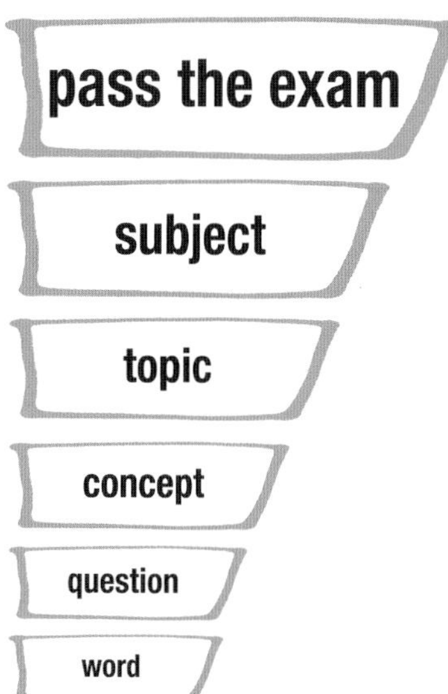

So, apart from numbers you will find much of what you need to learn, and, in turn, memorise, is far easier if you break it down into its component parts. For example, chunk subjects like history into time periods, people or events.

Times

- AD 43 Romans
- 450 Saxons
- 793 Vikings
- 1066 Normans
- 1485 Tudors
- 1837 Victorian
- 1939 World war II

British Prime ministers

- Harold Macmillan
- Sir Alec Douglas-Home
- Harold Wilson
- Edward Heath
- Harold Wilson
- James Callaghan
- Margaret Thatcher
- John Major
- Tony Blair
- Gordon Brown

If studying parts of the body in biology or medicine, chunk them into where they are located in the body or all words that begin with a certain term or expression. And if studying accountancy break the accounting standards down under the subjects to which they relate. For example, Tax standards – FRS 19 Deferred tax and FRS 16 Current tax, Business combinations - FRS 6 Acquisitions and Mergers FRS 2 Accounting for Subsidiary Undertakings.

Chunking leads naturally into organisation and association, this is discussed further below as a principle of memory.

Memory is more like cheese

Imagine that what you have learned (and so remembered) looks like a triangle. With the starting point being at the bottom: when you begin to learn your subject, you know nothing. Gradually you develop a broad base of understanding, a platform, if you like, on which all future knowledge is built. You then step up into the higher levels of the subject, level one and level two. You pass exams at these levels and so prove that you have the necessary expertise. The assumption often made is that because you have passed an exam at that level you will forever retain the same level of knowledge and have the same skills you had at the time of passing the exam.

Memory is more like cheese

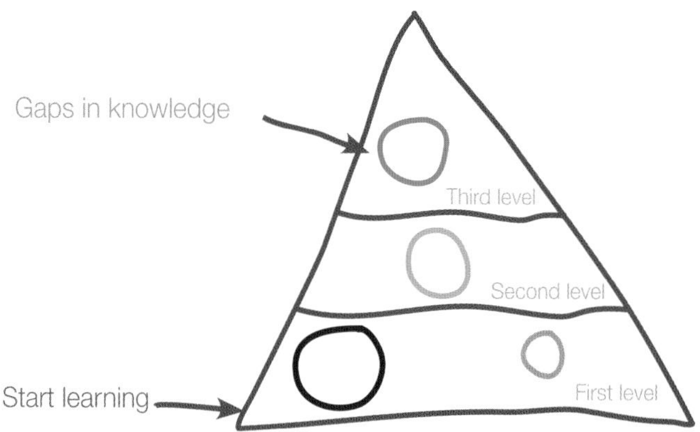

This of course is simply not true, you may remember how to do something, procedural memory, but be unsure about the facts, semantic memory. You may remember having been able to do something in the past, episodic memory, yet not be able to do it now. You may, of course, remember nothing. The reason is simple: if you do not use what you have learned on a regular basis, you will often forget. When it comes to memory, your understanding of a subject decays over time unless it is somehow refreshed. Think back to our example in chapter five as to how the neurons are linked, fired by an electrical impulse. Yet the power of this relationship diminishes without repetition and practice.

From a learning and memory point of view, this is not a complete disaster. Notice the triangle still stands; it's just that it is full of holes. Things you could once do may well need revising. This is one of the reasons that revision is so important. Without it, you are in danger of being asked a question on something you could do, even very well. Yet, on the day of the exam, you may fail to remember because it has become a "hole in your piece of cheese".

This can be very frustrating and there are few things worse than knowing you once understood something but don't now. It often prompts people to say that they are going backwards with the subject, not forwards.

Principles of memory

Now that we understand a little more about what memory is and how memories are constructed, let us now consider the process we go through in memorising. Although examples are used here to illustrate the points being made, specific examples of how to use the techniques are in the next section, Memory Techniques.

Principle one - It's all about input

The first principle of memory: how you record (input) the information in the first place is critical if you want to remember it later.

Take a look at the diagram below and imagine you are trying to memorise a list of the wives of Henry the Eighth.

- Catherine of Aragon
- Anne Boleyn
- Jane Seymour
- Anne of Cleves
- Catherine Howard
- Catherine Parr

This list of wives, we will call the event. In order to remember the event, we need to encode it in such a way that, when we come to retrieve the information, we know how to find it. You see, it's all about input: if you put the information in your head in the right way then, when you come to look for it, if it has been labelled properly, you are more likely to find it.

Memory process – it's about input

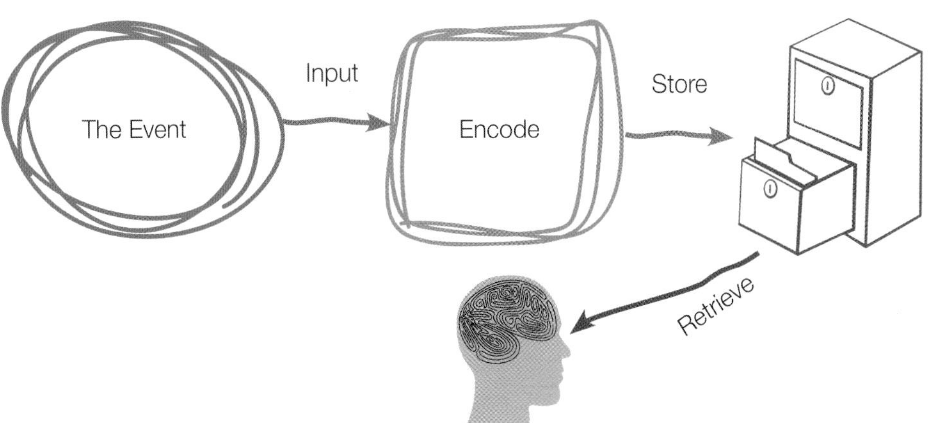

For example, think about the wives of Henry the Eighth. If I asked you to list them, what process would you go through to retrieve them? Do you see the words? Do you see pictures of the wives? Is it difficult to think of one of the wives without the others?

Now think what you did perhaps many years ago, to get them into your head in the first place. Did you write the names out several times? Did you put their names on a time line and put it up on your wall so that you could look at them every morning? Did you chant their names in a rhythmic fashion? Or, ironically, can't you remember?

We can look at the many different ways there are of encoding events; all I want to establish for the moment is that you did encode them. This may have been by visualising the words, the faces and using repetition to reinforce the experience to make sure the events stayed with you. In simple terms, the more powerful the encoding system, the easier it will be to find the information when you need it.

Ways to Input

The way you input the information is key to your ability to recall it latter.

1. Get into the right mood

The way you feel, your emotional state, the mood you are in all create powerful ways of encoding information. Take for example the classic memory question: can you remember where you were when Kennedy was shot? Or more recent events: when the Twin Towers collapsed or when Princess Diana or Michael Jackson died?

The reason you tend to remember these events is partly because of the initial state of shock you were in when you first heard it. It was an event that was unexpected, something you never imagined possible. Of course, the event was reinforced by a huge amount of media coverage so that you may well be able to recall very clear images of what happened. Also, everyone would have been talking about it, including you. Nevertheless, it is still the emotional input that created the most powerful part of the memory.

Remember those neurotransmitters, the chemicals that enable the synaptic gap to be bridged? The relationship between the two neurons will be strengthened or weakened by the type of chemical released at the time and the release of that chemical will be determined by the mood you are in.

From a practical exam point of view, the best state to be in when studying is curiosity. When in the revision period, the heightened sense of tension you will feel, as a result of the actual exam date getting closer, will naturally aid your ability to retain information; you will be sharper more alert and more focused. However, as mentioned before when discussing state, there is a potential downside. You may begin to feel that you cannot rise to the challenge and your state changes from one of nervous tension to stress. This can have a negative effect on memory, as the body begins to behave in a way more suited to physical survival rather than to sitting down and passing an exam.

2. Use your imagination - exaggerate

Something that is imagined is, by definition, not real: it is made up, created by you and can be an image, a sound, a smell, a taste or a feeling. For most people, an imagined event will probably be visual or auditory. We have a much greater ability to recall events if we play a part in their original construction. For example, if you were asked to remember that Anne Boleyn was executed on the 19th May, 1536 at 8.00am, you should use your own imagination to create a way of remembering this event. The event should be large, loud and unusual, do not go for something that is ordinary, ordinary is never easy to remember.

Using my imagination I would create the image of a women dressed in black but with a huge sign around her neck and it is flashing "**8AM**" "**8AM**" in a bright neon sign. She is walking towards a tree, a hawthorn tree, known as the **May** tree, its large white flowers are falling to the ground, yet the minute they hit the ground they fly into the air propelled by a huge gust of wind. Ann looks up at the bright blue background and can see that the flowers have drawn the number **19** in the sky. A crowd has gathered to watch her being beheaded yet they shout "**1536** hit her with bricks", "**1536** hit her with bricks".

Now I know that some of this sounds strange but this is my story. Have a practice and create your own, but remember let your imagination run wild. The more bizarre, the more exaggerated the events the easier they will be to remember.

3. Use your senses

As all information is fed into the brain through the senses, it should come as no surprise that they play an important part in what we can remember. They are effectively the input system. The combination and use of as many of your senses as possible will help create a unique event and, as was said earlier, the more unique the event, the easier it will be to remember.

Some people don't get a choice in this: they have something called synaesthesia. This condition, said to occur in 1 in 25,000 people, is the result of the senses getting cross wired. For example, a person with synaesthesia may see colours when they hear a sound, or can actually taste words. One very famous synaesthetic was Solomon Shereshevskii, the famous Russian memonist, who, it is said, had a memory so perfect that he could recall every minute of his life in graphic detail. He once told someone that they had a "crumbly yellow voice" and experienced another person's voice like a "flame with fibres protruding from it".

Your sense of smell and taste are of course related, ever had a cold and been unable to taste your food? From the perspective of remembering it is your sense of smell that is the most important, largely because smells feed directly into the limbic system, which if you remember is where memory is stored. Not many people use smells when it comes to learning and memorising, largely because it is difficult to think how you can do it. You can however buy scented marker pens which could be used to create an association between a topic and a smell. Or use the spray of a perfume, to create a similar effect.

But from a practical perspective the two most important sensory forms of input are your ability to visualise and to hear.

Visual – the big one

This is the big one for me: your visual memory is huge. Inputting information (events) into your head using pictures and images is one of the most powerful techniques you have.

Here is a question, what colour is your toothbrush?

How do you know? If you don't know, go back and reconstruct getting out of bed, look at the room around you, which foot did you put on the floor first? Move into the bathroom and reach down and take a look at your toothbrush, lift it closer to your face, rotate it. Now answer the question: what colour is it?

Your ability to recall events in pictures is a clue as to the most powerful way of memorising.

This ability to replay large parts of our life in pictures is a gift that we all possess, and one that we should use more if we want to increase the amount we remember. Advertisers understand this only too well; they use images to create strong associations with products. Think of any leading brand: it almost certainly has a logo, a picture, a colour and, where the marketing is really clever, even a sound. They will then repeatedly show this image and anchor it to a particular emotion, normally positive. They are effectively creating a link between the logo and the memory. The idea is that when you see the logo, you will feel the emotion.

The lesson for us is that we need to use visual images more when we input the information in the first place. Reading a textbook, for example, and then asking your brain to remember everything you read is asking a lot. The text is logical and normally black and white; it flows from left to right and on the whole is generally unexciting as a form of input. Neither is it unique, and the more unique an event, the more likely you are to remember it. Only when you begin to visualise what is happening in the text, only when you begin to create pictures in your mind, will this be something you can remember at a later date. The next step would be to use images and colours to record what you are seeing: these pictures will be much easier to remember and a simple glance at them will bring the information flooding back.

Auditory – rhythm and rhyme

Mary, Mary quite contrary
How does your garden grow?
With silver bells and cockle shells
And pretty maids all in a row

If, when you read that, a tune or, at the very least, a rhythm came into your head, that is an auditory memory. Although visual images are powerful, there is something absolutely amazing about our ability to remember sounds. But, once again, they won't be the sounds of a conversation you had yesterday about the weather with the person sitting next to you at work. This is an ordinary event that you experienced without any emotional context and it is unlikely to be unique. The result: you won't remember it. No, the type of auditory memory you are more likely to recall is something that was repeated many times, probably with rhythm, when you were experiencing a particular emotion and it may well be musical.

Many people will remember what happened to the wives of Henry the Eighth from this simple rhyme. "**Divorced, beheaded, died, divorced, beheaded, survived**"

The brain has a natural affinity with music; it satisfies many of the rules to create a unique form of input. It can be repeated, yet not seem exactly the same, it can change the way you feel and so change the emotional impact. Although we had the written word long before Johannes Gutenberg invented the printing press in 1436, one thing is for sure: large chunks of knowledge were passed from one generation to another by the use of language and song.

One way you could improve your ability to memorise using sound, would be to take the information you are trying to remember and simply say it out loud. In fact, if you say it out loud in a strange voice, it will have even more impact. Other ideas would be to record your notes onto your iPod or CD. Not only will you be able to listen to this on the move, giving you more opportunities to go over it but it is obviously in an auditory format. And finally, why not record your notes using music in the background or make up a song incorporating the key words? Classical music works best for this and there is some evidence that the music of Mozart or from the baroque period is the most effective.

You know it's funny what a young man recollects? 'Cause I don't remember bein' born. I don't recall what I got for my first Christmas and I don't know when I went on my first outdoor picnic. But I do remember the first time I heard the sweetest voice in the wide world.

Forrest Gump, movie

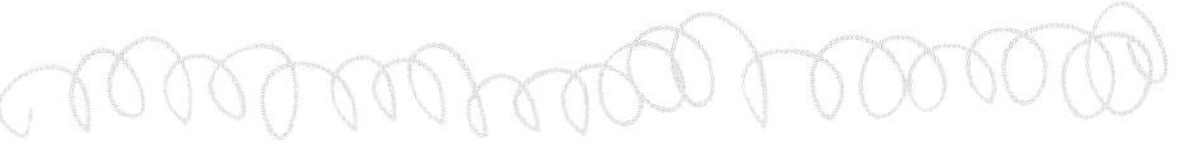

Principle two - Association and organisation

The second principle: it must be organised and associated.

Although you may remember something in the form of a visual image or sound, it will become increasingly difficult to retrieve that image unless it is stored in your memory in an organised and structured way. One of the best ways of storing images is to associate them with something that you already remember. For example, it is far easier to remember the name of certain trees if you imagine a tree with branches and on each of the branches you hang the name of the different types of trees.

Types of tree

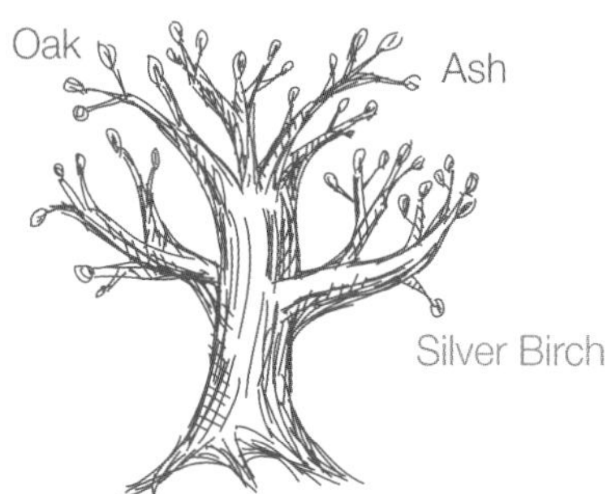

Almost all of the memory techniques use some form of association in order to create the memory. For example the number rhyming system (see below) uses numbers (the existing information) and links these to the new information by the use of sound. These are often known as *peg systems*, where the existing information acts as a peg on which you hang the new information. One of the most famous of these is the roman room or loci method, which is said to have been invented by a Greek poet named Simonides in 500 BC. Simonides was entertaining a group of wealthy noblemen who were all attending a banquet to celebrate a victory by the host in a wrestling tournament at the Olympics. He was asked to step outside but, as soon as he did, the roof of the banquet hall collapsed, killing everybody inside. The mangled corpses could not be identified until Simonides stepped forward, pointed to the place where each victim had been sitting, and said each name in turn. He did this by mentally recreating the scene of the banquet, visualizing each person in their place. When he saw the places, it helped him remember the person who had been sitting there.

Principle three - Repetition

And the last principle: repeat, repeat, repeat!

And lastly we are back to repetition. I have said much about why repeating things helps with both learning and memory. The need to continue to fire those electrical impulses across the neurons is what creates the memory in the first place. All methods of input will benefit from some form of reinforcement by repeating the process over and over again.

We can be a little more sophisticated by using what we call *spaced repetition*. This works on the principle that we tend to remember recent events. If you were asked to remember that Anne Boleyn was 36 when she died, in a couple of days you may well have forgotten, but if I asked you in, say, five hours from now, almost at the point when you were just going to forget, this would help reinforce the memory. Then if I asked you in 2 days, then 1 week, then six months, each time it would reinforce the memory.

In Summary

In order to create a memory, you need a sequence of events. Firstly, you need to input the information in the most suitable way. This might be by using images or sounds. Make sure you are in the right mood or state when you do this, and the more you exaggerate the event, the more likely you will be to remember it later. But creating a powerful memory using images or sounds is only part of the process. Think of the memory as a piece of paper. Yes, you have recorded the information, but you now need to make sure it is filed away so that you will be able to find it. This is why you need to organize the memory: it needs to be labelled and, where possible, associated with some existing information. And, finally, go over the process several times just to reinforce it.

These are the principles of memory. Below are some practical memory techniques and systems that use these principles.

Memory techniques

A memory technique or mnemonic is effectively anything that will help improve your ability to remember. The word mnemonic comes from the Greek word Mnemosyne which means "remembrance" and is the name of the goddess of memory. The fact that the Greeks had a goddess of memory gives you some idea as to how much importance they placed on the ability to memorise. Remember, before the written word, all knowledge was passed down simply by word of mouth.

When it comes to passing exams, you will be required to remember a whole host of different things ranging from definitions, formats, formulae, and, of course, the specific content of the subject. In chapter six, in the section ***Effective note-taking***, we reduced the content from the text down into bullet points or key words. When it comes to the revision period, it is these key word notes that we will need to commit to memory. Although you can obviously memorise at any time, I would suggest that you use memory techniques during the later stages of your studies, perhaps in the last week before the exam. Up until then, most of your time would have been taken up with practising exam questions and making your notes, so having time to devote to memorising would be limited. Equally, until you get to a certain stage in your studies, you don't really know what is important enough to memorise in the first place.

Before we look at any of the memory techniques, let's see how you get on with remembering the following, a sort of "before and after" test.

Memory test

Can you take a look at the following formulas, formats, definitions and content? Give yourself about five minutes. Then shut the book and see how good you are at remembering them. Although each section has an explanation as to what they are, it is only the figures in italics that you are required to remember.

1. Formula

There are lots of situations where a formula is needed to help solve a particular problem. Sometimes they are given in the exam but often they are not. One of the problems with formulae is that often they appear to be a sequence of random unrelated symbols or letters, so it is necessary to create some form of relationship between these to help you remember them.

Here we have the formula for calculating something called a corporate beta and the weighted average cost of capital or WACC. These terms are important if you are studying corporate finance. It is obviously far easier to remember technical content like this if you understand what these formulae do and why you need them. However, from a pure memorising perspective, we should still be able to commit them to memory.

Corporate beta $\beta = \frac{Pjm,\sigma j}{\sigma m}$

Where
β = Corporate beta
Pjm = Correlation with the market
σj = Standard deviation of equity returns
σm = Standard deviation of the market

$$WACC = Ke_g \frac{E}{E + D} + Kd\,(1-t) \frac{D}{E + D}$$

Where
WACC = weighted average cost of capital
Ke_g = Cost of equity
Kd (1–t) = Cost of debt after tax
E = Market value of equity
D = Market value of debt

2. Formats

Think of a format as a structured table of data. Very often in an exam you will be asked to answer a question that requires you to produce the answer in a standard format. This may be a legally agreed, or at least industry-specific, format, as with the example below which shows how you must produce an income statement in accordance with accounting standards. It could equally be a format that, if followed, will help you calculate the "right" answer or at least get close to it. It starts with one figure at the top of the page, you then deduct the next figure and add the next, etc. If you can reproduce the format in the exam, all you have to then do is slot the figure in next to the specific heading, making what

might be a very complicated calculation easy, as long as you can remember the format in the first place. Formats of this nature are often used when computing clients' tax charges. Over time, these formats can become best practice and accepted by everyone.

XYX Group – Income statement for the year ended 31 December 2009

	2008	**2009**
Revenue	X	X
Cost of sales	(X)	(X)
Gross profit	X	X
Distribution costs	(X)	(X)
Administrative expenses	(X)	(X)
Profit from operations	X	X
Investment income	X	X
Finance costs	(X)	(X)
Profit before tax	**X**	**X**
Tax expense	(X)	(X)
Profit after tax	**X**	**X**

3. Definitions

It is standard exam practice when answering certain types of exam question that you first state the definition of some of the key terms within your answer. This not only proves that you have knowledge of the definition but the definition can help you explain and structure your answer more effectively. Here we have, from economics, the definition of Gross Domestic Product:

The total market value of all final goods and services produced in a country in a given year, equal to total consumer, investment and government spending, plus the value of exports, minus the value of imports.

4. Content/narrative

Obviously you will need to remember large chunks of content or narrative. As stated earlier, in many instances, much of this should come from your own key word notes. There is a clear process here:

- take the material you have to learn and identify the key examinable topics
- make key word notes on the key examinable topics
- practise exam questions on the key examinable topics
- reduce your notes down even further and memorise.

It is the material in these final notes that we should be committing to memory. I should say that you do not need to be able to remember everything, just enough to give you a fighting chance of answering the question should this topic come up.

Here we have two examples, one from Steven Covey's book, ***The Seven Habits of Highly Effective People***, and those key word notes from chapter six where we learned about share capital and compared limited company with a partnership:

Steven Covey 7 habits of highly effective people

1. Be proactive
   Being proactive means taking the initiative, not waiting for others to act first, and being responsible for what you want.

2. Begin with the end in mind
   This is the habit of personal leadership; setting long term goals that lead you in a direction that you want to go.

3. Put first things first
   This is about organising and implementing activities in line with the aims established in habit 2.

4. Think win-win
   Win-win is based on the assumption that there is plenty for everyone, and that success follows a co-operative approach more naturally than the confrontation or win-lose.

5. Seek first to understand and then to be understood
   The habit of good communication. By listening to the other person's concerns before offering advice you will increase your chances of influencing.

6. Synergize
   This is the habit of creative co-operation and follows the principle that the whole is greater than the sum of its parts.

7. Sharpen the saw
   This surrounds all the other habits, enabling and encouraging them to happen and grow. It is a recognition that we all need to put time aside to learn.

And from chapter six

Equity share capital - Types of company

Two forms of association

- Partnership
- Company limited by shares
- Limited Company V Partnership
- Asset/liability are company's V Partners liable
- Members not agents V Partners are agents
- Limited engagement V Partners decide engagement
- Statutory provisions V Partnerships much less
- Perpetual succession V Partnership death ends

Okay, that's the end of the test. Close the book and see how much you can remember.

The memory techniques

The techniques below have to have some connection to the principles of memory we discussed earlier. So you will find that they all use, to some extent, a combination of images, rhythm and rhyme with large doses of imagination and exaggeration, held together with a structured and organised framework helping you to associate one piece of information with the other. They will all benefit from you being in the right mood or emotional state when you want to memorise them and by going over them again and again and again.

1. Acronyms

An acronym is an invented combination of letters. Each letter is a cue to, or suggests, an item you need to remember. It works on the basis of associated knowledge i.e. you already have the alphabet in your memory, so all you are doing is using your existing knowledge and associating new knowledge with it. In memory terms, this is known as the "tip of the tongue" rule. You do know the answer but can't find it. Prompting your memory with the first letter gives you enough of a clue where it might be. Incidentally, this does not work if you have the last letter, only the first! These are best used for things like lists and tables where some form of completeness is needed.

E.g. 1 Colours of the spectrum

ROY G. BIV is a very popular acronym in order to remember the colours of the visible spectrum:
Red, Orange, Yellow, Green, Blue, Indigo, Violet

And from the memory test above, how can you remember the difference between a Limited Company V Partnership?

E.g. 2 Limited company V partnership

SEA SAL

- **A**sset/**L**iability are company's V Partners liable
- Members not **A**gents V Partners are agents
- Limited **E**ngagement V Partners decide engagement
- **S**tatutory provisions V Partnerships much less
- Perpetual **S**uccession V Partnership death ends

In order for you to remember this, you would need to write it out next to your key word notes. It is important with all of these memory techniques that you have a very close association with the original text and the context from which the extracts were taken. Notice also **that you do not need the detail**: you do not need to know that this is the comparison of limited companies with partnerships. Simply remembering the acronym S will trigger Succession which in turn will remind you that a company can effectively live forever and has perpetual succession but a partnership ends with the death of the partner and so succession ends. Take a couple of minutes to associate these letters with the text.

2. An acrostic

An acrostic is different to an acronym in that it is not simply a list letters that stand for words, it is an invented sentence or poem with the first letter of the word acting as a cue to something you need to remember.

This is probably one of the most popular mnemonics and, like the above, is best used when you need to remember a list of words.

E.g. 1 sequence of musical notes

Every **G**ood **B**oy **D**eserves **F**ruit

This is an acrostic for remembering a sequence of musical notes: E, G, B, D, F.

And from the memory test above, how can you remember the format for an Income statement? For this one I will use a great example illustrated by my friend and colleague Clare Finch in her book "A student's guide to International Financial Reporting Standards".

E.g. 2 Format for an income statement

Really **C**ute **G**uys **D**istract **A**ccountants **P**reventing **I**nfatuated **F**ools **P**assing **T**he **P**aper!

Please substitute guys for girls, whichever you find easier to remember

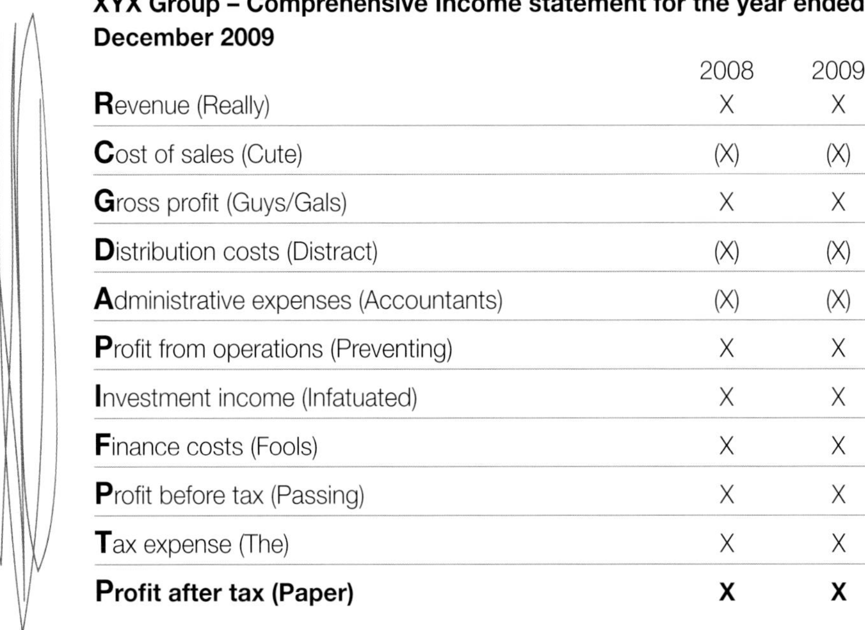

XYX Group – Comprehensive Income statement for the year ended 31 December 2009

	2008	2009
Revenue (Really)	X	X
Cost of sales (Cute)	(X)	(X)
Gross profit (Guys/Gals)	X	X
Distribution costs (Distract)	(X)	(X)
Administrative expenses (Accountants)	(X)	(X)
Profit from operations (Preventing)	X	X
Investment income (Infatuated)	X	X
Finance costs (Fools)	X	X
Profit before tax (Passing)	X	X
Tax expense (The)	X	X
Profit after tax (Paper)	**X**	**X**

Remember we are not looking for too much logic, just a bit. This has context, in that it makes some sense; however, it uses words that you would not normally use in the same sentence, words like Cute Infatuated and Paper. There is also some evidence that words associated with the opposite sex are more memorable. Once again take some time and commit this to memory.

3. Stack and link

As the name implies, this technique links each item, each key word to another. It does this by way of a story. The story enables you to create pictures and so use your visual memory. The linking creates an association between each of the key words.

As with most of the memory techniques, you should use images, making them as vivid as possible, using humour, exaggeration, colour and motion. Sounds and smells should be built in to make the event unique, smell and hear the bacon sizzling. Link items together so that each affects the other: the **rain** falls into a bucket and in the bucket is a **boat** and on the boat is… etc. This will enable you to start anywhere in the list and move in either direction.

And finally you will need to go through your new linked stack several times, embellishing the details if needed, until you have the connections and links memorised. This is best used when you are able to pick out some key words from the text, as in the definition of demand example below. And by simply remembering those key words you will be able to gain sufficient understanding to make the point required. There is not such a need for completeness of information as for lists or tables.

From the memory test we were required to remember the definition of Gross domestic product (GDP)

E.g.1 Definition of GDP

The total market value of all final goods and services produced in a country in a given year, equal to total consumer, investment and government spending, plus the value of exports, minus the value of imports.

First we need to select the key words. I am going to select the following; market value, goods, country, investment and spending.

Then stack them on top if each other and create a story using as many sensory words as possible

MARKET VALUE
GOODS
COUNTRY
INVESTMENT
SPENDING

A man walks in to a shop and asks "what's the MARKET VALUE of that watch you're wearing?" to the attractive girl in the bright red dress. She looks directly at the man who has one green eye, one blue and smells of tobacco and says, "the watch is not for sale, can you see any other GOODS you might want to buy?" The man smiles and starts to sing a COUNTRY and western song called I-N-V-E-S-T-M-E-N-T, the famous Tammy Wynette hit. The girl in the bright red dress says, "if you are not SPENDING get out of my shop."

Go over this several times and imagine you are in the shop, sing the song but with the words *investment*.

This time stack and link with a twist. If what you are trying to remember is not a word and does not easily bring an image to mind then you may need to create a new image. The interesting thing is it does not have to be an image that relates to the content of what you are trying to remember.

E.g.2 Formula for the calculation of a beta

$$\beta = \frac{Pjm, \sigma j}{\sigma m}$$

Pjm = Pyjamas

σj = OJ Simpson

σm = Mattress on a bed

Imagine you have just got up and have folded your bright red striped pyjamas and placed them neatly on top of your mattress. You turn away, but for some reason you turn and look back at your bed and to your surprise you can see OJ Simpson sitting on the bed, cross–legged, next to your pyjamas.

4. The Roman room (Loci method)

This technique was mentioned earlier and uses your visual memory to the full; it is also particularly good for kinaesthetic learners. This can be used to remember almost anything but works particularly well when remembering items in sequence i.e. things that follow on from the next, as with the formula example below.

Select any location that you have spent a lot of time in and know well, perhaps your house or a walk that you have done many times. Imagine yourself walking through the location, selecting clearly defined places. For example, if you chose your house think of the hall, the kitchen, the lounge, the study and the cloakroom. Imagine yourself putting objects that you need to remember into each of these places by walking through this location in your mind's eye. It is probably true that this technique works better with lists of words, nouns and less well with verbs. But with a large amount of imagination and creativity which are both essential ingredients for remembering anything is possible. When you first start to do this it is best to go the same way around the house but with practice you will be able to start and finish anywhere.

Remember, do not look for too much logic, more right brain than left brain. The more unusual and visually powerful the images the easier they will be to remember. The first time I came across some of these techniques, I was very sceptical and thought there was a lot of effort involved just to remember a simple formula. As a result I found myself rewriting the formula over and over again, using repetition to get the information into my head. I was in fact spending more time doing that than it would have taken to come up with some simple visual images that are required for the Roman room method.

I also thought that some of the methods just seemed a little odd. This was partly because I did not understand why and how the techniques worked, there seemed no logic, and I needed a left brain explanation. When I began to learn more about the brain and how it works a lot of the techniques made sense and so I began to use them with confidence.

From the memory test you were required to remember the formula for the weighted average cost of capital. Here is how you might remember this using the roman room method.

$$WACC = Ke_g \frac{E}{E+D} + Kd\,(1-t)\,\frac{D}{E+D}$$

E.g. 1 The WACC

Imagine walking up to your front door and opening it into the hall. Think what your hall looks like, visualise it. In the hall, sat on the floor, is a bright yellow fat little duck. It has an orange beak. It looks at you but instead of going quack is says WACC, WACC, WACC. It points with its wing to the lounge and you enter the lounge. See your lounge, the colour of the wallpaper, the texture of the carpet. In the bottom left hand corner of your lounge is a large **Keg** of beer, moving your eyes towards the top left hand part of the room you can't but help notice a clock over the fireplace, showing the **Time(s)**. In the top left hand part of the room is a very small baby called Edward he is balancing three wooden bricks. The one on the top has the letter **E** for Edward the two underneath have a **D** and an **E** on them. See the bricks and the small baby sat in the top left part of your lounge.

You walk from the lounge into your kitchen and pass a snake on the way, an **adder** in fact; its forked tongue is red. In the kitchen, in the top right hand corner, pinned to the wall, is a bank statement. It shows the bank rate, which is the cost of debt (**Kd**) and as you move your eyes towards the bottom right hand corner you once again notice a clock, the same clock that you saw before, it is showing the **Time(s)**. In that bottom right hand corner of the kitchen there is a large baby called Debbie and she is balancing three wooden bricks. The one on the top has the letter **D** for Debbie and the two underneath have a **D** and an **E** on them.

5. Number rhyme

The number rhyme system uses our natural sense of rhyme to associates existing numerical information, one, two, three etc with the words that rhyme with those numbers. It is one of the few techniques that uses rhyme to create recall. Yet many people will remember using rhyme so as to remember their times tables, one times one is one, two times one is two etc.

Rhyming type memory systems are particularly good for remembering things where there is a degree of repetition as with the the times table. This is because the repetition allows the brain to get used to the rhythm you have created. The number rhyme system itself is really useful for remembering lists and is best used when you feel that you have exhausted all the acronyms and acrostics or they are becoming confused.

Rhyming type memory systems are particularly good for remembering things where there is a degree of repetition as with the times table. This is because the repetition allows the brain to get used to the rhythm you have created. The number rhyme system itself is really useful for remembering lists and is best used when you feel that you have exhausted all the acronyms and acrostics or they are becoming confused.

E.g.1 Improve your spelling

This is a very simple example of using rhyme without key words I before E, except after C

E.g. 2 Steven Covey's 7 habits

This time an example using the number rhyme, from the memory test, Steven Covey's 7 habits of highly effective people.

This example already has a natural number sequence, being Steven Covey's 7 habits; if not, you simply put numbers in the first column equal to the amount of items you need to remember. Next to the number put the rhyme and in the last column the information you want to remember:

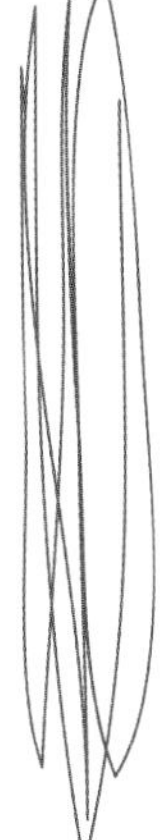

Number	Rhyme	New information
One	Wand	Be proactive
Two	Shoe	Begin with the end in mind
Three	Tree	Put first things first
Four	Boar	Think win win
Five	Hive	Seek first to understand then to be understood
Six	Sticks	Synergize
Seven	Heaven	Sharpen the saw

Now for the creative bit. For each of the numbers, you now need to link the rhyming word to the new information by way of a story.

Be proactive

Your first day at Hogwarts is not going well, not only were you late arriving on the first night but now you can't find the classroom for your first lesson. You look straight ahead and see a corridor that has thousands of doors, large wooden doors with no numbers, just a sign that says ***"Stay where you are."*** Suddenly, before your very eyes a huge WAND appears, yellow at the top but mostly black. The WAND then speaks in a sharp pointy little voice, "What are you doing standing there? You really need to be more PROACTIVE. Stop staring at the sign be PROACTIVE and get to class." The Wand then disappears.

Begin with the end in mind

Whilst walking down the high street you stop to look in a shop window. You don't seem to know why you are looking in the window, you just are. You stare at the shop window for what seems like hours and hours, still with no idea what you are looking for. Then suddenly a six foot red SHOE kicks you from behind, it knocks you through the glass window. You still don't know why you are there so decide to retrace your steps from when you woke up that morning. In your mind you go backwards until you get to the start of your day. You think what you wanted to do YOU START WITH THE END IN MIND. And remember you wanted to buy some SHOES.

Put first things first

It was a hot sunny day and a lone man stood in the middle of a wheat field. There was nothing else in this field except a very large oak TREE. The man was standing under the oak tree and was scratching his head; he looked puzzled. He had 3 blocks of wood, and chiselled on one of the blocks were the words FIRST THINGS and, on another block, the words second things, on another third things. The man looked up at the tree as if looking for inspiration; he was trying to put the blocks in some sort of order, but what order? To his amazement the TREE spoke, in a slow TREE-like voice, it said "If I were you I would PUT FIRST THINGS FIRST and second things second and third things third."

Think WIN WIN

There is a really good Chinese restaurant called the wild BOAR and what makes it very special is that everyone in the Chinese is Chinese and they serve wild BOAR; it's their signature dish. Normally the service is absolutely first class and the food is really tasty. They bring out the wild BOAR on a huge plate, the head is shiny and covered in honey, the eyes glazed and still. Like the haggis on New Year, music is played to announce its arrival at your table. Well, except for last Friday, my birthday. Win Win the Chinese waiter was new, not only did he forget the music, but he actually forgot the wild BOAR. The owner came out in a rage, he shouted at the new waiter:"You know your problem? You don't THINK WIN WIN, you don't THINK WIN WIN." I still had a great birthday.

Get the idea? Oh okay, one last one.

Sharpen the saw

The world log sawing championships were taking place in HEAVEN. The two dead competitors were both keen to win. The whistle went and the Canadian and Russian started sawing. They were neck and neck, saw for saw, when the Canadian suddenly stopped. The Russian could not believe his luck and began sawing twice as fast believing the Canadian was already tiring. Five minutes later the Canadian started again. God blew his whistle and the Russian was confident he had won as he had not had a break. On counting who had sawn down the most trees God announced that the Canadian had won. The Russian said, "This is not possible; you had a rest and I was sawing all the time you were idle." The Canadian said, "What rest? All I was doing was SHARPENing MY SAW which meant I could saw much faster."

I know this seems a lot of effort but remembering these seven principles could well be worth 15 marks in an exam and that could be the difference between passing and failing. After a while you will not need to go through the story and will remember ONE WAND, you may even see the Wand and experience the indecision before remembering the need to be PROACTIVE.

Read through these several times and really explore the environment with your imagination. The more you feel you are there, the easier it will be to remember.

6. Mind mapping

We introduced the idea of mind mapping in chapter six when looking at the different ways of making notes. Having read through the section on the principles of memory, it should now become clear as to why mind maps are a great way of helping with recall. A mind map has a central theme and so very easily associates and links each piece of information with the other. It uses colours and images and so creates very strong visuals which are easy to remember. They can be altered changed and rewritten, each time showing new and improved links, some that may not have been apparent when first created. And they are created, getting the learner to use their imagination, as ever the more unusual and exaggerated the better.

By having larger images for some topics that are more important, you can more easily see what is important and so focus on those areas. When it comes to revision, they can be pinned up on walls in the house, perhaps in the bathroom so that when you brush your teeth, you can look at the map each morning. This clearly helps with repetition. And a mind map does not take very long to review. In the same way that your eye can scan a whole series of images as it would if looking at a friend's photos, you can take in the whole mind map recalling large amounts of detail in a flash. You should use a mind map when you need to get an overview of the whole topic, or parts of it when you want to be able to see how it all fits together.

Why a mind map is an effective memory technique

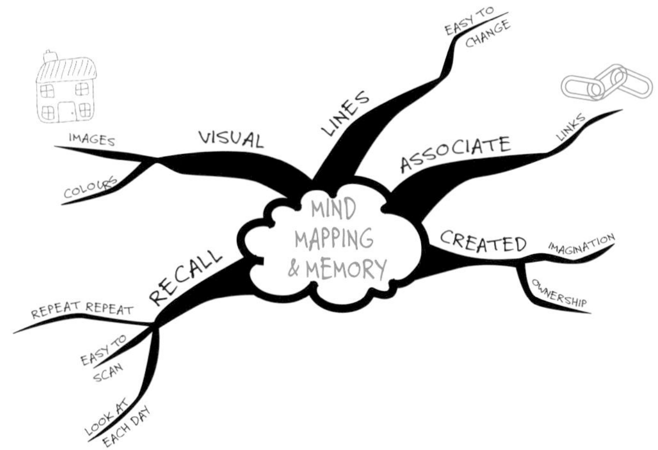

What is possible?

These techniques really do work but like many things they need to be practised. Every year approximately 85 competitors from 20 countries compete in the world memory championships.

The competition consists of 10 events that take place over two days. Competitors are invited to memorise separate packs of cards in one hour, a single pack of cards in under five minutes, random digits in one hour etc.

They do this using some of the memory techniques outlined in the section above. Here are some of the current records, they are amazing.

Challenge	Record
To commit to memory and recall a single pack (deck) of 52 playing cards in the shortest possible time.	24.97seconds
To commit to memory as many random digits (1,3,5,8,2,5, etc) as possible and recall them perfectly in 15 minutes	396
To commit to memory and recall as many random words as possible in 15 minutes	280
To commit to memory and recall as many separate packs (decks) of 52 playing cards in one hour.	1,404 cards

Source the world memory championships

Dominic O'Brien the World Memory champion, (he has won it at least eight times), can memorise seven packs of cards in ten minutes, and then recite each card in order. But give him an hour and he can memorise 27 packs!

Let's leave the final word to him about memory

It is all down to training the memory, says the 32-year-old accountant from Derby, who adds "Anybody can do it. You don't have to be some sort of natural born genius, I'm certainly not."

Dominic O'Brien, 8 times World Memory champion

Now have another go

Go over them all one last time then look at these memory joggers and write down how much you can remember of the original content.

1. **Limited company V partnership**
   SEA SAL

2. **Format for an income statement**
   Really **C**ute **G**uys **D**istract **A**ccountants **P**reventing **I**nfatuated **F**ools **P**assing **T**he **P**aper!

3. **Definition of GDP**
   A man walks into a shop

4. **Formula for the calculation of a beta**
   OJ Simpson

5. **The WACC**
   Walk into your hall what do you see, it's yellow.

6. **Steven Covey's 7 habits**

   One rhymes with
   Two rhymes with
   Three rhymes with
   Four rhymes with
   Seven rhymes with

Some of you may not invest the time needed to make these techniques work but if you do, you will be rewarded with the ability to remember whatever you wish. And if you want or need to pass exams, that can't be a bad thing.

In conclusion

Being able to remember what you have learned is an essential exam skill. In fact, some examinations only test your ability to recall facts. Sometimes all you need is a little reminder, a hint, maybe the first letter, and then the detail comes flooding back. That's how many of the memory techniques work: they act as a trigger, a key link into where you have filed all the knowledge needed to answer a particular question. I hope that by understanding a little about how the brain stores information and what is needed to make a lasting impression will make you less dismissive of some of the techniques. I have tried to give you a left-brained argument why a story involving Hogwarts might be a great way of remembering the first of Steven Covey's habits.

If I can just suspend that natural scepticism, which has served you well, for long enough to fully engage in some of the techniques described, I am confident you will reap the benefits. Please give them a go.

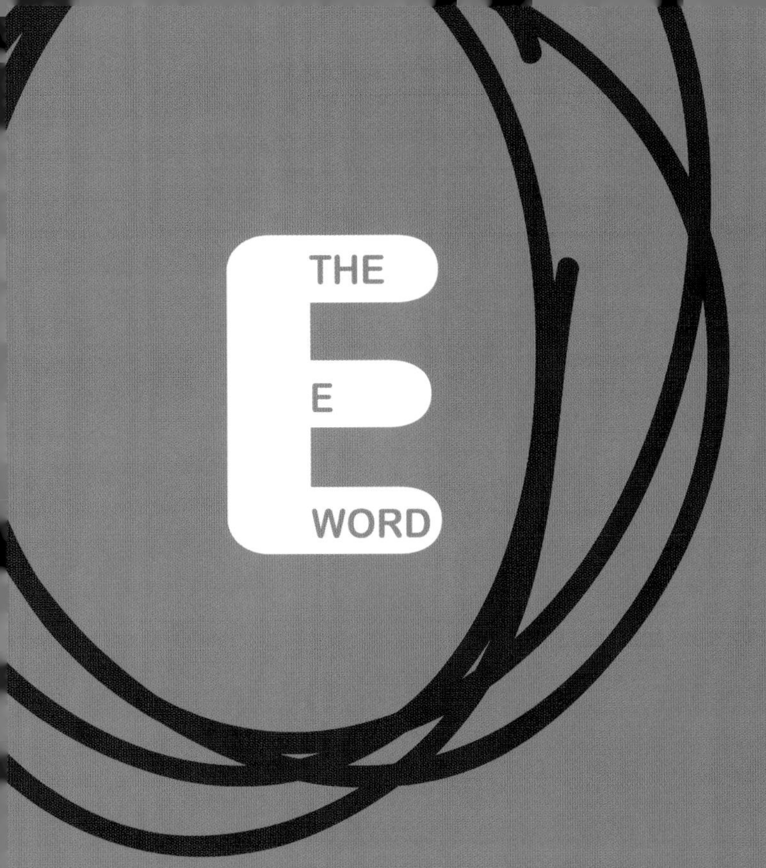

chapter 8 Techniques to improve exam performance

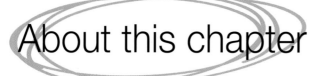

About this chapter

This chapter is about what you do in the revision period, including what to do in the actual exam. In theory you have been taught ***everything*** relating to the subject. Of course it's not really possible to have been taught ***everything,*** so let's assume you have been taught *most* of what was required. What do you do next?

This is when you need to start revision. In simple terms, you need to go back over what you have learnt, reminding yourself of the key points sufficiently so that when you are in the exam you will be able to answer the questions set. But what exactly should you do and what is the best way to revise? If the course took 9 months, how can you possibly go back over it in, say, four weeks?

This chapter is broken into three sections. Firstly, a section that clarifies what we mean by revision and what you are trying to achieve. Secondly, we look at how you get ready for the actual exam day, what should you be doing before the exam? And lastly, what should you do during the exam: specific exam techniques that will help increase the marks you get and make it more likely you will pass.

This book is about exams and how to pass them and, although this is almost the last chapter, it is perhaps one of the most important when it comes to passing. For me, revision is vital. No matter how hard you have worked in the year, poor revision and poor exam skills on the day of the exam can and does result in failure.

One of the reasons I think exam skills are so important is not because they help "poor or lazy" students to pass; they stop good and hard working students from failing.

What exactly is revision?

In simple terms, on tuition you learn, and on revision you "re Vision", you go back over what you have learned with a fresh pair of eyes. But to be effective, it has to be far more than a read-through of the notes that you prepared during the tuition period.

Rather than defining revision, let's think more about what you will be able to do if your revision is effective. You should be able to walk into the exam, open the exam paper and answer the questions. The answers should come easily to you and the knowledge needed should be fresh in your mind. You should feel confident in what you know. You should understand the questions being asked and be able to write an answer that is in line with the examiner's expectations. In all, the paper should hold no real surprises. Easy really.

All we need to do now is come up with ways in which we can learn how to do the above. What, for example, do we have to do to make sure the information is fresh in our minds?

Well, having looked at it recently would be a start, or having memorised it using some of the memory techniques from chapter 7. What do you have to do to understand the question being asked? How about looking at several past questions? That way, when you are faced with a similar question you see familiar terms. How do you write an answer in line with what the examiner wants? Looking at past exam answers would be great for this.

A theme is emerging and a plan becomes a little clearer. It involves looking at and working through past exam questions and answers. We also need to go back over the material already learned in a methodical way, making new notes and using memory techniques so that the content is not only fresh in our minds but also easy to recall when we need it next, in the exam room.

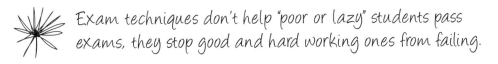

Exam techniques don't help "poor or lazy" students pass exams, they stop good and hard working ones from failing.

Attitude

I hope you have enjoyed this book so far and that I have managed to explain things clearly, inspire you where you have had self-doubt, and even make you smile at times. I consider this to be a serious book about how to pass exams and the revision period is so important that you need to take it seriously so that you devote sufficient time to it to give you the best chance of passing. I fully appreciate that different people have different approaches to revision: some leave it to the last minute whilst others are incredibly organised, planning everything to the last detail. How often I have heard the comment that "I perform better under pressure" – which is really just another way of saying that they find it difficult to motivate themselves; the proximity of the exam provides the catalyst for action.

I just want you to put your revision above almost everything else you do. I say "almost" because you do need to take a break and you do need time off and you do need to have fun. This might mean having very little or no social life in the next 2 to 6 weeks, but it is only for a relatively short period of time, and, after that, normal service can be resumed. During revision, your studies come first and your social life comes second.

Attitude changes over time

One thing that changes as you get closer to the exam is your attitude and mood. When you begin learning a new subject, although you will be aware that ultimately there will be an exam, you will focus more on each individual topic, taking each day as it comes and on the whole will be relatively relaxed. But as the revision period gets closer and so the exam, your attitude will change, your mood will become more serious and the pace of study more frantic.

Attitude changes closer to the exam

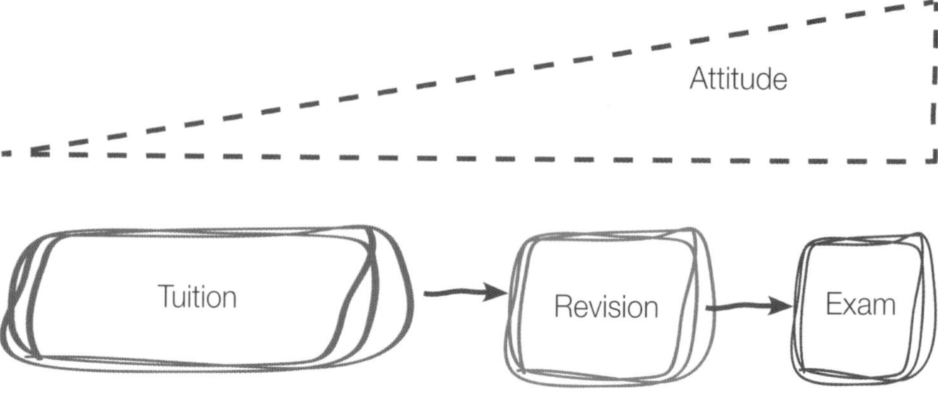

Now this is not necessarily a bad thing as the added pressure provides a catalyst for hard work and the change in mood can be very effective in helping you retain the information being learned.

This change in the way you feel is one of the main reasons revision is so effective.

I believe that this change in the way you feel is one of the main reasons that revision is so effective and why you can't begin the process of revising earlier. Many educationalists will argue that you can revise as you go along; learning something and then going back over it, but as long as your state of mind remains unchanged it will never be as effective as revising, knowing that the exam is just around the corner .

There are some things you learn best in calm, and some in storm.
Willa Cather

When to start

It is difficult to be prescriptive about when to start revision as it depends on many things: the length of the course, the level of complexity of the subject, the time you have before the exam and how many exams you are doing at any one time. But we do need a rough idea, so I am going to assume that revision has to start somewhere between two and six weeks before the exam. For some people, starting 6 weeks before the exam may sound early, but if you are studying more than one subject and or are working full time, when you actually break down the amount of hours you are revising, anything less than 6 weeks will be insufficient for an effective revision program.

The revision period 2 to 6 weeks before the exam

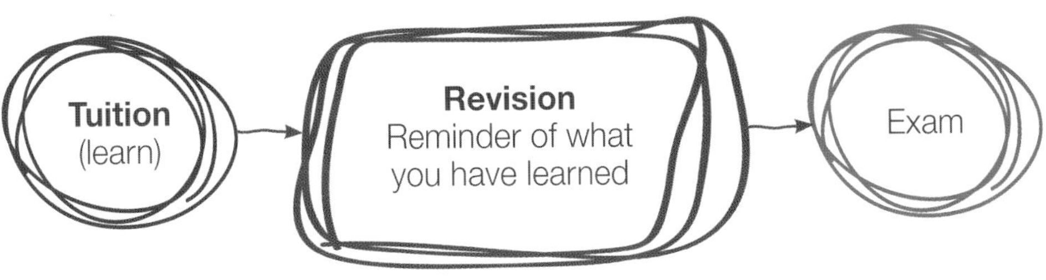

Revision is the period between the end of tuition but before the exam.

Before the exam

Imagine that you have just finished tuition and there are 6 weeks before the exam. You will have prepared a set of notes during the tuition course, or from the textbook if you are working on your own. I will assume that you have not read chapter 3 and so these notes are not particularly exam focused. If they are, the revision phase will just be that much easier.

The notes that you have, let's call them tuition notes, will probably be reasonably thick as they will often include many worked examples and illustrations and as a result are almost impossible to revise from because of this. During the revision period, you will need to make a new set of notes, these will be much shorter and more focused. Although your tuition notes, in theory, cover everything you need to know, you may find that this is not the case. This will probably depend on the type of exam you are taking: for example, if you are taking an internal exam (one that is examined by the school, college or university) then what is taught, and so what you have notes on, should very strongly correlate to what is going to be examined. If, on the other hand, you are taking an external exam (one that is set by a body independent of the school, college or university) you may find that what you have been taught includes too much on some topics and not enough on others. During revision, we will need to find out where the gaps are and plug them.

Apart from your notes being too thick and potentially not complete, your knowledge will probably be a little sketchy. There will be topics that you studied and, if truth be known, never really understood. Others you understood at the time but now they don't seem to make any sense at all, which is very frustrating. And some that, although you understood, you now can't remember.

Put all this together and you begin to see why revision is so important and that there is much to do.

Get organised

The first step in revision is to get organised. You need to know what you have to do and when you need it. And the best way of getting organised is to produce a timetable.

Timetables

The timetable is just for you and so can be as detailed or as simple as you would like. Specifically what you will do depends on many things, so in order to provide some guidance I am going to make some assumptions. One, that you are studying four subjects; two, that you are not going to enrol on a publicly organised revision course, and three, that you may be working and so for 4 out of the 6 weeks you don't have all day i.e. you will have 2 weeks off work that you can devote to your revision, full time. Obviously, if you are in fulltime education, you will be able to devote much more time to each activity. This might mean you can start revision a little later, but be careful – don't leave it too late.

If you were to enrol on a formal revision course, many of the things you need to do will probably be done for you. For example, the course providers should already have a good idea as to what the key examinable topics are. They will probably provide you with revision notes and even a mock exam. And on the revision course, you will almost certainly be required to practise past exam questions under both exam and non-exam conditions.

However, on the assumption that you are not on such a course, before we can begin to prepare our timetable, we need to list down the activities that need to go into it.

What should you do during revision?

- A - Produce an analysis of past exam papers so as to identify the key examinable areas
- E - Find out if your examiner has produced any specific examiner guidance or any technical articles
- N - Read through existing notes and make new revision notes based on the key examinable topics
- P - Work through past exam questions from the key examinable areas
- M - Take a mock exam
- B - Take a break

In order to give you some idea as to how much time you need to spend on each activity and when you need to do it, I have produced a mock-up of a revision timetable. Each task has a symbol, see above for the key.

A 6 week revision timetable

Week 1							Week 2							Week 3							Week 4						
A	A	A	E	E	B	B	N	N	N	P	N	N	B	N	N	N	P	N	N	B	P	P	P	P	P	P	P

Week 5							Week 6							Exam week						
P	N	P	N	P	P	N	N	N	M	M				X	X	X	X			
P	P	P	P	P	P	P	P	P	M	M										

The shaded areas are weekends and X denotes the actual exams. Week 5 and 6 assumes that you are not at work and so have a full day to devote to your revision. As you can see of the last 5 days 2 are taken up with mock exams and the last 3 are left blank. This is because there are two parts to revision.

The first is very much to do with making notes, practising questions based on the key examinable topics and continuing to learn but in a much more focused way than on tuition. Equally, what you are learning is far more about application, how the topic will be examined rather than what the topic is about.

The second is more about recognising that there will be some topics that you won't be able to master in the time you have left and others that you have mastered but can't remember some of the key prompts, definitions or formats. In this second period, we need to start committing things to memory.

At some point you need to accept there will be some things you can't do, but what do you do then?

Accepting that there are topics that you may never understand is not about giving up; it may all click into place the night before the exam. It is more about saying, "Okay, at this point, having spent some time on this topic, I still don't get it, what do I do if it's examined?"

You should memorise some key points around this topic so that if it you do get a question on it in the exam you can at least do something. Given that you have spent more time on the examinable topics, this will hopefully be less examinable and so not as likely to be examined on the day. Also in this second part of revision, you need to be producing a third and final set of notes (memory notes) and, if you have time, continue to practise past exam questions.

What to do each day

For some, the very idea of having a timetable of what you need to do in one and a half hour chunks will seem far too detailed. For others, it will seem an obvious next step and they may even break it down into smaller sessions. I have included a sample below, showing how you could break up your day. At the back of this chapter is a larger version that you may wish to photocopy and use as part of your own revision, filling in the blanks with questions and specific activities.

A single day timetable

Day one	Hours	
Session 1	9.00 - 10.30	1.5
Break	10.30 - 11.00	
Session 2	11.00 - 12.30	1.5
Lunch	12.30 - 1.30	
Session 3	1.30 - 3.00	1.5
Break	3.00 - 3.30	
Session 4	3.30 - 5.00	1.5
Dinner	5.00 - 7.00	
Session 5	7.00 - 8.00	1.0
Break	8.00 - 8.15	
Session 6	8.15 - 9.15	1.0
		8.0

This is obviously just a guide, but it does show that you can work reasonably effectively for 8 hours in a day. If you follow the assumption that you are attempting 4 exams, but only have two weeks off work to study full time, then the available hours to devote to revision would be 184 – or 46 hours per paper. (10hrs week1 + 18hrs week 2 and 3 + 26hrs week 4 + 56hrs for weeks 5 and 6).

This equates to roughly 5 days per subject and may sound a lot. But dependent on the complexity of the questions, your grasp of the subject during tuition, and the fact that you may be sitting more than four exams, even this may not be sufficient. If you started revision 4 weeks before, rather than 6, the time you have per subject is roughly 4 days and if you only leave yourself 2 weeks, then you will be down to 3 days. I have assumed that you cannot work flat out for 14 days, 8 hours a day; you must have some time off in that 2 week period.

One word of caution, if you ask people how much time they devote to revision, some will understate what they are doing, so as not to appear too keen, whilst others may overstate almost as if to convince themselves they are working hard. So take it with a pinch of salt and focus your attention on what you are doing and less on others.

The second part of revision - five days before the exam

Take a look at the diagram below. It shows what you need to do when you are about 5 days away from the exam. First you need to practise mock exams, one per subject under exam conditions. A mock exam is, as the name suggests, a simulation. In a perfect world, it would include the same topics that will be examined on the day, in reality it will just be a best guess as to what those will be. It should be in the same style as the real exam i.e. if there are four 25 mark questions in your exam paper, then the mock should reflect this.

The revision period 5 days before the exam

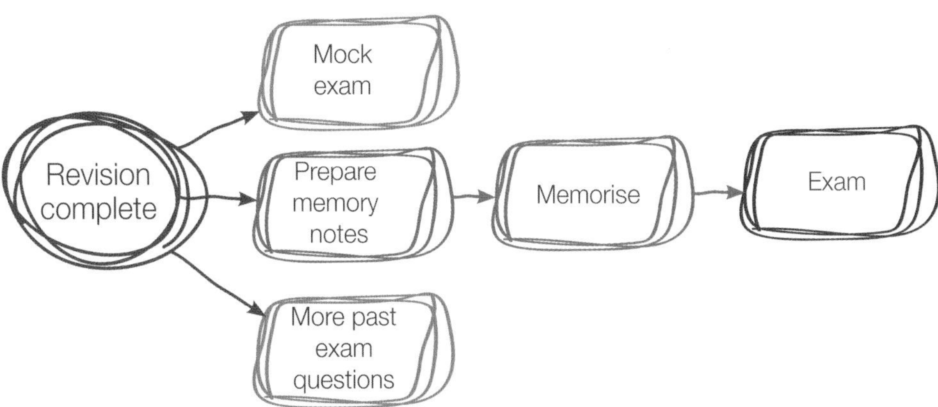

Secondly you need to begin to make your third and final set of notes. These *"memory notes"* need to contain even less information than your revision notes. They should be colourful, visual and include many of the other memory techniques outlined in chapter 5. Any time in between is taken up practising even more past exam questions, perhaps some that you have not attempted before or going back over some that you did not fully understand.

Folders and notes

As you can see from the timetable, preparing and summarising notes is a key part of revision. The more organised these notes, the better. You should have a separate folder for each subject and each subject should be divided up into a number of sections. There should be a section labelled "notes for self". This section is for you to jot down reminders of things you have to do, questions you might want to practise or questions that you need answering in order to better understand something. The second section is a reworked version of the mind map you prepared at tuition. By now you should have a much better idea as to how the subject fits together and which topics are the most difficult and link with others. If you don't like mind maps, simply prepare a list of the most examinable topics with some thoughts and observations next to each one. For example, you might have a note saying how easy or hard each topic was.

But by far the largest section will be taken up with the notes you will make on each key topic. These are your revision notes.

Organising notes

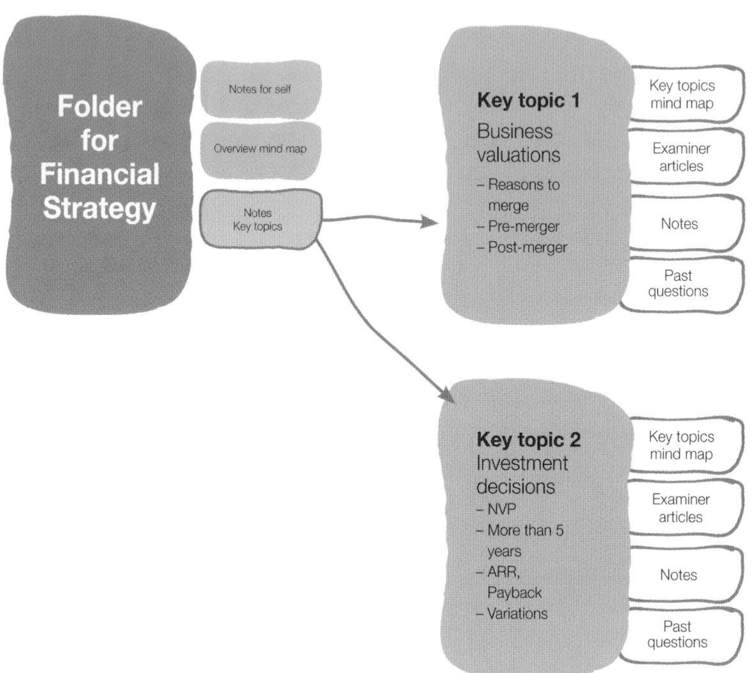

These revision notes are themselves broken down into several sections. Firstly, a section devoted to a key topic mind map. This is a summary, not of the whole subject, but of the individual topics within each subject. Notice that although there may well be 10 or more individual topics that are identified on the mind map, the three most important, in this instance, reasons to merge, pre-merger and post-merger are shown separately on the front cover. This just gives further clarity as to the areas that you simply must look at. This process of breaking down the subject into sections is key to the exam focused approach.

As before if you don't wish to do a mind map, do a list. The second section is for the examiner's articles, of course there may not be an article for each topic. But if there is, it will need filing and working through. You then have the notes on the key topic itself. These are effectively your revision notes. They are made by you working through your tuition notes, but with added focus being given from the analysis of past questions which makes it possible to identify the most examinable topics. As you attempt the past questions, file them in the final section. You should amend the revision notes with anything you have learned from working through these questions. As a result you will be able to identify the gaps in your knowledge from tuition.

Memory notes - five days before the exam

As the exam gets even closer we move into the final stage. As shown in the timetable above when there are only 5 days left before the exam we need to fit in mock exam practice and prepare our final set of notes. We are not making notes because it is a good idea and it gives us something to do. It is the process that is important, not the notes. We start making notes in the classroom or from the text book, recording new facts as part of the process of learning. We then make new exam focused revision notes as part of the process of focusing that knowledge around the key examinable areas. We now need to make notes as in order to help with the process of remembering.

Take out your revision notes and go through them from the beginning, but this time only record what you can't remember or don't understand. The notes should also be written in a more short hand style, we only want **key words** not whole paragraphs. You can do this either in a mind map or linear format. The notes should be no more than 10 pages in length. They should be structured in the same way as your original revision notes wherever possible.

Once prepared your objective is to memorise, we are no longer looking for an understanding, but don't be surprised if during this process something suddenly makes sense, a eureka moment. Use the memory techniques outlined in chapter 7 to help. The point is this, time for learning in the traditional way is over, you now need to commit as much to short term memory as possible. The night before and on the morning of the exam you just keep going over these 10 pages of notes. Use colours and images as much as possible and be creative, remember how memory works it's all about the input. The more powerful the form of input the easier it will be to remember.

Less is more - Tuition to revision to memory notes

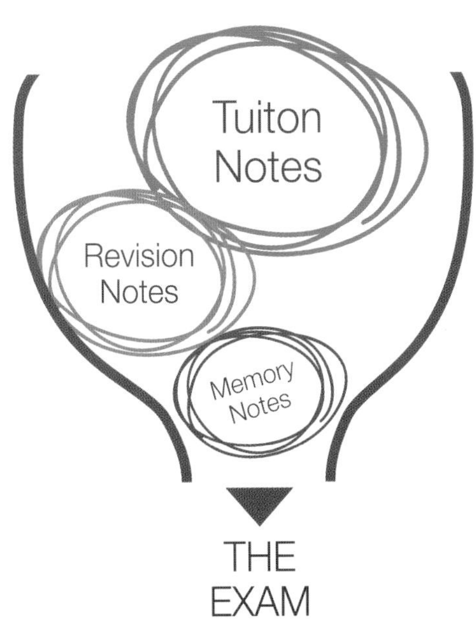

The exam focused approach to revision

Much of what has been described above is part of the exam focused approach to revision. In chapter 3 we introduced the concept of exam focused learning, which could be described as a method of learning that places a much greater emphases on looking at specific topics rather than the whole syllabus. Examination answers are used as both a way to learn and a focus of attention. Exam focused revision follows on from those principles, the difference being that we are less interested in learning about the subject and more interested in learning how to pass the exam.

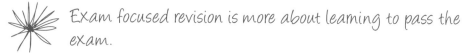

Exam focused revision is more about learning to pass the exam.

The timetable above follows a very exam focused approach, look at the activities. It includes producing an analysis of past exam papers and finding out if your examiner has written any specific guidance or technical articles so as to identify those all important key examinable areas. You are then required to work through past exam questions on those areas. These are all activities promoted in chapter 3. The approach on revision is, however, slightly different. In tuition we are just looking for a rough idea as to what has been examined in the past. We would still expect to study reasonably broadly around those areas. But as we enter the revision phase we want to be far clearer about the *specific topics* we think will be in *next time's* exam.

Analysis of past questions

On revision the analysis of past questions needs closer scrutiny. What you are looking for are patterns, patterns in the way certain topics have been examined for example, how long has it been since a particular topic has been examined? If it has been a long time, you may need to make a judgment call, does it mean it is likely to be examined again or is it a fringe area? Perhaps there is a topic that used to get examined every sitting, but has not been examined for two sittings? This might indicate a very likely examinable area for this times exam. If a topic has been examined in every single exam, then you must make sure you look at this. You may need to tabulate the possible exam topics and then mark when they last came up. Going back about three to four years should give you a reasonably good idea.

Analysis of past questions

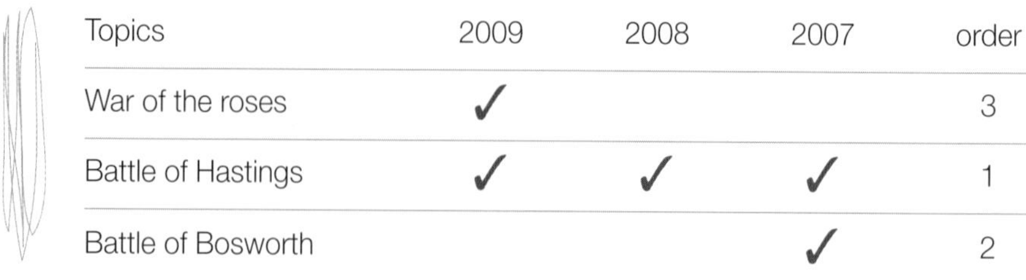

Topics	2009	2008	2007	order
War of the roses	✓			3
Battle of Hastings	✓	✓	✓	1
Battle of Bosworth			✓	2

What we are looking for is to identify a list of topics that we think will be examined **this sitting**. Your revision should be based on these areas. From the table above we would make sure that we revise the battle of Hastings as it has been examined each sitting, so is likely again. The War of the Roses was examined in 2009 so is perhaps less likely but The Battle of Bosworth is possible as it has not been examined since 2007.

It will be impossible to avoid the criticism that this is **question spotting**. I prefer to think about it as a better way of prioritising the time that you have. If you had limitless time, you could of course look at all the past questions. But if you had limitless time, it would not matter which questions you looked at first, as in theory you would be able to look and work through them all. But you don't have limitless time. So what would you prefer, spend your time practising questions based on the belief that you will look at them all, but not do so, or start by practising questions on the areas that are most likely to come up in the next exam?

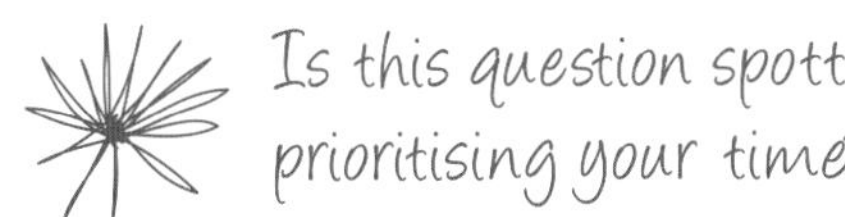

Is this question spotting or simply a better way of prioritising your time?

To me it is clear, pick the questions that you think are most likely to be examined and work through those first. Then work through the next most examinable questions and so on, until you run out of time. If of course you don't run out of time then you will have covered every topic anyway.

Sit a mock exam

One of the other tasks identified in the timetable is to sit a mock exam under timed conditions. This is not so much about assessment, trying to find out if you will pass, but more about giving you the experience of working against the clock and learning from that process.

You may know that managing you time is important, but until you practise a question under timed conditions you cannot be sure you will actually manage your time when it matters, in the exam. There is always the temptation to spend more time on a question that you can do and keep trying to get it right. You need to practise leaving questions you can do so that you can move onto other questions. It is always easier to score marks early on in a question and much harder later.

More revision tips

The main approach to revision is outlined above but there are many other things you can do in the revision period. Below is a list of hints and tips as to how to make your revision even more effective.

1. Where to study

You need to find an environment that is conducive to learning. Some people will prefer a location that is quiet and devoid of any distractions, they will probably wish to study alone. Others may like to be in a room with students, somehow soaking up the atmosphere around them, finding it inspiring. Interestingly you don't need to be studying the same subject, just in the same situation. This is a personal choice; the trick is to find the one that is best for you. Perhaps try both and look back at the end of each day over the amount of work you have completed. Remember it is not how much time you spend revising but how much you have learned.

2. Use your common senses

Don't forget how you learn and what was discussed in chapter 5 about learning styles. After all you are still learning during revision, just different things. Why not record your memory notes, turning them into an audio file. This is ideal for auditory learners, it is also very mobile so can be listened to on the move. Be creative with this, record them over music that you are already familiar with so as to further help with recall. Use strange voices to highlight topics that you find hard to remember. Using your voice in this way may sound a little strange, but is the equivalent of highlighting a key word in a set of notes; it simply makes it stand out. Making these recordings is a whole lot easier with modern technology. And mobile phones and MP3 players have made listening convenient and practical. One additional benefit of doing all this is that just reading notes out loud can be a great way to revise.

Put some of your key examinable topics on cards so that you can organize them, ideal for kinaesthetic learners. Don't just use black and white, add colour and images. Try to use some of the memory techniques discussed earlier. In the illustration below I have used a simple acronym (OPEC) to help remember 4 techniques that might be examined in Investment Appraisal. These cards can be hand-written or typed, it's up to you.

Key topic cards

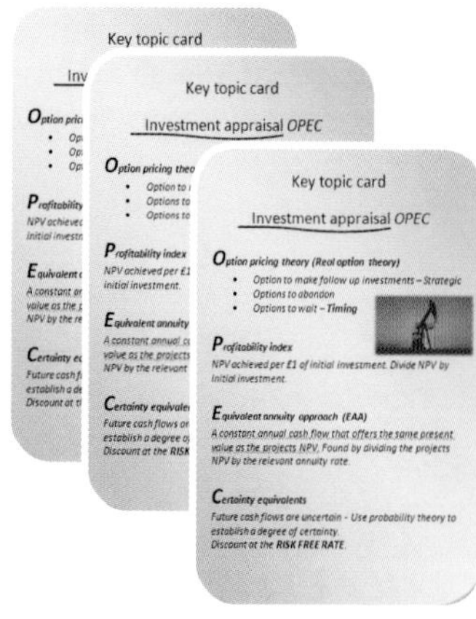

Why not make some posters of the key words, but don't forget to use colour even if you don't do a mind map. Put these in a place that you look at every day. Below is an example of what can be done. Notice the notes are next to the light switch, something that is used every day.

Lucy's wall

3. Become a marker!

This is a great revision technique. Remember that you can often get access to examiners' answers and in many instances marking guides. Find someone or a group of people who are also studying towards the same exam. This will be easy if you are in a classroom environment, but if not, why not post a request on a discussion forum and ask if anyone else wants to do this. You will need some past exams and as mentioned the answers and marking guides.

You each attempt the question(s) and give it to the others in your group to mark, a group of 5 would be ideal. Apart from gaining a very good insight as to the technical element of the question, you will also begin to understand more about what the examiner wants. You will perhaps need to read the requirements again, as well as looking at the marking guide so that you can identify exactly where the marks need to be awarded. When you do this you may be surprised as to how easy some marks are to earn, yet how hard it is to earn others.

You may also pick up how hard it is to give marks to an answer that you just can't read!

4. Teach or explain to someone else

There will be topics that you understand, or think you do, better than your friends. And in turn there will be topics they will understand better than you. Why not get together and teach each other. I have to admit I always think that this sound like something you would do at primary school. But if I think about my own learning experience, one of the most powerful ways of learning has been when I have had to prepare a lecture in order to teach something to someone else. To do this you don't need a rough idea how it works, you need to know exactly how it works. Developing different ways of looking at the topic and coming up with examples to explain to others will in fact do more to improve your understanding than it will to your potential students.

Explaining something to others is a great way of making sure you understand it!

5. Diet and exercise

I am far from an expert on diet, so will keep this section reasonably short. But what you eat and drink will have some impact on your performance in the exam room.

There seems little disagreement that water is good for you. The brain is made up of 80% water and when dehydrated your mind can begin to play tricks and becomes far less effective. So during the revision period drink lots of water. It is recommended that you should drink around 2.5 litres of pure water a day. But please do not think the more water you drink the ***cleverer*** you get, believe it or not it is possible to drink too much!

And as for drinking coffee, there has been some research from the US to suggest that although caffeine may keep you awake and give the impression of being more alert, your ability to recall is impaired. A far better solution to improve both mental sharpness and memory is to take a nap. So the advice would seem to be drink less coffee, more water and get a good night rest.

Increasing your intake of omega 3 could be helpful. Omega 3 oils are beneficial because they provide fluidity to cell membranes and improve communication between brain cells. There is some evidence to suggest they may help boost learning power and also enhance mood. Foods rich in omega 3 oils include oily fish such as sardines, salmon and mackerel.

In the biggest study so far on the effect of Omega 3, the Oxford Durham Trial took 17 primary school children with conditions like dyslexia, ADHD and dyspraxia and asked them to take fish oil supplements over a 6 month period. The results saw improvements in confidence, perception, reading and writing and memory.

These results are far from conclusive with critics suggesting that although there were improvements in the children's performance in this study, there is no evidence that it would improve the performance of children without the conditions described. But as I see it, if we don't manufacture these essential fatty acids, they have to be taken in from what we eat. The best way to do this would probably be to have a diet that gives us these naturally or to take a supplement. So if you have a balanced diet with a reasonable amount of omega 3, one portion of oily fish a week, you should be fine.

We should take exercise for so many reasons, not only does it makes you feel good, it is a natural antidote to stress. It increases the blood and oxygen flow to the brain, helps create new nerve cells and increases the amount of chemicals generated that help with cognitive tasks. And that seems to be a lot of good reasons to get to the gym. Don't forget when putting your timetable together, make sure you block some time in for regular exercise.

During the exam

If you read as many examiners reports as I have, there are only so many things that you can get wrong in the exam. And sparing the obvious ones like not knowing the subject or not knowing enough about the subject, most involve, **not reading the question** properly, **not writing a good enough answer** and **not managing time**. So if you want to improve your chances of passing, these are the areas to focus on. The idea is not just to identify what the mistakes are but to offer advice on what you should do to improve.

How to read exam questions

You would think that reading an exam question would be easy. After all you just read it, don't you? Well yes, but it is not reading that's the problem, it is understanding what the examiner is looking for. As multiple choice questions are relatively easy to read I have ignored them in this section.

1. Break the question down

When you are looking at an exam question for the first time, don't read it from the top of the page, look down until you find the requirements and read these first. It is important that you identify what you are being asked to do before you start to read the question. Then begin to break the question down by identifying the key words and underlining them. The first key words we should look for are the **technical ones**.

e.g.

> ***Requirements***
> *Calculate the NPV and equivalent annual costs for each project, using the discount rate obtained in your answer to (a). Make whatever assumptions you think necessary but base them wherever possible on information provided in the scenario.*
>
> ***(15 marks)***

This question clearly requires knowledge of NPV (net present value) and equivalent annual cost. I appreciate that too many people reading this, the specific content will have no meaning; however the principle will be the same in any question. Take for example the economics question below.

> ***Requirements***
> *How do you think the economy will be affected by the introduction of a national minimum wage? Give economic reasons for your answer.*
>
> ***(10 marks)***

In this question the technical content requires that you have knowledge of the national minimum wage. Having established what you need to know the next stage is to find out what you need to do and to do this effectively we need to understand the action words (verbs) being used.

2. Understand the action words

Understanding the action words means understanding the verbs. What is the question asking you to do? In the (verb) table below is a sample of words that are likely to appear in exam questions. The list is not meant to be exhaustive; it is just to give you some idea. The different examining bodies will often publish their own verb list. The table not only includes the definition but an extra column to provide some guidance as to how you can do it, not simply what you should do.

The "*how you can do it*" column is very easy in some instances. For example, for definitions you simply have to memorise them, but how do you describe something. What exactly should you do? Here I have suggested that you visualize, create pictures in your mind's eye of the event. Imagine yourself in a specific location if that helps, or if asked to describe a process as "*describe how this would be calculated*" imagine yourself actually doing the calculations and talk about what you are doing.

Verb table

Verb	Definition	How to do it
Low order		
Define	Give the meaning of. Translate into language anyone can understand	Memorise, use memory techniques to help
Describe	Communicate characteristics and features	Write down what you can see. Thinking about the order in which you see it might help
Demonstrate	Show by way of example	Provide an example either from memory or by writing down what you see when you go through the process you are demonstrating
Middle order		
Calculate	Mathematical solution	Use numbers to solve the problem
Explain	Make clear	Identify the components and any cause and effect they may have. Give reasons why. Talk through the images in your head and consider using an example. Just say more…
Compare and Contrast	Show similarities and or differences	Identify the components and talk through what looks the same and what looks different
High order		
Analyse	Identify components and the relationships between them	Take apart the key components and identify cause and effect if possible
Evaluate	Appraise or asses the value	State the criteria, then choose which one is best in accordance with that criteria
Discuss	Examine in detail by argument	Identify issues and provide points for and against. You need at least two sides of the argument to discuss
Recommend	Advise a course of action. What should they do?	Visualise the situation and think about what you would do in these circumstances. Write them down

One of the most difficult words to explain is the word explain. To help I suggest that you break down what you are trying to explain and identify the parts or components. Then state what makes or causes that component to do something and what impact or effect it is having on what you are trying to explain. This is beginning to sound too abstract and far too complicated. So let me give a simple **example**, which is of course an excellent way to explain.

Requirements
Explain how to boil an egg.

Firstly boil the water for the egg, (the **components** are the water and the egg) *the water needs to be boiling before you put the egg in or the egg may be undercooked*. (This is a **clarification** of what you are doing with an **effect** of what might happen if you do not do this, it is a **reason why**. It is also an example of how you would **talk through** the process).

Get the idea. There will probably be lots of visualization going on in your head, so as before use those images and talk about them.

To illustrate this point further let's look at the NPV question again.

Requirements
Calculate the NPV and equivalent annual costs for each project, using the discount rate obtained in your answer to (a). Make whatever assumptions you think necessary but base them wherever possible on information provided in the scenario.

(15 marks)

We have a very simply verb here, "calculate" but a further action "to make assumptions". But can you see how, by underlining the key words and then the verbs, what is being asked gets clearer.

3. The rule of AND

Once you have identified what you need to know and what you need to do to answer the question, the next step is to further break the question down making sure that you clearly answer all parts. The rule of AND is a simple yet effective technique to make sure that you don't miss part of the question. Take a look at the question below and read it through, thinking about what you need to do. Once again I appreciate that the content may be a little distracting, but it will avoid you thinking too much about the answer when for this exercise you need to think about the structure.

Requirements
Explain the shortcomings of using the CAPM in the circumstances of the scenario presented here and comment on an alternative method of evaluating uncertain cash flows.

(8 marks)

This is a classic rule of AND question. Whenever you see an AND in the questions simply put a line through it and place a full stop at the end of the previous section. Then make the first letter after the AND into a capital, in effect creating a new sentence.

> ***Requirements***
> *Explain the shortcomings of using the CAPM in the circumstances of the scenario presented here. ~~and~~ Comment on an alternative method of evaluating uncertain cash flows.*
>
> ***(8 marks)***

Now read the question. It should become very clear that there are in fact two questions, one that is asking you to *Explain the shortcomings of using the CAPM* and two, *Comment on an alternative method of evaluating uncertain cash flows.* The reason I would suggest you actually cross the AND out is because it makes it absolutely clear what you have to do. Just thinking you will do this in the exam often doesn't work due to the many other things you are thinking about and the frame of mind you are in at the time.

After a while it becomes difficult not to look at questions without breaking them down in this way. For example I can't read this question without wanting to underline the word CAPM (what I need to know) and the explain (what I need to do).

This also leads very nicely into our last rule, guessing the marking guide. By breaking the question down you not only improve your understanding of what is required but you are preparing the ground so that you can spot the marking guide.

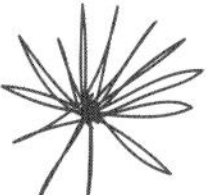

Break questions up using the rule of AND.

4. Guess the marking guide

The rule of AND really helps with this. Using the example above once more, but this time breaking it up into the separate sections.

> ***Requirements***
> *Q1. Explain the shortcomings of using the CAPM in the circumstances of the scenario presented here.*
>
> ***(Say 4 marks)***
>
> *Q2. Comment on an alternative method of evaluating uncertain cash flows.*
>
> ***(Say 4 marks)***
>
> ***(8 marks)***

Now of course we won't know if there are 4 marks for each part of these questions. But it's not a bad guess and it at least gets us to think about answering them, forcing you to devote a reasonable amount of time to both. Now it may be possible to refine this further by looking in more detail as to what you need to do and changing the mark allocation accordingly, giving more time to the harder and more involved task. Equally you will get better at guessing the marking guides the more examiner's answers and marking guides you look at.

Guessing the marking guide is all about allocation of time. Knowing what the marks are in the exam really does not matter particularly. What does matter in the exam is how much time you devote to a particular question.

Let's finish this section with a history question and apply all of the rules learned so far. I have deliberately chosen a question that for all sorts of reasons is difficult to answer, so as to help illustrate the whole process.

Requirements

Answer both

The Wars of the Roses, 1455-85

(a) Why did rivalry between Lancaster and York lead to war in 1455?

(25 Marks)

(b) Explain how seriously civil war affected the economy, society and culture of England between 1455 and 1485.

(25 Marks)

Let's begin to break by breaking up the question.

Requirements

The Wars of the Roses, 1455-85

(a) Why did rivalry between Lancaster and York lead to war in 1455?

(25 Marks)

(b) Explain how seriously civil war affected the economy, society and culture of England between 1455 and 1485.

(25 Marks)

What knowledge do you need - this is clearly about the War of the Roses (1455-85)

What are you being asked to do - for part (a) we are required to say W*hy* the rivalry led to war. Why is a justification verb and so we need to give lots of examples.

For (b) we are being asked to *Explain* how this war affected the economy, society AND culture.

Once you have broken the question down you can now think about guessing the marking guide.

These are large essay style questions of 25 marks each and so require a very full explanation to score well. Part (a) is particularly difficult as the question is very open and little can be gleaned by underlining the key words. As a result it is not possible to break the marking guide down any further. Part (b) is much easier and you can see we could guess that there are three questions of 8 marks each.

When faced with a question like part (a) where breaking the question down is not easy, you will need a good answer plan to give you the structure necessary to score the marks. How to approach questions like this is shown below in the section on planning.

The best we can do at this point would be to guess that the marks would be split as follows:

- Why rivalry led to war 25 marks
- Explain how seriously civil war affected the economy 8 marks
- Explain how seriously civil war affected the society 8 marks
- Explain how seriously civil war affected the culture 8 marks

5. Dealing with scenarios and case studies

Often exam questions are far more involved than a few sentences and require you to read a scenario or case study on which the questions can then be based. This brings with it more complexity and further opportunity to misread the question. As with the questions we have looked at so far we need a simple process that will help clarify what we have to do.

Below is an example of a typical scenario/case study. The requirements have been underlined and the questions broken down as per the guidance above. It has a number of paragraphs separated only be white space and has no formal headings. The shading has been added to help make it stand out in the book. One of the problems with this style of question is that the words all tend to blur into one, so it is important to put some structure in place.

Step one – read the requirements first.

Step two - break the paragraphs up into separate sections. If there is no white space to separate the headings, find an appropriate place, perhaps where a new topic is being discussed or a new theme introduced. Number each section. The numbers have been added in the example below and were not in the original question.

Step three – As before underline the key words and write in the margin any points that may help clarify the scenario or help you in gaining a better understanding as to what is going on. Remember from a learning perspective writing on the question paper can help not simply because it makes the words stand out but also because it is a kinaesthetic activity. It is tempting to underline most words as they may all seem important given that the case itself is new to you. But try to underline as few words as possible, picking the key themes from the requirements in the question can help.

Step four – forget that this is an exam and make it as real as possible. Visualise the events taking place and put yourself into the situation being described. This will help when you get the, "*what do you think*" and "*how will this work*" style questions.

Example - scenario/case study

1st Paragraph is about the history

1. MLD began over a century ago as a family-run business producing confectionery (sweets or candy). Since this time there has been considerable change. The company is now publicly listed and has grown rapidly over the past five years. This growth has been achieved through acquiring a number of smaller manufacturers of packet foodstuff and bottled drinks. MLD has, up until now, operated each acquired manufacturer as a separate division.

They have grown by acquisition

2nd Paragraph is about the structure

2. As a consequence of past acquisitions, MLD now has three additional head offices in different parts of the country. It has different systems and support structures, as well as many middle managers performing a wide diversity of roles. For instance, whilst personnel specialists assist managers of all levels in the main confectionery division, in other divisions there is no such support. Middle managers in the packet foodstuff and bottled drinks divisions are responsible for all the 'hiring and firing" of the divisional factory workforce in addition to their other duties and responsibilities.

This paragraph is just giving an example

3rd Paragraph is about what they want to do

3. MLD now wants to consolidate its business by simplifying its operations. This will involve centralising finance, payroll, marketing and human resource functions into a single head office. MLD believes that improved efficiency and cost savings will result.

Sounds like change, redundancies?

4th Paragraph is about the HR strategy & technology

4. Middle managers and those employed at the additional head offices are fearful of losing their jobs. However, MLD has assured them that there will be no ill-considered job losses. Instead MLD states that a proper Human Resource (HR) strategy will be developed that will focus on the future needs of the company as a whole. MLD's technology currently lags behind that of its competitors and it has established a budget aimed at renewing equipment and modernising and standardising systems, although the majority of this budget will be spent on manufacturing applications,

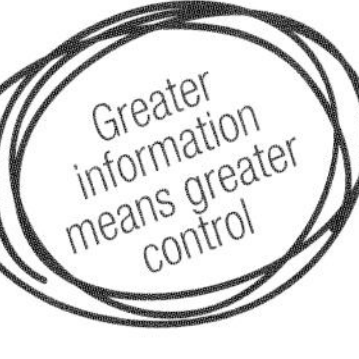

HR strategy focuses on the company not the staff?

5th Paragraph is about what the new system will do

5. MLD has engaged a software developer to advise on the replacement of its many outdated administrative and management systems with the most advanced available. MLD has supported the software developer's recommendation to introduce a central People and Payroll system. Within this system a web browser would allow managers to have immediate access to information on their staffs' diaries, overtime, holidays and sickness, as well as being able to submit timesheet entries directly into a central payroll system instead of relying on manual entry systems.

Greater information means greater control

Required:

(a) Explain the difficulties associated with the way in which MLD has, up until now, dealt with HR issues in the packet foodstuff and bottled drinks divisions.

(5 marks)

(b) Identify the advantages and disadvantages of MLD's strategy of growth through acquisition of smaller firms.

(5 marks)

(c) Explain how the proposed People and Payroll system could benefit MLD.

(5 marks)

(d) From the alternative implementation systems available, recommend, with reasons, which MLD should use when introducing the new People and Payroll system.

(5 marks)

(e) Explain the key stages involved in developing an HR strategy for MLD.

(5 marks)

(f) Using Mintzberg's five part categorisation for organisations, - how MLD supports its operations.

(5 marks)

(30 marks)

How to write an answer

And so to the second area we need to improve in the exam room, how to write an answer. This section is more about how you can use exam skills to improve your answers rather than how to improve your writing style. Writing style is something that develops over several years and is partly to do with your education and to a certain extent your background. To write well you need to think clearly, that little voice inside your head needs to be making sense. So in effect you are simply translating what is in your head into the written word. It is also difficult to give advice about writing style when some styles may be specific to the exam, for example how a particular exam board or examiner prefers to see something presented. So although some guidance on writing style is given, it is generic and so relevant to most exams.

There are lots of reasons as to why people write poor answers in the exam.

- Lack of knowledge

  One, you may not know the answer and so don't know what to write, or what you do write is not very good. A bit obvious perhaps but might just need stating. This is more to do with knowledge and less to do with writing and so will be ignored in this section.

- Poor planning

  Two, you may know the answer or at least think you do, but when you come to write it down you are not sure how to do it. This is more than likely the result of poor or no **planning** and can be improved.

- No clear structure

  Three, you know what to write but don't seem to be able to write very much. This could of course be the result of insufficient knowledge. I will assume however that this is more a lack of understanding how to **structure** your answer as a result of the question providing little guidance. A good structure is not only helpful for the marker it is helpful for you. Having some headings in place will prompt you to think what to say.

- Poor presentation

  Four, you know what to write and how to write or so you think. Unfortunately no one can understand it or worse, read it. Sounds like a problem with your **presentation**. Don't assume just because you know the answer the marker or examiner will give you marks, if they can't understand or read the answer, how can they?

Planning and structuring your answer

To some extent the way you plan an answer is an extension of how well you have read the question in the first place. If you have underlined the key words, including the key verbs then to some extent you already have a plan. However where questions are less specific in what they require, planning is very important. Take for example the history question looked at earlier.

Requirements
The Wars of the Roses, 1455-85

(a) Why did rivalry between Lancaster and York lead to war in 1455? ***(25 Marks)***

We already know that this is about the Wars of the Roses and that you are being asked a why question. Why is a justification question, it is asking you to come up with ***reasons*** as to why the rivalry led to war. But it is a 25 mark question and the answer needs to be reasonably comprehensive to score well. If this were a 3 hour exam you need to spend 45 minutes on this one question. The problem is it gives very little guidance as to what you need to do in that 45 minutes.

Whatever you do, don't answer the question

One of the commonest mistakes in answering this type of question is to try to answer it all too quickly. This would be a helpful technique for questions that are worth 2 or 3 marks. For these shorter style questions it is useful to get to the point quickly and add the word BECAUSE at the end.

So the structure becomes; *rivalry between Lancaster and York lead to war in 1455 BECAUSE.........*

The problem with this is you will answer the question or to be precise you will answer the question too quickly without demonstrating the depth of knowledge the examiner requires. This is a 25 mark question, so we don't want to answer the question too quickly, we don't want to get to the point too fast, and we don't want to be too concise. In order to do well on a 25 mark question you need to say much more and to do this you need a plan.

How to plan

The plan is needed to give a structure to your answer. This structure will effectively be a series of headings that will act as prompts, reminding you of what you need to say.

Planning is a creative process and we may need a little help to be creative. There are many ways to plan an answer, in this example we will taken some advice from Rudyard Kipling.

I keep six honest serving men, they taught me all I knew, their names are what and where and when.

And why and how and who.

Use these words to help develop your answer plan.

- WHAT was the house of Lancaster and WHAT did they want to achieve
- WHO were the key people, HOW did they become so important
- WHAT was the house of York and WHAT did they want to achieve
- WHO were the key people, HOW did they become so important

This gives us a background to the situation a way of understanding perhaps that rivalry was inevitable if they wanted different things.

- WHAT was the nature of the rivalry, be specific
- WHY was this rivalry so strong that is would ultimately lead to war

Expand your questions to further develop your answer but moving more towards the actual exam question, which of course must be answered.

It is important that you explain some of your answers and give lots of examples supporting your comments. In fact one of the most important aspects of writing answers is to provide lots and lots of examples.

The define, explain and illustrate rule

For essay style questions where there is very little structure but a lot of marks, the approach described above works very well. But for shorter questions it can seem a little too involved and time consuming. So for these questions we need another method, it's called the Define, Explain and Illustrate approach. Let's look at one the questions from earlier in this chapter.

Requirements
How do you think the economy will be affected by the introduction of a national minimum wage? Give economic reasons for your answer.

(10 marks)

By underlining the key words, we already know that this question is about a national minimum wage. But by using the define, explain and illustrate approach we can develop a plan as to how to write a more structured answer.

Firstly **define the technical words** or make some comments/statements about these technical words. It is important that we start off with a definition of what the national minimum wage is.

Secondly we need to **explain** more about the national minimum wage and how this will affect the economy and, as the question suggests, give reasons.

And lastly we need to give examples in order to help us **illustrate** the points we are making. Where possible the examples used should be from the question or scenario.

The define, explain and illustrate approach will help you write a lot more, when you are required to do so by the question. Marks are not given for volume, they are given for content, and where essay questions carry a lot of marks you will not score well with a brief answer, and writing a lot is on the whole better than writing very little.

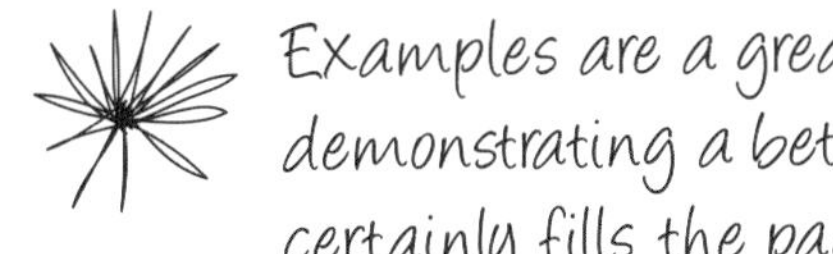

Examples are a great way of explaining and demonstrating a better understanding. And yes it certainly fills the page.

I cannot stress the importance of giving examples; it is such an effective way of demonstrating a deeper understanding of the subject and gives the depth often required by examiners.

Presentation

How you present your answer may on the face of it seem trivial or relatively unimportant. A student will not pass an exam just because their handwriting is neat or because they have clear headings and good referencing. No of course not, but you can put in hours of work, have a very effective revision period, yet fail the exam because the markers could not read or understand what you are saying.

A marker could be faced with 200 or more scripts at any one exam sitting, so by the time they have marked, say 20, they have probably seen all the different ways possible of answering that particular question. They will become very quick judges of good and bad answers and will make up their mind within seconds of seeing the script; presentation is one of the factors they will notice.

White space

White space is a term used to describe a space between paragraphs. Using white space is a very effective way of forcing the marker to take stock of what you have just said. This breathing space gives the marker time to reflect and so decide if what you have said is worthy of marks. Which of the two examples below do you prefer? I we assume each tick equals one mark; the first answer will score 2 and the second 4.

White space

Using white space is a very effective way of forcing the marker to take stock of what you have just said. Using white space is a very effective way of forcing the marker to take stock of what you have just said. Using white space is a very effective way of forcing the marker to take stock of what you have just said. Using white space is a very effective way of forcing the marker to take stock of what you have just said.

Or

Using white space is a very effective way of forcing the marker to take stock of what you have just said.

Using white space is a very effective way of forcing the marker to take stock of what you have just said.

Using white space is a very effective way of forcing the marker to take stock of what you have just said.

Using white space is a very effective way of forcing the marker to take stock of what you have just said.

I am not suggesting that if you simply insert white space between each sentence you will get more marks; your content has to be good. What I am saying is that if you present it in this way it will help the marker by not missing valuable points you have made.

Make it easy to mark

The overall advice with presentation is to make your script easy to mark. Make sure you show all your workings and cross reference them. This will help the marker follow your logic, even where your answer may differ from that of the model answer.

Have a clear layout and use headings and sub headings where appropriate, this will not only give structure to your answer but will also show the marker what you were trying to do. Make sure you label each part of the question so the marker can see where one question ends and another begins.

And where you are not sure what you should have done and so may have made assumptions, make sure you write them down. Once again just because you have a different answer to the model answer does not mean that your answer is wrong. If the marker can understand what you were thinking, and if your assumptions were valid and your answer is based on those assumptions, then you can still score highly.

Poor handwriting can make it very difficult for the marker. Although you may have made some very valid points, if the handwriting is illegible or even difficult to read it can seriously effect your chances at passing. How would you like to read pages and pages of writing like this?

How to manage time

One of the commonest criticisms made by examiners is that students have managed their time poorly. This of course is very easy to resolve. Just make sure you finish each question on time. But if it were that easy then it wouldn't really be a problem. As with many things, knowing what you should do is useful, but we need some techniques to help become more effective.

Something that it very easy to do, take of your watch and put it in front of you in the exam. Focus on the fingers of the watch for a second noting where they will be when you finish the question. As a way of reinforcing this write down the time you will finish on the question paper.

Mark allocation = time

Using the marks from the question as a guide as to how much time you should spend answering the question is probably one of the most valuable things you can do to make sure you finish on time. In fact I have often wondered why examiners bother with marks and don't just put the time.

Before you enter the exam room you should know how much time you have for each mark so that it becomes a simple multiplication exercise on the day. For a standard three hour exam it is 180 minutes divided by 100 marks, giving 1.8 minutes per mark. So for a 10 mark question you will have 18 minutes. Now you may not need to spend all the allotted time on each question. Some questions may be more difficult to solve and so the marks reflect the extra thinking time required. But if you can solve these quickly, perhaps because it is on an area that you are particularly good at or have seen before, you will be able to free up time for other questions. The point is this, it is only a guide, but it will avoid you falling into many traps, like spending too much time on your favourite question, or on an area that you can't do but want to get right. For Peter Perfect (see chapter 3) sticking to the mark allocation would be incredibly helpful.

I have answered three questions and that's enough.
Lewis Carroll

Easy marks first

When those all important words are uttered by the invigilator, "You can now start the exam," your heart may begin to race a little faster in anticipation of what may be on the paper. You look at the first question and glance through the individual topics, "that's not too bad", the next one "that's okay" and then you find what you're looking for, the most difficult part of the question, this is where you will start. It may be human nature to start with the most difficult question first on the basis that you are fresh and you will know that once you have solved this one everything else on the paper will be easy.

But from an exam technique point of view it is not a good idea to start with the hardest question first. In trying to get the question right you may go over on your time allocation, it may frustrate you, so putting you in the wrong frame of mind for the rest of the paper and worst of all you may find that you can't do it! So start with the easiest questions first and leave the hardest ones until the end and with a bit of luck you will run out of time. How good is that running out of time on the question you couldn't do anyway!

If you are going to get it wrong – do it quickly

This is about recognizing that you may not be able to do something. You couldn't do it before the exam and you will almost certainly not be able to do it in the exam. It may be your worst topic, but it may also be worth 10 marks. You must have a go at questions like this; you can't leave a 10 mark question completely. Your target mark however will be about 2 or 3 out of 10. Re-focus and look at the question again, not asking "can I do this" but "how can I get 2 to3 marks". You may know the definition of some of the terms or some pre remembered facts, just put them down and then move on. Don't spend a long time on questions you can't do, make some assumptions and leave it. Don't spend a long time getting something wrong that you could in fact never do. I like to think of this as **managing ignorance**.

Do the things you can do, not the things you can't do, because you can't do what you can't.

Stuart Pedley-Smith

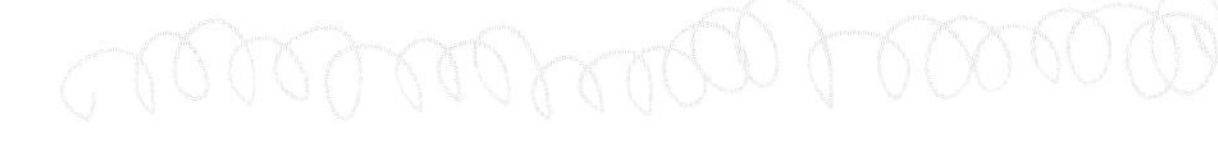

In conclusion

This has been an important chapter, what you do in the revision period and how you approach the questions on the day of the exam can often be the difference between success and failure. So having a good strategy for revision and practising those exam techniques is vital.

I can still remember being told at school that I should start revision; it was about two weeks before the exam. I don't remember asking anyone what to do so I made it up. My revision consisted of reading through the notes about two days before the exam. I didn't have a timetable, I didn't make any revision notes and the very idea of looking at past exam papers or practising questions could not have been further from my mind.

My recollection as to what I did in the exam room is a little hazy, but I am pretty sure that I would not have underlined the key words or looked carefully at the mark allocation to give me guidance as to how long I should spend on that question.

I hope that this chapter gives you some useful pointers as to what you can do to avoid most of my mistakes.

The E Word Interviews.

A Student

Q Could you introduce yourself and tell us about your interest/involvement in the exam process?

I have been studying for 11 years as a mature student, five years at AAT, a year break and then five years at CIMA. I never found studying easy at school, but was always encouraged by my teachers' statements of "if you work hard you will do well". I fell into an accounting role in the 80's, found I enjoyed it and decided to study AAT as a first step towards helping me to climb the career ladder. The lower level exams were easier to study as they involved learning facts and regurgitating them. As my studies continued, it became more difficult to pass the exams. I often missed the point of some of the questions and found I was just brain dumping all my topic knowledge into the question being asked. I found practising past exam questions and attending exam technique courses a good way of breaking this habit. The techniques learnt gave me a process to follow and the exam practice, enabled me to manage my time during the exam itself. This gave me the confidence on the day of the exam that I could tackle any question.

Q Belinda do you see a clear distinction between tuition and revision? How would you define revision?

There is a distinction between tuition and revision. Tuition is more about learning the course content, facts, techniques and theories. Revision is contextualising the facts, techniques and theories based on a scenario and the question asked. The only way to learn how to contextualise and apply the facts is by practising lots of past questions and papers.

Q How far in advance of the exam would you startrevision?

At the lower level exams I found crash revision worked, but as I progressed through my studies I found that I needed to allow more time for the facts and practice questions to sink in. I had found that 4 weeks revision was just about enough to see me through however for the final level papers I am finding I have already started the revision and exam technique process and there's still 6 weeks to go!

Q Did you find that your attitude or mood changed the closer you got to revision/exam?

Yes, I find that I take things much more seriously the closer to the exam I get.

Q Have you ever found yourself feeling stressed, the result of sitting exams?

Initially I did. But the magic word is PLANNING. I normally found that I got stressed and blamed the lack of revision on the ironing not being done or the housework not being done. I have now found that I plan and do the ironing 6 weeks before the exams, Yes I know 6 weeks worth of clothes!!!!

Q Are you an organised student when it comes to revision, do you produce a timetable?

I am an organised student but I don't have a timetable. Having read chapter 8 I will probably start using one, although self analysing myself I know that I will only be able to cope with 6 hours study a day.

Q Do you focus on past questions or do you have a different way of refining what you spend your time on?

Definitely past questions, normally old exam papers.

Q What benefit do you get from looking at past questions and answers?

It helps me to contextualise and get used to the examiner's style of asking questions, and the expected answers.

Q Did you sit a mock exam, if so what did you learn if anything?

I always sit any progress papers or mock exams. It helps with the time management if nothing else. It also helps with what formats work and don't work for the exam day.

Q Do you think that exam techniques made any difference to your exam performance?

I am not the quickest of readers, so the exam techniques definitely worked for me.

Read the requirements before reading the scenario helps to pick out the relevant points right from the first read through. Also the time management of mark allocation helps to give discipline as to whether you should be writing half a page or 3 pages.

Q What would be your top exam tips, which ones really made a difference for you?

Its only an exam. No one is going to die if you fail. Don't take it too seriously you can only do your best. If you don't know something you don't know it. Just do the best you can and if you fail you can always re take it. LEARN TO WRITE QUICKLY IN BLOCK CAPITALS FROM THE START. IT MAKES HANDWRITING EASIER TO READ ESPECIALLY WHEN YOUR BRAIN IS WORKING FASTER THAN YOUR HAND WILL WRITE.

Q Do you think that passing exams means that you are good at what you do, if not what does passing an exam prove?

Passing an exam proves that you have a certain level of competence, but like any skill if it's not used it is easily forgotten. An exam can help you see the bigger picture and how things fit together that you would not ordinarily be exposed to in the work place .

Q Is there anything you would like to add that we haven't discussed?

Oily fish and no alcohol does help during the revision period. It also means you have something to look forward to once the exam is finished.

Daily timetable (to copy)

Day one		Activity	Questions
Session 1	9.00 - 10.30		
Break	10.30 - 11.00		
Session 2	11.00 - 12.30		
Lunch	12.30 - 1.30		
Session 3	1.30 - 3.00		
Break	3.00 - 3.30		
Session 4	3.30 - 5.00		
Dinner	5.00 - 7.00		
Session 5	7.00 - 8.00		
Break	8.00 - 8.15		
Session 6	8.15 - 9.15		

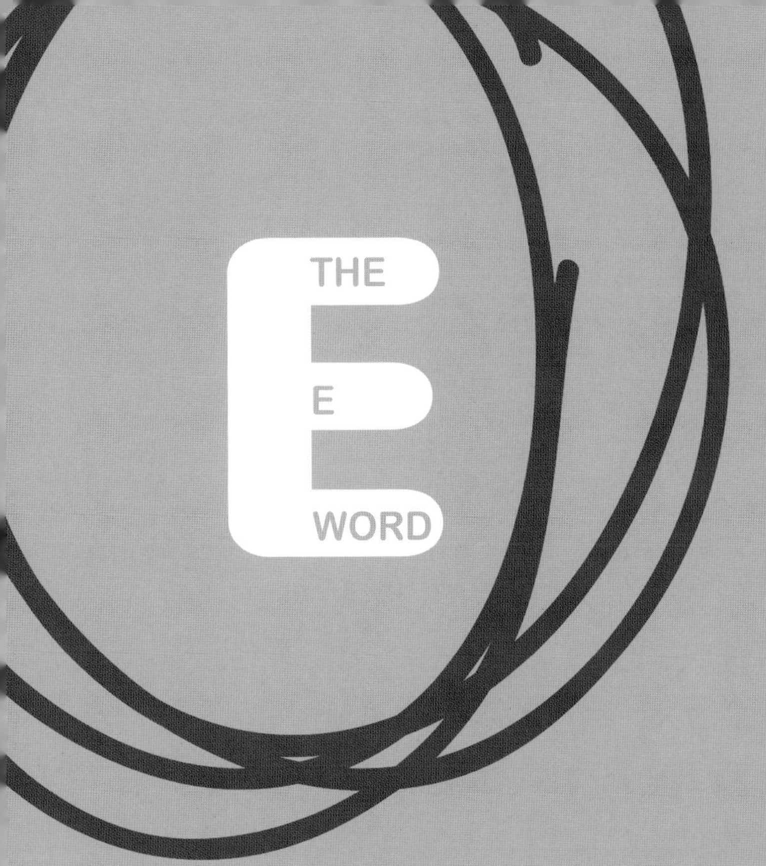

chapter 9 Conclusions and reflections

About this chapter

Reflection is an important part of the learning process. To reflect you have to think back on what you have already studied, when you revise you have to reflect. The best way to reflect is to think with a purpose. There will be much internal dialogue and probably some visualization, asking why and how questions will help. The result of this reflective learning will be that you will begin to make connections and in turn those connections will lead to a feeling that sometimes even takes you by surprise, a feeling that you finally understand.

This chapter is my turn to learn something, to go back and re-read what has been written and summarise the key messages and lessons as much to reinforce my own understanding as it is to provide some conclusions and final thoughts for you.

Final thoughts

The system – how examinations work

One of the motives for me in writing this book is evident in some of the arguments put forward in this chapter. Examinations do matter because of the way people use them to form opinions about you and because of the self respect and confidence you develop as a direct result of passing the exam. And yes, they do make you stand out from others, not because of what you know, although that should not be ignored, but because they show that you have the ability to work hard, concentrate and focus on a goal.

I have at times been guilty of making light of the content/knowledge that you have to learn. This is not because content does not matter or that passing the exam does not show you are knowledgeable about that subject, of course it does. It is just that this is a book about passing exams, not about being right, or about how much you know, it is not about being an expert or a genius. It's about passing, and many people fail, not because of lack of knowledge but because of how they studied, revised and what they did on the day of the exam itself.

As for the sacrifices you have to make in time, energy and mental anguish, is it worth it? You will only be able to answer this honestly after the event, for my own part and for many of the students I have taught, the answer has to be yes.

I still have concerns about how easy it is to get caught up in the whole *exams are everything world*, where people form opinions as to the future of a 14 year old or worse, consider them a failure simply because of an answer they gave to a question in an exam.

So I will give the last word on this to Howard Gardner.

Pay one's respect to school and test results but do not let them dictate one's judgment about an individual's worth or potential. In the end what is important is an individual's actual achievements in the realms of work and personal life.

These judgments can and should be made directly, not via the proxy of a test score.

What's stopping you from passing?

Recognising how you think and gaining a deeper understanding of who you are, requires a level of maturity worthy of an exam pass in its own right. The first step is probably to have a little laugh at some of the characters in this chapter, the second an appreciation that some of them might be you.

The exam focused approach on one level is so simple that there are times when I think it is not even worth mentioning, everyone knows that looking at past exam questions will help you pass! But when you are trying to learn something it is easy to get caught up in ***the knowledge trap***, the trap that you have to learn everything to pass. And although knowledge is essential (remember no amount of exams skills will help if you don't know anything) focusing on learning everything can often make the subject seem impossible and begin to create destructive self doubt.

The exam focused approach is about direction, it is both simple and profound. The best way to pass an exam is to produce an answer that is considered correct when compared with the model answer, and the best way to do that is to look at the model answer, simple. When there is so much to learn and the volume itself appears daunting, you simply need somewhere to start and for me, that has to be the most examinable topics. With limitless time you would learn and understand everything, but just in case you don't have limitless time, having studied the most examinable topics has to give you a better chance of passing.

Motivation and Attitude

This chapter is about the energy you put into your studies and the direction from which you choose to look at events. Having the right attitude is a key part of exam success. It is in some ways the magic dust that can be sprinkled to change the result in your favour. You may not be top of the class, but if you are motivated and have the right attitude you can still achieve whatever you want.

Although motivation is primarily about setting positive goals, how can you be motivated, if you don't know what you want. The fear of failure can be equally powerful, and in my experience is a significant factor in motivating people to pass exams. Watch for the reaction when someone gets their exam results, if they punch the sky and shout out, it is probably something they really wanted and they are motivated towards it; if they breathe a sigh of relief, it is more than likely they were motivated by the fear of failing. When the exam result drops through the letter box or pings into your email account, my guess is there are more sighs than whoops.

Attitude is the frame of mind you have, it is how you look at problems and deal with setbacks, including stress and exam failure. The key message here is to have a positive attitude, not because everything will turn out right, but because it forces you to keep coming up with solutions to problems, it stops you wallowing in self pity and feeling sorry for yourself, it keeps you moving in the direction of your goal and ultimately towards success. Attitude is so much about how you look at something, it's directional.

And finally, if you find that when you compare yourself with others, you feel they have a much better chance of success because you think they are ***brighter, smarter or more intelligent,*** then take heart from what is written in this chapter. Your attitude and level of motivation can more than compensate for this. Please never lose sight of this fact.

Learning

Being intelligent is often confused with knowing things, knowing the capital of *Ghana or the year *John Keats died perhaps. Yet being able to list all the countries that have won the World Cup in order and knowing the final score would probably be considered trivia and so somehow less worthy a demonstration. However as these include only a very small element of problem solving they have less to do with intelligence and more to do with memory.

There is of course no doubt that if you "know things" you will stand a better chance of passing exams, but at higher levels of the exam process you are required to do so much more than regurgitate facts, you need to do things, solve problems and communicate this knowledge so that others can understand.

This chapter has a simple message, if 60% of your intelligence is predetermined, don't beat yourself up about how intelligent you are, focus on the things you can improve. Work with the remaining 40%, build those neurological connections and learn how to learn more effectively. Learn about memory skills, learning styles and how your beliefs can affect much of what you do.

And never underestimate how intelligent you are, recognise that to simply exist and survive in modern society requires a significant level of intelligence. To pass most exams, you only have to be intelligent enough, and if 75% of people are of average intelligence and above, chances are you already have what it takes.

**The capital of Ghana is Accra. John Keats died 23rd February 1821*

Learn smarter – techniques to improve how to learn

It doesn't matter how good your exam skills are, you will not be able to pass the exam without the required knowledge. So I wanted to include something on what knowledge is and some of the ways you could think about it. My main intention was to create a visual framework that can be used to help explain how knowledge is structured and how it develops and links together to form an understanding of a subject or topic. I hope that this structure will be useful in helping you think about learning and how we acquire knowledge so that it makes the process seem less mysterious and as a result, less daunting.

The remainder of this chapter is dedicated to providing practical hints and tips as to what you can do to learn more effectively. Learning is obviously a key part in passing exams and if it is possible to make it easier, that has to be a good thing. Please give the techniques a go, and remember as with many things, it often takes a little practice before you are able to realise the benefits.

Memory

Memory techniques are essentially exam skills. They are part of a whole range of skills that can be learned in order to help improve your mark and so your exam result. The ability to remember is essential if you are to be successful in the exam room.

Most people think they understand what memory is, yet often confuse having a good memory with being intelligent and perhaps fail to appreciate you need to remember different things. For example not only will you need to remember ***facts*** such as, names, dates and formulas, you will also need to remember *how to do things* like, draw diagrams, solve problems and make calculations.

However, whatever you are trying to remember there are some simple principles of memory that will help. I think they are so important. I will repeat them again in this final chapter.

1. Input – how you record the event or experience is vitally important.

2. Association and organisation – In order to remember something it needs to be linked and organised.

   Think about a piece of information that you need to remember, very much as you would a letter that you have read, but may need to be found later. If it has been clearly labelled and filed in a well organised system, finding it will be easy.

3. Repetition – This for me is the most important principle of all. If you go over something time and time again, you will remember it.

The specific memory techniques included in the second part of this chapter all use these three simple principles, please give them a go.

Techniques to improve exam performance

This is the last chapter because it takes you up to the period six weeks before the exam and into the exam room itself. Although explaining what revision is may seem a little basic, having sat in a meeting recently and heard this question being discussed by several very experienced tutors, who to some extent actually disagreed, I feel it is necessary. The process of going back over what you have learned is essential, but for my mind it can't be done at the end of each section, chapter or topic, it has to be done in the period just before the exam. The reason? Because you and your attitude are different then. The level of concentration is higher as you suddenly realise the exam is just around the corner and it is this heightened sense of urgency that makes revision so effective.

The exam focused approach is revisited here, simply because it becomes even more important to spend your time focused on the most important areas. If you were short of time when you were learning the topic, you will certainly be short of time when you only have a few weeks or even days to go before the exam itself. There is only one thing you should be doing at this time and that is practising exam standard questions on the most likely topics for that sitting.

I honestly believe that the advice, hints and tips given in this final chapter could make the difference between passing and failing, particularly the section on how to read exam questions and managing time.

And finally

If you put all of these chapters together you will get the formula we first started with.

Knowledge + Examination skills + Mental attitude = Exam success

A formula that may not make you happy but I hope will bring you exam success, what you do with that is up to you....

Forrest Gump: What's my destiny, Mama?
Mrs. Gump: You're gonna have to figure that out for yourself.

Forrest Gump, movie

chapter 10
References

References

Essentials of Human Memory – Alan Baddeley. Psychology Press (1999)

Using your Brain for a Change – Richard Bandler. Real People Press (1985)

Losing My Virginity: The Autobiography – Sir Richard Branson. Virgin Books (2002)

Use your Head – Tony Buzan. BBC Active (2006)

Head First! – Tony Buzan. Thorsons (2000)

Mapping the Mind – Rita Carter. Phoenix (2000)

NLP in Business – Peter Freeth. Communications in Action (2005)

Words that Change Minds – Shelle Rose Charvet. Kendall/Hunt Publishing Co (1997)

The 7 Habits of Highly Effective People – Stephen Covey. Simon & Schuster Ltd (2004)

A student's guide to IFRS – Clare Finch. Kaplan Publishing (2007)

Learn Faster and Remember More – David Gamon and Allen Bragdon. Allen Bragdon Publishers (1999)

Five Minds for the Future – Howard Gardner. Harvard Business School Press (2009)

Extraordinary Minds – Howard Gardner. HarperCollins (1997)

Frames of Mind – Howard Gardner. Fontana Press (1993)

Outliers – Malcolm Gladwell. Penguin (2009)

A Manual of Learning Styles – Honey, P., Mumford - London: P Honey (1982)

Fish! – Stephen C. Lundin, Harry Paul, John Christensen. Hyperion (2000)

Routes to remembering: the brains behind superior memory – Maguire, E.A. and Valentine, E.R. and Wilding, J.M. and Kapur, N. Nature Neuroscience (2003)

Guinness Book of World Records, 1989 – Donald McFarlan. Sterling Publishing (1988)

A Case of Unusual Autobiographical Remembering – Elizabeth S. Parker; Larry Cahill; James L. McGaugh. Neurocase, Volume 12, Issue 1 (2006)

Introducing NLP Neuro Linguistic Programming – Joseph O'Conner. Thorsons (2003)

NLP Workbook: A Practical Guide to Achieving the Results You Want – Joseph O'Conner. Thorsons (2001)

The Magic of Metaphor – Nick Owen. Crown House Publishing (2001)

Knowing-Doing Gap – Jeffrey Pfeffer, Robert I Sutton. Harvard Business School Press (1999)

How the Mind Works – Steven Pinker. Allen Lane (1998)

The Woman Who Can't Forget – Jill Price, Bart Davis. Simon & Schuster (2008)

A Golden Age – Steve Redgrave – Sir Steve Redgrave, Nick Townsend. BBC Books; New edition (2001)

Richardson, A.J., Montgomery, P. Paediatrics 115 (5) 1360-1366 (2005)

Awaken the Giant Within – Anthony Robbins. Free Press (1992)

Learned Optimism – Martin Seligman. Pocket Books (1998)

The Mind Gym: Wake Your Mind Up. Sphere (2005)

Wikipedia the free online encyclopaedia

THE E WORD

chapter 11
Index

Index

A

B

C

D

E

F

THE
E
WORD

L

M

N

O

P

Q

R

S

T

U

V

W